BOOM, BABY!

My Basketball Life in Indiana

BOBBY "SLICK" LEONARD AND LEW FREEDMAN

TRIUMPH
BOOKS

Library of Congress Cataloging-in-Publication Data

Leonard, Bobby, 1932–
   Boom, baby! : my basketball life in Indiana / Bobby "Slick" Leonard and Lew Freedman.
      pages cm
   Includes bibliographical references and index.
   ISBN 978-1-60078-859-8 (hardback)
   1. Leonard, Bobby, 1932- 2. Basketball players—United States—Biography. 3. Sportscasters—United States—Biography. I. Freedman, Lew. II. Title.
   GV884.L46A3 2013
   796.323092—dc23
   [B]
                                                         2013030144

This book is available in quantity at special discounts for your group or organization. For further information, contact:
   Triumph Books
   814 North Franklin Street
   Chicago, Illinois 60610
   (312) 337-0747
   Fax (312) 280-5470
   www.triumphbooks.com

Printed in U.S.A.

ISBN: 978-1-60078-859-8

Design by Amy Carter

I dedicate this book to Nancy, my wife and love of my life—a beautiful, smart, loving, funny gal, tough and a little feisty, who always thinks of others before she thinks of herself.

At the time of this writing, we have just celebrated our 59th year of marriage after starting our journey as freshmen at Indiana University.

Nancy's been an inspiration to me and our five children—Terry (our only girl), Bobby, Billy, Tommy, and Timmy. Okay, Bob, Bill, Tom, and Tim! Through all the ups and downs of everyday living, there's no doubt she's always had our backs.

Nancy is the first to admit she's a little demanding. Her philosophy—everything you say or do affects somebody else—either good or bad. No gossiping, no lies, don't cheat, be respectful, give it everything you've got, love everyone, and always go to church on Sunday.

Now, to our kids. Thanks for enriching our lives with four great daughters-in-law: Tami, Susie, Kristin, and Kristy. And Larry, one super son-in-law. And the best grandkids, in order: Katie (Patrick), Elly (BJ), Bo, Nick, Tyler, Briana, Allison, Maizie, Hannah, Timmy II, Wyatt, Stella Mae, and our first great-grandchild, Aubrey Lynn.

Love you all!
Bob Leonard

CONTENTS

Foreword *by Larry Bird*   vii

Acknowledgments   ix

Introduction   xi

Chapter 1 **GROWING UP IN TERRE HAUTE**   1

Chapter 2 **HIGH SCHOOL HOOPS**   11

Chapter 3 **GOING TO IU**   27

Chapter 4 **PLAYING FOR INDIANA**   37

Chapter 5 **VARSITY BREAKTHROUGH**   45

Chapter 6 **NATIONAL CHAMPS**   55

Chapter 7 **GOING FOR TWO IN A ROW**   65

Chapter 8 **BEING DRAFTED AND BEING DRAFTED**   73

Chapter 9 **GOING PRO**   85

Chapter 10 **BECOMING SLICK**   97

Chapter 11 **GO WEST, YOUNG MEN**   111

Chapter 12 **OFF TO THE WINDY CITY**   121

Chapter 13 **OUT OF THE GAME**   131

Chapter 14 **CALL FROM THE INDIANA PACERS**   141

Chapter 15 **PACERS BECOME CHAMPS**   153

Chapter 16 **BIG WINNERS IN INDY**   167

Chapter 17 **THE WINS KEEP ON COMING**   177

Chapter 18 **INDIANAPOLIS TITLE TOWN**   189

Chapter 19 **CHASING A FOURTH CROWN**   199

Chapter 20 **ON TO THE NBA**   211

Chapter 21 **NBA STRUGGLES**   221

Chapter 22 **END OF THE COACHING LINE**   231

Chapter 23 **BOOM, BABY!**   237

Chapter 24 **AS SERIOUS AS A HEART ATTACK**   247

Epilogue: **BROADCASTING FOREVER**   255

Appendix   261

Sources   265

About the Authors   267

Index   269

FOREWORD

By Larry Bird

I first met Bob Leonard when I was attending Indiana State in Terre Haute and playing basketball there. Bob was the coach of the Indiana Pacers at the time, and he wanted to meet with me to talk about possibly playing for the Pacers. I was eligible to be drafted because of the rules at the time, but I still had one more year to play for Indiana State and I wasn't thinking about the pros yet.

We met at a Hyatt Regency in Indianapolis. He knew a lot of people that I knew because he grew up in Terre Haute. I knew a lot about him from those people. I knew his background. We had similar backgrounds growing up in Indiana and had a lot in common.

I never played for Bob, but we became friends. I went to him for a lot of advice. He is an Indiana basketball historian. He can name all of the great high school players. He'll go down in history as one of the great Hoosier basketball minds. I went to him for a lot of things, and we both liked to drink beer and golf together. I've had a lot of fun with Bob.

I'll see him and golf with him and visit with him in the summer.

One thing that was unbelievable to me about his athletic ability beyond basketball is how Slick won a high school tennis championship. He didn't even own a racket at first, and he practiced just by hitting the ball off the wall.

Sometimes after games people will stop and talk to him. They recognize him and just want to talk about the Pacers. Slick is a friendly guy.

He never forgets your name when he sees you, and everybody knows him. There's no question that he is the face of the Indiana Pacers. They wouldn't be here without Slick—and without the help of his wife, Nancy. They ran a telethon to help save the Pacers when the team was having hard times. Everybody knows that.

And "Boom, Baby!" He's got that tradition going. If you say Slick Leonard, you're saying Indiana Pacers.

———◯———

Larry Bird grew up in French Lick, Indiana, was one of the best Indiana high school basketball players in history, and was an All-American at Indiana State in Terre Haute, Bob Leonard's home town. Later, Bird was a many-time NBA All-Star for the Boston Celtics and is in the Naismith Basketball Hall of Fame. After retiring as a player, Bird coached the Indiana Pacers, at one time was named Coach of the Year. He now serves as the Pacers' president of basketball operations and won the NBA's Executive of the Year award. Leonard was a Pacers broadcaster during Bird's tenure as coach and team executive.

ACKNOWLEDGMENTS

ACKNOWLEDGMENTS OF THE JOURNEY

First, Ray and Hattie Leonard. Mom and Dad gave life a battle when times were really tough.

Donna (Max) and Darlene (Don)—two great sisters.

The Marines in the predominately Catholic neighborhood who came back from many beachheads in the South Pacific. Their return to Gerstmeyer Tech to finish high school. The basketball goal they built down the alley. It's where I really started the journey.

Howard Sharpe, the great fundamental basketball coach at Gerstmeyer. All the teachers and my high school teammates.

Branch McCracken—the Big Bear—who coached us at Indiana University to two Big Ten Championships and the 1953 National Championship. Lou Watson our freshman coach, Ernie Andres our varsity assistant coach, and my outstanding IU teammates.

Reverend Merrill B. McFall of Bloomington's United Methodist Church, who baptized me at the age of 19.

The Reserve Officers Training Corp of Indiana. As Cadet Colonel, I was given the opportunity to advance my leadership skills.

All my army buddies at Fort Leonard Wood, Missouri.

Nancy's parents, Roy and Roberta Root, and sister Joyce (Joe), my home away from home.

Teammates and coaches during my playing years with the Minneapolis and then Los Angeles Lakers.

The owners who invested their time and money to bring Indiana a professional basketball team. The stat crew, all the fans, TV and radio personnel, unbelievable community support—all contributed to the early glory days of the Indiana Pacers.

The exceptionally talented Pacers players who brought us three American Basketball Associations championships. It has been a privilege and honor to be their coach and friend.

My pals at Plum Creek Golf Course in Carmel, Indiana.

And last, all the fun years doing radio with my broadcasting partner and Hall of Famer, Mark Boyle: "Boom, Baby! The Wicked Witch is dead!"

Bob Leonard

INTRODUCTION

Bob Leonard is a basketball lifer, one of the few lucky enough to spend virtually his entire life involved with the sport he loves and a huge percentage of his time within the state of Indiana, where he grew up, attended college, and experienced his greatest professional success.

The genial and popular Hoosier icon nicknamed "Slick" was born in the state that loves basketball the most, and he has contributed mightily to the lives of those who consider hoops to be the most important element in their lives aside from inhaling and exhaling.

Basketball led Leonard out of a life of childhood poverty and provided him with opportunities that relieved hard times and carried him to state and nationwide respect and fame.

A graduate of Terre Haute Gerstmeyer where he was a high school star, the 6'3" Leonard became one of the cornerstones of Branch McCracken's "Hurryin' Hoosiers" teams that won the 1953 NCAA basketball title for Indiana University. Those Hoosiers finished 23–3, defeating Kansas for the crown in Kansas City. Leonard scored 1,098 points for the Hoosiers from 1951–54 during an era when freshmen were not eligible for the varsity and there were no three-point shots.

Leonard was chosen for All-American teams in 1953 and 1954, and his picture adorns walls at Assembly Hall in Bloomington, Indiana, where the team plays its home games. Leonard was a first-team Big Ten selection in 1953 and 1954.

Slick was drafted to play in the NBA during that league's growing pains of the 1950s and split his time between the Minneapolis
Lakers 1956–60, the Los Angeles Lakers 1960–61 in their first year
on the West Coast after the franchise shifted from the Midwest,
the expansion Chicago Packers in 1961–62, and the Chicago Zephyrs
for the 1962–63 season after they changed nicknames. In 1962, Leonard
became a player-coach for Chicago in time for the club to move to
Baltimore for the 1963–64 season when they became the Bullets. Over
the course of seven NBA seasons, Leonard averaged just about 10
points per game.

In 1968 Leonard was named head coach of the Indiana Pacers, and
during his 12-year reign he presided over the greatest successes in franchise history, which included the team winning three American Basketball
Association championships. Since the mid-1980s Leonard has been one
of the voices of Pacers basketball, serving as a color commentator and
analyst on TV and radio broadcasts.

Leonard's down-home style and smooth tones play well with listeners, but his signature call of "Boom, Baby!" when a Pacers player nails
a three-point shot is what fans enjoy most about his game observations.
The phrase has become so identified with Leonard that strangers who
recognize him on the street shout it out to him. Fans love to hear "Boom,
Baby!" so much perhaps because the more Leonard says it, the better
their team is faring in the game.

The one time coach and current broadcaster is one of the enduring
faces of the Pacers franchise, spanning generations of players. He has been
honored with a banner hanging in the rafters of Bankers Life Fieldhouse
along with the retired jersey numbers of players he coached.

When Leonard walks the arena hallways, he is invariably stopped
again and again by fans who wish to chat, obtain autographs, or pose for
pictures with him, and he is always obliging.

Leonard has crossed so many lines in his basketball life that when
he is addressed it is not always easy to predict what's on the fan's mind.

Sometimes the fan knows Leonard from his broadcasts. Others know him from his coaching days. Still others best recall his playing days.

Anyone who spends much time around Bob Leonard, however, knows that his No. 1 interest, the only thing that rates above basketball to him, is family. He and his wife, Nancy, have been together for more than 60 years since their freshman year as students at Indiana University, and they are the parents of five grown children, one girl and four boys. All of the children live in Indiana, and all of them rave about what a great dad their father was when they were growing up despite the demands of his job and the amount of time he was on the road with his teams.

Spending time shooting the breeze with Slick, or just hearing him delve into his storehouse of memories on the radio, led many of his friends to urge Leonard to write them all down. For a long time he resisted, but then he decided that it was not such a bad idea after all. He thought it might make a fine legacy for his children and grandchildren. Over a period of months Leonard and I rendezvoused at his home while he picked his own brain, trying to recall all of the salient details of a life long-lived. Although we regularly referred to record books for statistics and the man is past 80 years old, I learned that Bob Leonard's memory is pretty darned good.

When it comes to basketball, Leonard is an encyclopedia of knowledge in the sense that he has teamed with, watched play in person, or coached just about every great hoops player of the last 60 years. He can just flip to a page in his mind and tell you about so-and-so's game. Even in high school Leonard observed rival Terre Haute Garfield's Clyde Lovellette, a future Basketball Hall of Famer. In college he played with other Indiana legends, and he played against other great college stars of the era.

Whether it was sharing the court with them, watching them play, coaching them, or coaching against them, Leonard can discourse on the talents and styles or personalities of everyone who shone in NBA history from George Mikan and Bob Cousy to Bill Russell and Wilt Chamberlain, from Elgin Baylor, Jerry West, and Oscar Robertson to Roger Brown,

Mel Daniels, and George McGinnis, to Michael Jordan, Charles Barkley, Magic Johnson, and Larry Bird. Bird is an Indiana icon himself, of course, and he is a Leonard pal.

Leonard can weave a yarn. He can tell a joke. And certainly that's the way his listeners on the radio like it. But he has a serious side, and no one goes through life without setbacks. He has had his health scares, some of them well-publicized and dangerous enough to leave a mark, but he has always bounced back from them.

Except for the occasional hard times, Slick Leonard has to admit that on most fronts it's been a wonderful life. And in his own way he's still out there hitting those three-pointers. For which there is only one reply: "Boom, Baby!"

Lew Freedman
September 2013

CHAPTER 1

GROWING UP IN TERRE HAUTE

The basketball player nicknamed "Slick" was born William Robert Leonard on July 17, 1932, in Terre Haute, Indiana. The youngster was born into the Depression that was afflicting his home town in the same manner as it insidiously diminished life and caused hardships in much larger cities across the United States.

Terre Haute is located near the western border of Indiana, almost on the Illinois state line, about 75 miles mostly west and slightly south of Indianapolis. It is home to Indiana State University, which boasts a long basketball tradition. Among the school's coaches was John Wooden, who is regarded as the finest college basketball coach in history. The school's biggest star player was Larry Bird, who led the Sycamores to the NCAA Championship Game in 1979 and later became a friend of Bobby Leonard.

The city is situated along the Wabash River and is the hub of the Wabash Valley. In Terre Haute, the intersection of 3rd Street and Wabash is known as "The Crossroads of America." The name Terre Haute means "high land" in French because the settlement was located above the Wabash River.

In the 1930s, when Bobby Leonard was growing up there, Terre Haute's population was about 63,000. It is now about 61,000.

One of Leonard's overlapping contemporaries in Terre Haute was another famed basketball star. Clyde Lovellette was a senior at Terre

1

Haute Garfield when Leonard was a sophomore, and they never played against one another in a varsity game but grew to know one another well in ensuing years. Lovellette went on to an All-American career at the University of Kansas, won an Olympic gold medal, and was an NBA star with the Minneapolis Lakers, Cincinnati Royals, St. Louis Hawks, and Boston Celtics. Lovellette and Leonard even played on the Lakers together long after both had left Terre Haute.

"Terre Haute was a railroad town," Lovellette said. "We had all kinds of trains going through. They had huge yards there. We had big manufacturing plants. It used to smell quite a bit. It wasn't always a pleasant odor. It was big enough for small-town boys like Bobby and myself when we were growing up."

Because of the few-year age difference and the fact that they attended different Terre Haute high schools, Lovellette, who also still lives in Indiana, and Leonard did not become closer friends until a little bit later in life when they were teammates on the Minneapolis Lakers.

"Bobby was a nice kid," Lovellette said. "When we were in college, we came back in the summer and socialized, and we'd play ball."

BOBBY LEONARD

I was born at the end of the Depression, but it was a struggle for my family. Life was a struggle all the way. We lived in what they called shantytown in Terre Haute. A shantytown was basically poor people, but you didn't notice it because everybody was poor and the house we lived in was called a shotgun house. That was because if you fired a shotgun, the shot would go right through it from end to end. Anyone who grew up poor in most parts of the country knows what a shotgun house is.

There was a front room with a pot-bellied stove and a bedroom in the middle. Everybody slept in that bedroom. There was one bedroom for the house. The kitchen had a wood stove. Outside the back door was a pump where you got your water, and a little bit further away, about 20 or 30 yards away, was the outhouse. If you had to go to the bathroom at night, we had a chamber pot and one of my first jobs to do in the morning was to empty the pot at the outhouse.

My mom was named Hattie Mae and she was raised in Glasgow, Kentucky. My dad was Raymond Albert. He was from Staunton, near Brazil, not far from Terre Haute and there was no work there, so he came to Terre Haute. I had a step-sister, Donna Mae, and another sister, Darlene, who was four years younger than me. We had Hattie Mae and Donna Mae, and now I have a granddaughter, Stella Mae.

I had other chores, too. One of the main things I did from the time I was small was to handle the coal bucket. We were right on the railroad tracks. I never could get away from those darn railroad tracks. A lot of that is torn down now because Indiana State built there. I was right around those trains all of the time. I used to go out with a coal bucket and the coal cars went by and dropped coal. I'd fill up the bucket with coal that fell off those trains. That was free fuel for us.

The bucket was a big round thing, but it had a spout you could use to transfer the coal from the bucket into the little door on the stove. I used to stand out front and watch the Dixie Limited go through. They had a really big depot down the road, which is also part of Indiana State University now. I used to stand out there, and by the time the train got to the area where we lived, it was slowing down and the conductors were standing down on the steps of the cars. The tracks were no farther from me than from the back porch to the front porch of the house I live in now.

We had all kinds of trains coming through. Some of them were passenger trains, some of them were freight trains, and we had the coal cars. I was about six or seven years old, and I liked the Dixie Limited, a passenger train. That was special to me because the conductors always waved to you. The big thing to me was wondering where they were going. When the dining car and the club car passed, I'd wave at people and they'd wave back. The Dixie Limited.

3

Times were tough financially. The Depression was over, but it wasn't that easy to tell. It may have been over technically the way the government measures things, but unemployment was high and it took a long time to get people back to work and making a living wage. My dad was a ditch digger. By 1938 or so when I was six or seven, he made $12 a week. I always remembered that. Two doors away in shantytown there was a bar, and every Friday night when my dad got paid my mom was in there. They got paid in cash. He and all of the other workers, the poor guys who got paid in cash, ran a bar tab all week. Beer was a nickel or 10 cents a glass. At the end of the week, payday, they'd have to pay off their bar tab.

On Friday night my mom went to the neighborhood bar to make sure that he didn't spend more than he owed on that tab. It was the same at the grocery store. You ran a tab all week at this little dinky grocery store, McMillan's Grocery Store, and she had to pay that grocery bill. I don't know what the rent was. Rent couldn't have been more than $6 a month.

Terre Haute was called "The Crossroads of America" because Highway 40 ran west through there and Highway 41 ran north and south. Now Interstate 70 has pretty much replaced 40 West.

Terre Haute was always a working man's town, and the big money man in town was Tony Hulman. He was Hulman and Company, the Clabber Girl Baking Powder Company, and the Indianapolis 500. Hulman owned the Indianapolis Motor Speedway and ran the Indianapolis 500.

When I was little in the 1930s, there is no question the whole country was having hard times. We used to stand in commodity lines and they would give you a few cans of food and some flour, some basics. They took an old broken-down building to use, and my dad and I would take a gunny sack. You'd stand in the line and the government would give you things. That was when President Franklin D. Roosevelt was in office, and that was one of his relief plans.

In elementary school I remember families that were a little bit better off brought in used coats and they donated them for the other kids. I was in third grade and the teacher took me over there. I wasn't going to go. But she knew. "Come on, Bobby, I'm going to take you," she said. "I want you to pick out a coat." I picked out a coat, and I was really happy with it because it was warm. I took that thing home and my dad made me take it back. That's the pride he had.

Starting about when I was only four years old or so, I had a habit of running off and my parents and step-sister had a hard time corralling me. Once I got outside I wanted to see what was going on and I could go pretty far away before they found me. Well, my mom was pregnant and was going to have a baby, my sister. She had a midwife and she didn't want me running away and she didn't want me in the house with the midwife. So they tied me to the clothesline. A huge storm came up, and it was strong enough that it blew out the front window of the house. And here I was, tied to the damned clothesline. It was thunder and lightning and everything. They forgot about me when the baby was coming. I got more than a little bit wet that day, and scared, too.

Around the time I was 10 or 11, in the early 1940s during World War II, I got a job pushing an ice cream cooler with Eskimo pies and fudge bars. You'd get your cart and they filled it up and they cost a nickel apiece. You would get one penny for each one sold, and they would get four cents. The troop trains would come through that depot, so I just went to the train station and parked that cart. I'd sell out two or three times a day. I was selling so many I got the idea to start selling them for a dime. I was making more money than the guy who owned the coolers. I was making six cents a bar and he was making four cents. That was my territory, so I had no competition.

Then the prison trains began coming through. They carried prisoners of war, taking them east, I think to Virginia. I was out there on a hot summer day, and the cars were open air. The MPs stood there on the steps holding carbines in case anyone tried to escape. I was standing there and all of a sudden a big roll of money came out of the car. I guess they wanted a lot of ice cream. I no more than leaned over to pick up that money than an MP had a carbine right on me. He said, "Hey, boy, you give me that." I was going to give him a free ice cream bar, but I changed my mind then. The first time I saw a train with prisoners of war I was surprised. It amazes me now that they would bring prisoners all of the way across the water and all of the way across the country. I never thought about it then.

A lot of people around us got jobs with the Works Project Administration. They repaired sidewalks and roads. The president also came up with the Civilian Conservation Corp where people went out and planted trees and that kind of stuff. Things were tough, but that all changed.

I didn't have an older brother to show me, so I got into sports with my friends. There was an alley behind our house, and about a half block down was the Sullivans' backyard. This was a predominantly Catholic neighborhood, part of St. Anne's Parish. In the Sullivans' backyard they had an old leaning barn with a basketball goal.

The Sullivan kids were older than me, high school aged, and I was about seven years old going on eight. The first time I went over there it was baseball season. At that time you didn't concentrate on just playing one sport. If it was baseball season, you played baseball. Football season you played football, and basketball season, you played basketball. But I started playing basketball myself.

I never had a basketball, but the Sullivans did. They had a little bit better house than we did, and they had a basketball that they left on the back porch. I'd go up on the back porch and get their ball. All they said was, "Now make sure you put the ball back."

The backboard was wooden and there were times when there was no net. But when there was a net, at least you could see when the ball went through. I'd shoot for hours and hours by myself. I had a make-believe guy that I was playing against. It was one-on-one, and I beat him every time. I always made the last shot. It was some kind of life. I did this after school, and I spent almost all my time down there. Because it was another sports season, nobody else was playing but me. There were some older guys that were in high school that would play out there on Sunday afternoons, but that was about it. That was the start for me in basketball.

I got started playing baseball in a completely different way. The football coach at Rose Polytechnic Institute (that's what they called it before they changed it to Rose-Hulman Institute of Technology) was a guy named Phil Brown, and his son, Jeff, ran an ad in the newspaper looking for kids who wanted to play baseball. They didn't call it Little League yet, but it was the same type of thing for kids. I was 10, and we were good. The team was called the Terre Haute Jays, and we won two state championships in our age group.

The thing that changed everything for us, the whole family, and the whole country was December 7, 1941, the day the Japanese bombed Pearl Harbor. I remember it so well. I was walking down the street, and it was an unusually warm day. People had their screen doors open, and I could hear the radios blaring in those houses I was passing. It was about 11:00 in the morning, and that changed things.

The first way it changed things was because they set up defense plants to make ammunition, and my dad and a lot of the other workers around the neighborhood got jobs in them. They used to carpool to work. The money was different. The money was better than before. The bombing of Pearl Harbor sent us into World War II, of course, but I don't think I will ever see again during my lifetime the *esprit de corps* we had in the United States during the war.

Suddenly, people were working 24 hours a day, around the clock, in those plants. Everything was rationed like certain kinds of food, gasoline, and rubber. You couldn't get a pair of basketball shoes then even if you had the money to buy them.

At that age—I was 11—my heroes were the high school kids in the neighborhood who were playing football and basketball. A lot of them came to Sullivans to play, maybe 15 of them. They were high school juniors and seniors, guys like Charlie Mount the fullback, Joe Thornberry the quarterback, and others. They were my heroes, and when the Japanese bombed Pearl Harbor, they joined up. Twelve of them joined the Marine Corps. Joe Thornberry and Charlie Mount joined the army. Joe and Charlie both got killed in the Normandy invasion, the D-Day invasion of June 6, 1944. The other 10 or so guys were in the big invasions in the South Pacific, Guadalcanal, and Iwo Jima.

Once in a while they would get a 30-day furlough and they would come back and visit, and I would see them. There was an amazing thing about them—they all made it back from the South Pacific despite going through some vicious landings.

After the war they went back to get their high school diplomas. We had welding, woodshop, auto shop, print shop, and just about every other kind of shop. We were preparing guys in Terre Haute to work in the factories. This was after the defense plants weren't needed anymore.

After they got back, they tore down that barn in Sullivans backyard. But they also put in the nicest looking basketball goal you can imagine. They put it together at night welding class. There was a big oak tree and they put up a light so you could step out on the porch and turn the light on and play at night. That's when I started playing with them on Sunday afternoons. They were working during the week when I was in school.

We had just enough guys to play five-on-five half-court. Sometimes we broke it down to three-on-three and if you won you got to stay on the court and play again. I was much younger than they were, and they were much bigger and stronger. They were men. They knocked me around. It was quite an experience, but that was really how I got started playing basketball. It was a whole different ballgame when I was playing with those guys than when I had been shooting by myself. I was the youngest, and I was the last guy picked.

When we took a break we would go up and sit on Sullivan's back porch and old Ma Sullivan would make us some coffee. Those guys would tell stories about the islands from the war, and my eyes would be as big as saucers because it was vicious stuff. It was scary. They would tell stories about being in the trenches and the Japanese would try to infiltrate the lines with guys who spoke English and they'd send them right in with you and say, "Hey Joe." Then you would be trying to advance and you'd pass some of your comrades hanging from a tree skinned alive. That's how vicious it was.

After they got back from the war, they were still young and they had been through this fighting. They were pretty wild. They still had that young wildness in them. On Friday nights they would go out on the town and they taught me how to spit-shine shoes. They brought their dress shoes and a decent pair of pants with them and they always said, "If your hair is combed and your shoes are shined, you can go anyplace." They set their shoes out, and I'd shine all of their shoes for them and have them waiting for them on Friday night. It was about 10 pairs of shoes. They paid me a quarter a pair. Two dollars and a half. I was pretty happy about that deal.

Another way I made money back then was cutting lawns. An old lady in the neighborhood gave me an old push mower, and I went around trying to cut yards. Some of the people gave me a dime or 15 cents. Once I was cutting the grass at this one house and a lady came over and said, "Now, if you come over here and run that sweeper and empty the waste-paper basket, I'll play you $5 a week on Saturday."

That was astronomical. I was a naïve kid, maybe 13 by then. So I emptied the baskets, ran the sweeper, and cut the grass. One time I was walking out the door and here come four Marines from the neighborhood. One of them said, "Bobby, what are you doing in there? Don't you know that's a cat house?" And I said, "What do you mean? I've been working here all summer and I haven't seen a cat yet!" They all started laughing.

CHAPTER 2

HIGH SCHOOL HOOPS

On the Terre Haute Gerstmeyer Technical High School website, there is a list of alumni luminaries and one of them is Bob Leonard. There is a link summing up Leonard's life in basketball.

Among the other names included are Harley Andrews and Arley Andrews, twin brothers who also starred in basketball for the school and were friends with Leonard, as well as teammates, although they were a few years younger. Like Leonard, the brothers not only starred for Gerstmeyer but were later elected to the Indiana Basketball Hall of Fame in New Castle, Indiana.

Harley later played for Louisville, and Arley, who ended up in the class a year behind his brother's because of an injury during childhood, played for Indiana State. By the time the Andrews brothers were competing for Gerstmeyer, Leonard was nearing the end of his eligibility, and he was the local hero.

"He was an outstanding player," Harley Andrews said. "A great shooter. He was the team leader. He was the leading scorer and the team's go-to guy. "

Harley was a 6'3" forward on the junior varsity team and mostly watched Leonard lead the school to a sectional championship at the end of the 1949–50 season. During Leonard's days in high school, Indiana was known for its state basketball tournament, combining the largest and smallest schools in an event that mesmerized the state for weeks in the countdown to the title game. Winning a sectional title was considered a special achievement, and that was as far as Leonard's teams advanced.

Another highlight of the season for the Black Cats was always the Wabash Valley tournament, an immense annual basketball tournament that attracted 116 teams.

"It was huge," Harley Andrews said. "We won that three years in a row."

Another great athlete from the school, although he came along more than a decade after Leonard graduated, was Major League Baseball player Tommy John, who won 288 games in his pro career. Bob clearly remembers Tommy as a blond-headed crew-cut kid of five or six years who ran out on the floor and was the team mascot for the varsity games.

Tommy John Sr. played a big part in Leonard's life as he often took Bobby along in his pickup truck when he made service calls for the electrical company. Tommy had the first successful surgery to repair a pitcher's arm. Named after Tommy, it is known as the Tommy John surgery. Young Tommy and Leonard have remained friends.

Although the Andrews were a few years younger than Leonard, they all had in common a burning desire to improve. That meant they wanted to play in the off-season when the school building was locked up.

"We worked out together in the summer all the time," Harley Andrews said. "We practiced together. The gym was locked. Sometimes we had to go in through the window. It might be 105 degrees in there."

They were all just being true to their school because they wanted to win. Gerstmeyer also has a school fight song that encouraged that. The words go:

Gerstmeyer High
Oh, here's to Gerstmeyer High
Here's to the orange and the black.
Here's to the slogan
'Tech Fight Back'
Colors true to those who honor you.
Oh, here's to everything we've done.

Here's to every game we've won.
Gerstmeyer High!

One reason Gerstmeyer had the success it did in basketball was due to legendary Indiana high school coach Howard Sharpe, who was Leonard's coach. Sharpe won 724 games in a 47-season coaching career, 27 of them at Gerstmeyer. Also a member of the Indiana Basketball Hall of Fame, Sharpe was known nationally as a speaker at basketball clinics and forums where he spoke more than 1,000 times.

BOBBY LEONARD

I had a great, great high school basketball coach in Howard Sharpe, one of the winningest coaches of all time. He was fundamentally as good as they get.

His background was that he went to Indiana State when it was called Indiana State Teachers College, and the coach there was Glenn Curtis. Curtis coached John Wooden in high school in Martinsville and won four state championships. Sharpie learned from him. From Sharpie I learned the psychology of the game, and he helped me pick up the fundamentals at an early age.

I was only about 5'4" when I started high school in 1946, right after the war. Then I graduated in 1950. I grew to 5'10" as a sophomore and 6'3" as a junior. That was all in a short period of time. I was growing out of my clothes. Sharpie made sure I had a new pair of sneakers, though, Converse.

As a freshman and a sophomore I was on the B team, which is what they call junior varsity now. It was a lot different than playing by myself or playing pick-up games at Sullivans. It wasn't until my junior year that I began playing varsity. The first game of the season we went down to Evansville to play Evansville Bosse. We had older guys who drove us in cars, four or five of them. One of them was Tommy John's dad. We rode four guys to a car on the way to the game. They had the radio on and we heard the Bosse coach say, "We're going to play the first team in the first half and the second team in the second half." Well, it didn't work out like that. I scored 36 points, and we beat the heck out of 'em. They never did get their second team in the game. After that night, I was scoring big numbers every game.

From the time I had been playing on the junior varsity I had gotten a whole lot better. And I grew a lot. I was hungry all the time when I was growing, and I used to go down to McMillan's Grocery Store and steal candy bars (my favorite was a Milky Way) all the time. Years later I went back there and Buck McMillan said, "Bobby, I just want to let you know that all those times when you were taking those candy bars, I knew it." I said, "How much do I owe you?" He said, "You don't owe me a dime. I've always enjoyed the games." So I left $10 on the counter. At 5 cents a bar, that would pay for 200 candy bars.

I was also a football player in high school, and I was probably a better football player than I was a basketball player. I played tackle football on Saturdays and Sundays with those ex-army and ex-Marines, the older guys I played basketball with. They were all big Notre Dame fans. I was a bit bigger than I had been when I first started playing basketball at Sullivans backyard, but I still got the hell knocked out of me.

By the time I went out for football I was probably 6'3", but I probably only weighed about 160 lbs. I had played with the guys on the varsity football team in sandlot football, so they knew that I could play. We had a coach by the name of Freddy Wampler, and he talked me into suiting up. I suited up for my first game against Clinton High School and caught five touchdown passes and we won the game. Our quarterback was Billy Siler and he was a baseball pitcher, so he could really throw the ball.

But Howard Sharpe went bananas because I was playing. He said, "You're going to ruin your basketball career." He and Wampler got into a fight about it. He even came to the house and told the same thing to my mother. He had my mother crying. He was projecting all of these great things for me as a basketball player. He made the argument that I was good enough to go to college on a basketball scholarship, but if I played football I was going to get hurt and I'd lose out on the scholarship. I was really disappointed because I loved the game.

I wanted to play. But that was the end of it. No more football for me. One game and I scored five touchdowns and I retired.

This was the time period when I was cutting lawns with the push mower to make money. I was putting the mower back in the woman's shed and while I was in there I noticed a tennis racket on the wall. It looked like a snowshoe. The lady was looking at me and asked me if I wanted it. It had belonged to her son who got killed in the war. She gave me that tennis racket, and I went out and found two tennis balls somewhere and started hitting balls off the wall at the school. I had never played tennis before, but I was intrigued by it, and I became a pretty good tennis player. I played a lot of tennis. I taught myself how to play.

There was something about it in terms of hitting the ball over the net that felt like putting a basketball through the net. By my sophomore year in high school I was the No. 1 player on the team. Then I won some tournaments, and I became the state champion, though after I left high school competitive tennis was over for me.

I was a good athlete. I played some football and baseball and I was good at tennis and basketball in high school, but I don't know where the athleticism came from. As a matter of fact, my mom and dad never went to any of my games or anything like that. They were too wrapped up in trying to make a living. Later, when I played basketball at Indiana, my mom started saving the newspaper clippings. When she died my sister put them together and sent them over to me. But basically my parents weren't sports people. They weren't sports fans. They hadn't played.

It all came from playing on my own. I developed my own abilities, but I had good coaches along the way. I was pretty much an introvert growing up—I know a lot of people wouldn't believe that now since I talk for a living on the radio and have met thousands of people over the years. But I was. I focused most of my energy on sports. Eating all of those Milky Ways, my teeth went down the tubes. They were all rotten, and I was ashamed of that, so I wouldn't smile. I would put my hand over my mouth. The combination of that and not having nice clothes made me an introvert. I never had a date when I was in high school. I was shy. And Sharpie was one of those hardcore coaches. He would say, "No drinking, no smoking, and no girls." That's the way it was, tough rules.

One important and nice thing was done for me by my print shop teacher, John Valle. One day my junior year he called me into the print shop and said, "I'm going to do something. I've got a friend who's a dentist and a graduate of Indiana University. I want you to take this envelope and you take it down there to him. We're going to get your teeth fixed." In the envelope was $150. You know teachers at that time were probably making $2,500 a year, and he was giving me $150. It took me a while, but I got the $150 back to him.

The dentist was located in downtown Terre Haute, and I went in and he pulled all of my poor teeth, wisdom teeth, they were a mess. I suffered a lot with my teeth. This was in my early teenage years. After I had my teeth fixed I grew a foot, more or less, from 5'4" my freshman year to 5'10" to 6'3" as a junior. I gained a little weight and felt like a million dollars. I think there was an overall health connection involved there.

Think about it, though. You have a kid in those kind of circumstances, and it really hurts their personality. It does affect their personality and sometimes they never get over it. I call my wife, Nancy, a socialist. I don't mean that politically. She enjoys being around people, socializing. I'm just the opposite to a degree. I was introverted back then, and I'm still a very private person, but I am a little bit more outgoing. I'm okay once I get to an event, but my wife has to drag me sometimes. I don't know what I would have done in my life without her.

Having my teeth fixed changed my life, but the big thing that changed my life was basketball. The students all knew me because I played basketball. It wasn't that big of a school anyway. I think we had about 150 in our graduating class. It was a decent size and everybody sort of knew everybody, but they knew me because I played basketball. There was more emphasis on whether or not you were a good guy than a big athlete.

I got into trouble one time in high school when it was worth it. There were these Cushman motor scooters and boy were they nice looking. I always wanted one of those things really badly, but we didn't have any money. Nobody had cars in high school in those days, but this one kid had a Cushman and he rode it to school. He parked it out front, and one day I was looking at it and the keys were in it.

I took that Cushman and I rode that thing all over Terre Haute. If I had run out of gas I would have been in bad shape because I didn't have any money, but I rode it everywhere and missed school. Naturally, when I got back, this kid was irate and told the principal. I got punished. I got the old 10 whacks with the paddle and then I got seventh-hour detention. But at least I got to ride that Cushman. It was worth the trade—at least until I got back.

My coach, Howard Sharpe, had a lot of rules, "No smoking, no drinking, no girls." No girls. I didn't have the clothes or things, and I never had a date in high school. But come to think of it, my sophomore year at Gerstmeyer there was this one girl from the neighborhood who came to the door and wanted to go to a school dance with me. My mother opened the door and she said okay without even talking to me. The girl's name was Caroline and she came back on the night of the dance, I think it was Halloween, and when she came to the door my mom couldn't find me. I hid under the bed and nobody could find me. I didn't go to the dance with her. I was very shy, and I didn't know how to dance. I played basketball.

The first year that I played basketball on an organized team was my freshman year at Gerstmeyer, and it was great. I loved it. I was one of the starters, and we had great kids. I can still remember the starting five very well. It was Ronnie Brewer, Dick McDuffy, Keith Youngan, Denny Stevens, and myself. We had known one another before we were on the team. We played against each other, one-on-one, pick-up games. Ronnie Brewer and I used to show up at the school at 6:00 in the morning, and the old janitor would let us in the gym. I used to go in there before school and shoot, and Ronnie and I would play one-on-one full-court. This wasn't a really big gym. There was an old floor over the wood shop, and that's where we practiced.

We didn't have our own gym at Gerstmeyer until my senior year. We used to play our home games at Terre Haute Garfield. That was where Clyde Lovellette went to school. Oh, Clyde was a player. Clyde and I could have been teammates in college, long before we became teammates with the Minneapolis Lakers. Branch McCracken wanted him to come to Indiana, and everybody thought he was going to go to IU. Then old Phog Allen stepped in there and got him for Kansas. He would have been a senior when I was a sophomore.

Garfield was on the north side of Terre Haute. Gerstmeyer was in the middle. In 1947, Garfield with Clyde Lovellette was the first team to get to the final game of the state tournament undefeated, but they lost. Shelbyville beat them with Billy Garrett. They had Garrett and Emerson Johnson. Johnson killed them from outside. Bill was at IU when I was there. He was a senior when I was a freshman.

Those guys I played with on the Gerstmeyer B team all went on together to the varsity. We were teammates for all four years of high school. Most of them did well in life, too. Keith Youngan went to college, got a degree, and became a high school principal. Denny Stevens went to IU when I was there, got his degree, and became an officer in a huge insurance company. Ronnie Brewer had a big job with Bemis Bag Company, and Dick went to Chicago and got into a lot of things. His dad was in the construction business in Terre Haute, and he had some avenues. Dick was smart, and he went on and made a lot of money. Ron Brewer passed away. He had diabetes. He's the only one who died. The other ones are still alive.

When I was in high school, they didn't differentiate the positions like a point guard and a shooting guard and a power forward. I was just a basketball player. I was pretty much a forward in high school. I could bring the ball up like a guard, but they didn't ask me to. Branch McCracken made me a guard at IU. They called them playmakers then.

I improved a lot as a player in high school as I got bigger and with good coaching. I may have started as a freshman, but I was a short guy on the freshman team. I came a long way by my junior year when I was 6'3" and was a big scorer on the varsity.

We had a pretty good high school team. At tournament time, most people talked about the sectionals. It was like winning your local championship. The teams in the sectional were from the area. Those rivalries were intense. You were playing against your neighbors. Winning the sectional was like having local bragging rights. Sure, winning the state championship was a dream, but with every team in the state entered, it was always going to be a longshot. Winning sectional was always the first goal. People would go around town asking, "How did you do in your sectional?"

Junior year we got beat in the sectional. Senior year we won in the sectional and advanced to the regional. If we had won that, we would have played in the same old field-house that we had when I went to IU. The regional was played in Martinsville, which was the first town in Indiana to have a gym bigger than the population of the town. They built a lot of those after that. New Castle has the biggest high school gym in the world. The bigger the gym, the more likely you could attract a sectional or regional.

That regional was played in Martinsville, and a guy hit a shot at the gun to beat us. Broke our hearts. Winning the sectional was big, though. That used to be how things were really measured by the local fans. Winning sectional was big because it meant you'd beaten all of the area teams. That was true all around Indiana, but in our area the thing that was even bigger was the Wabash Valley Tournament. It was the biggest high school non-state tournament in the United States with 116 teams.

The Wabash Valley Tournament was played in January or February, and it included all of the teams within a 60-mile radius. We didn't win it while I was playing. It was a super-organized tournament. It had to be with all of those teams entered. It was broken down a lot like the state tournament where you had a sectional and advanced through various areas. Everybody stayed in their own immediate area until they advanced. It was a big tournament.

The first game my junior year was against Evansville Bosse. Starting for the first time on the varsity and scoring 36 points in that game was a big breakthrough for me. But I think I was like a lot of kids. It's the same thing that happens to so many kids. They grow and they get better if they work at it. You just keep working and shooting and practicing and this, that, and the other thing, and you gain from the normal progress and aging. That's how it was for me. I can't really remember what I averaged for the B team, but I think it was probably double figures, around 10 points a game.

I went from that to scoring 30 points in a game, or in the high 20s most of the time. It was a big jump, especially because the competition was so much better. I was a good scorer. I was shooting from beyond where the three-point line is now. But Sharpie was the one who taught me the hesitation fake, and I drove to the hoop a lot of times. I had a pull-up jump shot, too.

I had the outside shot, the drive, and the pull-up jumper. To this day I say if you're really going to excel in the pro or college game that you need to be a threat from the three-point area, you need to have the medium game, and you have to have the game where you can take it to the hoop. If the big guys are in there on defense, you can lay it off and make the assist. And you've got to be able to play defense.

You know what really helped me on defense? Tennis. The lateral movement and the backward movement. And I got quick. I got to the point where I was pretty quick. It helps all of the way around if you're quick. Playing tennis you really learn how to move your feet. Side to side and backward, you've got to be able to move your feet, and that helped me a great deal in my basketball game.

I was a 6'3" forward, but back in the late 1940s there weren't that many bigger guys I had to work on covering. The game has changed so much. That size was common for a forward, and in high school there were still 6'3" centers. Guys have gotten taller and they jump higher. We won a high percentage of our games, but the most important thing was that we won the sectional.

There were great games during my high school career, but the thing we all dreamed of, every kid's dream, every kid that ever came up through Indiana high school basketball, was to get to the Final Four at Butler Fieldhouse, which is now called Hinkle Fieldhouse. The Final Four—that was the name of the game. People don't realize that Indiana high school basketball had a Final Four before the NCAA ever used it. We didn't make it to the Final Four.

The biggest high school game I was in was the sectional championship. We beat Fontanet. Fontanet is in Vigo County, right near Terre Haute. They were called the Fontanet Beantowners. In the summertime then, and to this day, they have the big annual bean dinner there. You go out into a big open field area, and they have tripod pots sitting all over the place. They have games for the kids and all of that. It's a festival—the famous Fontanet bean dinner. They had a real good player when I was in high school named Don Maneely.

Sectional finals were at the Indiana State gym. It was the biggest gym around, and that's where all the big games were played, the Wabash Valley championships, everything. We got down to the end of the game, and we were losing to Fontanet. I hit a 20' jump shot, and that sent the game into overtime.

In the state tournament sometimes on Saturdays, you play two games in one day, one in the afternoon and one in the evening. We were young kids, but we were playing back-to-back. During the first minute of overtime or so the lights went out in the gym. The whole place went dark. The lights were out. We went over to our benches. We had been playing and playing, and you're so tired you could almost fall asleep. The lights were out, and they stayed out. Ten minutes passed. Fifteen minutes passed. Finally, they came back on and we had to finish the game. There were a couple of minutes to play when the lights came back on, and we went on to win the sectional.

BOOM, BABY!

I always remembered the lights being turned out on us. You remember when Don Meredith, the old Dallas Cowboys quarterback who used to do *Monday Night Football* games on TV? When it was clear who was going to win, he used to sing, "Turn out the lights, the party's over." Don was a great friend of mine, and we played golf down in Texas. I ended up doing that at Pacers games. I sing that. Part of the reason was that Don sang it, and part of it is me remembering that high school game. Sometimes I sing it a little bit too soon, and the other team comes back. But I never sang it and had it backfire on me.

It was kind of like Red Auerbach with the Boston Celtics lighting up that victory cigar of his with 30 or 40 seconds left in a game. That was a big deal. I know a lot of players who said, "Boy, I'd just like one time to shove that cigar down his throat."

We won that sectional game at night, but it had been a long day. I think we beat Blackhawk in the first game of the day. That's another school located near Terre Haute. We started playing at 9:00 in the morning, and I think I scored 52 that game. That was the most points I ever scored in a high school game. It was a long wait till the championship game later in the day.

I don't like the way they have changed Indiana basketball to the class system. For people who have grown up since it changed, they can't believe how important the sectional was. When I was in high school, there were 714 teams, and they all were in the state tournament. Every little town had a high school, and they each had a basketball team. On Friday nights the gyms were packed. That was true all around the state. That was before they consolidated a lot of the high schools and created regional high schools.

It didn't matter what size the school was—they filled the gym. Every kid was out playing in the barnyard and shooting wherever there was a basket. That's how I was, and that's the Indiana basketball story. I'm not talking about the organized games, but just playing every minute you could, like the Sullivans' backyard thing. As we went along and got older, wherever we congregated you played and played and played. It's always been that way in Indiana. Take Jimmy Rayl from Kokomo. He was a great scorer in high school and for IU and played in the pros. He was on the basketball court all of the time, shooting, shooting, shooting. Rick Mount from Purdue and the Pacers, too, over in Lebanon, shooting, shooting, shooting. You don't get that good overnight. It takes work to get to the level of shooting those guys had.

They spent a lot of time shooting the basketball, and so did I. High school was fun. I had a great coach. I learned a lot from Howard Sharpe that would carry me through. I had some great coaches. Branch McCracken at Indiana was a great coach. But by the time I got to that level, you were expected to know the fundamentals. The only thing the coach went over was what fit into his program. Sharpie taught me the fundamentals.

I had a good friend in high school named Billy Nasser whose dad owned the meat market. His dad bought a new Packard car, and one night Billy came by with a couple of our buddies and was going to take us for a ride out on old Highway 40. This was without his father's knowledge. He wanted to see how fast the car could go.

We pulled up to the cemetery right out of Terre Haute, the Highlands Cemetery, and when he said he was going to try to see how fast the car could go, I said, "Let me out." I just decided that I didn't feel good about it. I said, "I'm not going to get killed in a car out here." I stood by the cemetery that night and watched them buzz down Highway 40. When they came back, they said, "Boy, we got it up to 110 mph." His dad raised the devil with him when he brought the car back. Billy Nasser was like a C student in high school, but he turned out to be one of the great heart surgeons in the United States and he started the Care Group, a nationally known organization in Indianapolis.

It just goes to show you that people have dreams. Here's a guy who was a C student. His dad owned a meat market. They didn't have a lot of money, but look at what he ended up being. What convinced him was being in the Korean War and seeing all of those casualties. He came back, went to college, went to med school, and became a great man. He could afford any number of Packards then.

When Howard Sharpe stopped me from playing football and talked to my mother, I was just thinking about being a good high school basketball player. I had zero idea that I was going to go to college. Zero idea. Nevermind the idea of getting a basketball scholarship, I had never even thought about college. That didn't cross my mind until later when I began having recruiters start coming to me and Sharpie wanting me to go see their school. I didn't go look at very many of them.

College recruiting was a lot different 60 years ago. You didn't get all of these letters or phone calls, emails, or texts or whatever they do now. They would contact your coach first, for the most part. Recruiting pretty much didn't even start until your senior year after the basketball season was over.

Notre Dame was one school that was interested in me. Moose Krause, the famous athletic director at Notre Dame, tried to recruit me to South Bend, and I went there and visited. Everett Case, who was an Indiana legend for winning more than 700 games and four state championships, went to North Carolina State, and he recruited a lot of Indiana ball players. He was the guy who took North Carolina State to another level. I went down and visited North Carolina State. Then Adolph Rupp contacted me from Kentucky. Then I went over to Louisville, and I went to Indiana. They all had outstanding programs. This was all taking place in the spring and early summer of 1950, right about the time I was graduating from high school.

I remember the trip to Kentucky well. I went to Lexington and Harry Lancaster, who was Rupp's right-hand man, took charge of my visit. He made sure that I got meal money. We went over to the gym, and I was supposed to work out. So Adolph Rupp came in and they had this other kid there who was like the 12th man on their varsity. He was there because he was going to summer school and trying to make his grades. Adolph said, "Why don't we just have a half-court game here, you against…I can't remember the kid's name?" Well, I kicked his butt. Adolph Rupp said, "Get dressed. We're going downtown to the hotel."

Meanwhile, as I was getting dressed Rupp called two or three alumni, doctors, to meet us at the hotel. At dinner they made me an offer to go to Kentucky. It was more than anything I ever heard about from Indiana. The one thing that I remember Adolph Rupp said was, "Now, do you like horses?" He meant did I like to go to the race track and bet on horses. Lexington is the heart of thoroughbred breeding country. I said, "Well, I don't know much about them." Rupp said, "Well, we've got a race track out here called Keeneland Race Track, and if you ever want to go to the race track, you've got a $100 voucher to bet with."

Kentucky was offering me a little bit more than just a scholarship. There was a little more at Kentucky than at Indiana. Branch McCracken was very strict with everything at IU. Kentucky was willing to give me tuition, books, the horse track, and some spending money. Although I knew all of these programs were famous, I didn't know much about the college game, not the way I grew up. I was still educating myself. I knew Kentucky had a great program, though. I knew that. Later on in life, I got to know a lot of their former players like Alex Groza and Ralph Beard and Frank Ramsey and Cliff Hagan. But that was all later. They were all good ball players.

I came close to going to Kentucky. But when I was still in high school, I used to listen to some Indiana games on the radio, so I knew a few names of the players. And then I went to Bloomington to watch the high schools state semifinals that were held there then. I saw that silver-haired old man Branch McCracken. I kind of said, "That's the kind of guy I want to be around."

Coach McCracken attracted me as much as anything else about IU. One of my teammates at IU, Dick Farley, who played forward, came close to going to Kentucky, too, but he changed his mind and came to Indiana. I believe Dick had taken a visit to Lexington the week before I did.

Other schools contacted me, and there was no limit on the number of visits you could take back then. Those were all the schools I wanted to visit. They were all basketball programs with long traditions. They all paid for my visits, but I'm not sure the visits were as good back then as they are now. I think the NCAA rule book when I went to school was about half-an-inch thick. Now it's about 4' thick. It seems as if it is as tall as a person now with hundreds and hundreds of pages. They run everything. The NCAA has way too much power now.

I visited those schools, and Coach Sharpe would tell me that this was a great place and that was a great place. I got enough information. College basketball wasn't on television in those days. There wasn't much television in those days, period. It was Sharpie saying, "Go take a look at this one. Take a look." I did, but I didn't go to very many of them.

Until all of this began when colleges started recruiting me to play basketball and were offering me scholarships I thought I would graduate from Gerstmeyer and then go to work in a factory in Terre Haute. That was it. I thought I would finish high school and go to work. Had I not been a basketball player, that's where I would have ended up, in a factory in Terre Haute.

When Indiana was recruiting me, Branch came to Terre Haute. He sat down with Sharpie, and he barely even talked to me. It wasn't my parents, it was Sharpie. Sharpie felt really good about that. Branch was an All-American in two sports at IU—football and basketball—so he was kind of a big athletic name even before he became the coach. Although it wasn't quite as big a deal as it is now, Branch had already taken IU to one NCAA championship by then, in 1940. So he had a reputation.

After Branch left, Sharpie said, "I think that's a great program there. It's not that far from home. It's only 60 miles." To me, being that close to Terre Haute wasn't a big factor. After I enrolled at IU, I never really went back to Terre Haute much. My parents did not go to games, so it wasn't as if I chose IU that they would come to games and that if I chose Kentucky they wouldn't come to games because it was farther away. However, Terre Haute did have a big IU alumni club.

So that was it. I chose Indiana University. And everything good that happened in my life after that was because I went to school at IU.

CHAPTER 3

GOING TO IU

College sports and NCAA rules were a lot different in 1950 than they are now. Once Bob Leonard committed to attend Indiana University that fall, his coach-to-be, Branch McCracken, told him that if he wanted to get to Bloomington early he would find him a summer job. So Leonard left Terre Haute well before he started classes and moved to the city that was home to the university.

This was hardly a no-show job or an easy assignment where Leonard would work a few hours a day, take long lunch breaks, and have time to goof off. He went to work with a group of stone cutters. The Bloomington area, stretching toward the community of Bedford, is known for its lime-stone. The rock is dug out and used for buildings, and many of the structures on the Indiana University campus are constructed from limestone.

Partway through his freshman year, Leonard got to know a young woman who intrigued him. They shared classes, and he was attracted enough to ask her out. They talked and became friendly and eventually began to date. They became more serious about their relationship throughout their four years in college and eventually married. More than 60 years after they first met, Bob and Nancy Leonard are still together.

Nancy Root grew up in South Bend, in the northern part of the state, but also chose the state university where she was interested in training for a career in the health field. Some of her classes on anatomy and physiology were also classes for a physical education major like Bob.

"We were first semester freshmen at IU," Nancy said, "and were assigned to one of our required courses, along with a friend of Bob's. When I went to Bloomington, I was determined to first get an education, and second to not go steady with anyone. High school stuff! At one of the freshman activities, I met a really nice guy by the name of Charlie Kraak. Charlie was a friend of Bob's, and later one of his best friends on the 1953 National Championship team. The class size was small, and the three of us sat in the last row.

"I remember someone saying Bob was interested in taking me out, and my reply was, 'No way, I've been dating Charlie, and that's not fair.' Not the end of the story, only the beginning.

"One Sunday night, I was in my dorm room studying and there was a knock on the door. It was a couple of friends who said they were in a predicament and they needed a huge favor. They had set up a blind date with one of the girls—she was nowhere to be found, and the date was standing in the middle of the living room, waiting. Big dilemma! I always studied on Sunday evenings—no dates. I'm a nerd! Their song and dance was that they'd never ask anything again.

"So I went along and found out what they were up to, and I thought, *Oh my God, what kind of mess have I gotten myself into?*" It turned out Nancy was being set up for a blind date with Bob. But it wasn't a blind date by strict definition because they had already met. "We left with two other couples for hamburgers and lots of talk," she said. "I still have a very clear memory of thinking this is a very nice guy and thoroughly enjoying the date. Soon after that I got a phone call from Bob, and he asked if I wanted to go to an IU basketball game."

Bob had neglected to inform Nancy that he was actually a member of the basketball team and was going to be playing in the opening game with the freshman team. Nancy was a big basketball fan and in general a big sports fan. At that time students who wished to see games were admitted on a first-come, first-served basis and scrambled for seating. They didn't have assigned seats. She and her friends would go over to the home gym and try to grab the best spots they could. When a guy asked her out, naturally enough Nancy expected him to come pick her up and escort her to the evening's entertainment. But instead, Bob said he would meet her there.

From 1928 to 1960, including Leonard's tenure with the team, Indiana played in an arena that was simply called The Fieldhouse. It later became the Wildermuth Intramural Center.

"He said, 'I'll meet you,'" Nancy recalled. "It was going to be inside The Fieldhouse near the training room steps. I was stunned that he wasn't going to come get me, but I said okay because I was going to the game anyway. Meanwhile at my dorm I'm going around telling everybody about this stupid guy who didn't know enough to pick me up. I went to The Fieldhouse with my roommate and best friend from kindergarten through high school in South Bend, Kathie Barnes.

"We're walking up the ramp and we heard the public address announcer say, 'Two for Leonard.' I looked at Kathie and said, 'Oh no!' We went in and there he is on the basketball court. So that's why I had to meet him at The Fieldhouse. He met me after the freshman game and before the varsity game. I just thought, *Oh, my god.* I couldn't believe it. I had no idea he was a player. It was just really strange."

After that beginning, Bob and Nancy began dating more seriously and after only about a month together, Bob mentioned something about getting married. Nancy recalled thinking he surely seemed serious but had to be kidding. "It was a wee bit rushed, but it seemed natural. Obviously, we did not get married then. We dated all through college and got married the day after graduation." That was in June 1954.

However, there was one time during their college-length courtship when Nancy briefly considered breaking things off with Bobby. She cannot remember what the sticking point was, but their argument revolved around her belief that Bobby was staying out too late playing cards with the guys or something of that nature.

"I don't remember exactly," she said, "but I looked at it and assessed the situation and I decided, 'No, this is just not gonna work. I don't believe it will.'"

For a time Nancy refused to talk to Bob. This was their sophomore year, and they had been together through two basketball seasons. "I wouldn't talk to him," Nancy said. "He did something." At the time Bob was rooming with his sophomore basketball teammate Sammy Esposito, and Esposito played the middleman in attempting to patch things up. "Sammy called on the phone a couple of times and then finally he came over the house and said, 'Can I talk to you?' He said, 'You've got to talk to Bob. You've just got to talk to him. He's not as bad as you think he is. He's not the kind of person you think he is.' I just said, 'Sammy, I can't take a chance on it. I just can't.' I had already told Bob's mother goodbye at a basketball game. I was crying. Sammy just kept saying, 'You don't know what he's really like. You've got to talk to him again.' Finally, after getting bombarded, I said I would. And Bob came over and we talked and we made up."

It was a good thing that the tensions arose that year because after sophomore year Esposito wasn't around to help. He left Indiana to pursue a Major League Baseball career, which he spent mostly with the Chicago White Sox during the next decade.

Nancy was Bob's girl, but even before they met, Leonard had developed another new relationship with basketball coach Branch McCracken. Big Mac was one of the major influences in Leonard's life.

Emmett B. "Branch" McCracken was born in 1908. An Indiana University player from 1928–30, McCracken was an All-American selection his last season. He coached Ball State University basketball from 1930–38 and then took over the Hoosiers later that year. McCracken coached IU from 1938–43, was interrupted by World War II, and then coached IU again from 1946–65.

Under McCracken the Hoosiers won the 1940 and 1953 NCAA basketball championships. His overall record was 450–231, a 66 percent winning rate, and his IU clubs also won four Big Ten titles.

Nancy understood right from the start how much Bob revered McCracken. Even before McCracken invited Leonard to come to

Bloomington early for a summer job, the coach had done him one other big favor.

"He bought Bob a suit so he could graduate from high school," Nancy said. "If he had done that now and they found out about it, Bob would probably have lost his scholarship and IU would have been fined a million dollars. But those are the things you did in those days. That started the respect between Bob and Branch McCracken."

BOBBY LEONARD

Branch McCracken was a special guy. He was like a father to me. He was a great basketball coach because he did it a simple way. When I say a simple way, I mean things he could still do today. Branch believed in full-court pressure, rebounding, a fast break, and a simple offense. That was it. Because of the fast break, that's why they called us the Hurryin' Hoosiers.

Our offense was built around execution. We didn't surprise anybody. We had the talent, and we didn't have to surprise anybody.

Once I decided to go to IU, Branch suggested that I come to Bloomington for the summer. He said he would get me a job. He did, too, as a stone cutter. I spent the summer of 1950 working in those quarries. It was the hardest damned job I ever had. I did the nasty work, toting shale and that stuff.

I was wheel-barrowing around stuff. I did a lot of heavy lifting. But I got to know a lot of great guys, those stone cutters. It was tough, a tough job. You were outside working in the heat and the sun. Branch told me I was going to get very sun tanned. He said, "You'll be browner than a bear." The stone cutters cut, and I carried. I call it a wheel barrow, but I moved the shale in some kind of cart. The stone cutters were great guys.

One day during the summer when I was working at the quarry, Branch came up to me and asked me to take a ride with him. He was going recruiting. He said, "I'm going to take a trip down to southern Indiana. I want you to go with me." On the way to the town of Winslow, which is

31

a small place that had maybe 500 or 600 people (about 900 now), he told me what it was all about. Dick Farley came from the same kind of background that I had. His father was a coal miner, and they were poorer than hell. They have the Farley Bridge there, an old historic bridge.

When we got there, the family had the wash out on the line and Dick had just played in the Indiana High School All-Star Game and his No. 7 jersey was hanging on the line. We hit it off right away and became close friends. He scored more than 10 points a game for us at IU during his career.

I enjoyed the company of the stone cutters, but that got me in trouble one time. It was later on, during the school year. They had a six-card stud poker game that went on above a pool room in downtown Bloomington. I bumped into one of the guys and he said, "Why don't you come down and play with us?" It was a quarter a hand or a half-dollar, something like that.

They taught me how to play six-card stud, and at first they took my money, but then I started taking theirs. What got me in trouble with Branch was that one day we were playing the game and all of a sudden, BANG! The doors opened, and the police raided the joint. When they burst in, I started raking all of the quarters and half dollars off the table and stuck them in my pockets. The next day they had the names of all the guys who had been busted in that poker game in the newspaper, except they didn't put my name in. However, some of those guys' wives started complaining and saying, "How come Bobby Leonard didn't have his name in the paper?"

Soon after that Branch called me into his office. Boy, you knew when Branch called you in by yourself that something was going on. He telephoned me where I was living and said, "Leonard, I want to see you in my office at 3:00." I was in my dorm, and when he called I knew I was in trouble.

Of course he knew about the poker game, and he reamed me out bad. Branch was a big, raw-boned, 6'5". Some people called him "The Bear" and some called him "The Sheriff." But part of his lecture as he

32

sat me down in his office was how I could be a leader on the team, and I didn't want to blow it. That really started our relationship. We stood up and he was getting through with me and said, "I'm going to tell you something, young man. If I ever have to call you in this office again, only one of us is going to walk out." By that time I was up to the door and I said, "And I guess you know who that'll be, too." And I ran down the hall. I knew he was in there laughing.

I was out of the limestone business once classes started. After that I sold programs at the football games to make a little extra money. A lot of the basketball players did. The programs cost 25 cents. I remember the football team didn't do very well.

But that year we upset Notre Dame 20–7 in Bloomington, and that showed you how excited the student body could get. Beating Notre Dame, boy, the whole place was bedlam. Students are throwing stuff out the windows as if they had won the national championship. On the Monday after one of the students staged what we called a "walkout" and nobody went to class

Right there in the fall of 1950, I met Nancy. It was a physical education class. But first she dated Charlie Kraak, my basketball teammate. But by January 1951 we were dating regularly. I was over at the TriDelt House, and I gave her my Delta Tau Delta fraternity pin. We've been together ever since. I don't think she had any idea that she was going to spend her life in a basketball gym. She's seen more games than anyone I know.

When I look back and think of myself as one of the Delts, as they called the fraternity, sometimes it seems surprising. I was kind of a maverick coming out of Terre Haute. I didn't always do what I was supposed to do, and Branch knew he was going to have to square me around. I missed some classes. I'd go downtown in Bloomington and meet those stone cutters and have a few beers. We weren't supposed to drink.

You might say I was not the perfect model for behavior. This was a little bit later, but we did have one guy on the team named Jim Schooley.

He had been an Indiana high school All-Star from Auburn, Indiana. He was a brilliant student, and we'd be sitting around and Branch would be going over things and say, "Why can't you guys be like Jim Schooley? Jim never misses a class. He's a straight-A student. He goes to church on Sunday. Why can't you be like Jim Schooley?" And he preached that all of the time.

Well, one time we traveled to Wisconsin for a Big Ten game and after the game Branch took us to this famous steak house in Madison that was owned by seven brothers. We won the game and here we were in this fancy steak house, white tablecloths and the whole ball of wax. It was a very well-known steak house.

The next morning we were leaving to go back to Bloomington, and we came down from our rooms ready to go. We all carried a team player's bag with our uniforms and personal stuff in it. The equipment manager did not carry that stuff. Branch lined us up and said, "Set your bags down in front of you." Then he launched into this speech. "I'm going to tell you something," he said. "Last night somebody took six of those pearl-handled steak knives out of that restaurant. Does anybody want to raise their hand and admit who took it?" Nobody raised their hand. So he went man-to-man, just like an inspection in the army. He stopped and opened up everyone's bag, looked in, and said, "Okay, you're okay." Boom, boom, boom, one player after the other. He got to me, and I knew when he looked me in the eye, he thought I was the guy. He opened up my bag, and I wasn't the guy. But two guys down the line there was Jim Schooley, and Branch opened the bag and there were those steak knives in Jim Schooley's bag. We never had to hear about perfect Jim Schooley again.

But Schooley truly was a terrific guy. He went on to Washington, D.C., and headed up the Department of Weights and Measures.

One of the key players when we were freshmen was someone who wasn't with us anymore by the time we went on to varsity. My back-court partner was Sammy Esposito. Sammy was a heck of an athlete. We were roommates and very good friends, too. Sammy and I used to play one-on-one all the time, and he was a heck of a defensive player. Playing against him helped my game.

By the time our junior year started, though, he was gone. He was signed by the Chicago White Sox for a $50,000 bonus. He was in the major leagues by the time he was 21, and he made his career in professional baseball. Sam spent 10 years in the majors as an infielder, and he was on that 1959 White Sox team that won the pennant. Later he was the baseball coach at North Carolina State for a long time, 21 years, and I think he is in their athletic Hall of Fame.

Sammy was a great guy, and he was an assistant basketball coach for North Carolina State, too, I think in the 1970s when they had David Thompson. Actually, about as soon as Sammy broke in with the White Sox, he was drafted into the army. We were the starting guards on the varsity as sophomores.

CHAPTER 4

PLAYING FOR INDIANA

From the first time Nancy watched Bobby Leonard play basketball, she was able to recognize that he was a pretty good player. But there was a big jump from being a member of the freshman team to being a member of the varsity. She is much more knowledgeable about basketball now than she was as an undergraduate at Indiana University when she was worried that Bobby wasn't good enough to make the varsity squad as a sophomore and that he would become very depressed if he did not.

"I actually talked to my father about it," she said. "I wanted to know what to do if Bob went out for the team and he didn't make it. I thought, *He's going to be crushed. How can I help him deal with that?* I don't remember what my dad said, but I remember that being a big concern for me. It worked out."

It worked out because Bobby Leonard was a very good basketball player, easily good enough to make the team, and he soon became a star for the Hoosiers in Big Ten and national play.

"He did very well," Nancy said.

Nancy also did her part. She went to all of the games with her friend and TriDelt roommate, Marge Eckrich, and because there was competition for the best seats among the students, they had to get there early. But it also became a superstition that they had to sit in the same place every home game so the team would win and Bobby and Marge's boyfriend, Dick Farley, would play well.

"You had to get there right when the doors opened," Nancy said. "We had to sit in the same seats. That was the superstition. I always wore the same outfit, too."

After the brief flurry of worry about what kind of guy Bob really was, Nancy came to a conclusion that he was a pretty solid person. "He was very quiet," she said. "I was very comfortable with him. He was very nice. We talked a lot."

One of the friends Bob Leonard made in college who was involved with the IU basketball team but not as a player was Bobby Howard. Howard, along with John Heiney and Don DeFur, was one of student managers.

Howard said Leonard was the Hoosiers' leader in almost every way, on the court, in practice, and in huddles. He saw the team dynamics up close every season for several years, and one of his jobs was to handle the whistle in scrimmages.

"I refereed the practices for four years," Howard said.

What he observed was player interaction, and Leonard was always in the middle of things, the extension of coach Branch McCracken on the floor.

"One reason Bob was so good at shooting foul shots was that he practiced 100 free throws every day at practice," Howard said. "Leonard was the leader. When he spoke up, everyone listened to him. I remember one game there were about 19 seconds to go and we were a point down, and there was Leonard diagramming how he should take the last shot."

However, because freshmen were not eligible to play varsity at the time, Leonard's first basketball competition for IU was played not for Branch McCracken, the man who recruited him, but for assistant coach Lou Watson. Watson was from Jeffersonville, Indiana, and he had played for IU. Later, after McCracken retired, Watson started with the 1965–66 season and coached the Hoosiers most of the stretch between 1966–71. He died in May 2012 at age 88.

BOBBY LEONARD

Until the official start of practice under Lou Watson, all of us were able to go to the old men's gym and shoot, play two-on-two or three-on-three. There were maybe 10 baskets in that gym, and that was sort of our pre-season conditioning.

Lou was a tough guy. He survived the second wave at Normandy, the D-Day invasion. He was tough, but he was a great guy. The freshmen players were Sammy Esposito, Lou Scott, and Ron Taylor, from Chicago; Charlie Kraak from Collinsville, Illinois; Jim DeaKyne from Fortville; Goethe Chambers from Union City; Jackie Wright from New Castle; Junior Phipps from Kokomo; Otto Case from Jeffersonville; Dick Farley from Winslow; and me. We didn't even have a full freshman-squad schedule. We just played intra-squad games in those days.

Sometimes we played before the varsity in the big gym, and we would fill out the team with walk-ons in order to scrimmage before the varsity game. At one point that season, IU was ranked No. 3 in the country. They had Billy Garrett from Shelbyville, who was almost the first black player in the Big Ten. They had a good ballclub and Branch, who had never taken a freshman team down to scrimmage against the varsity on the big floor, said to Lou, "Why don't you bring those kids down here and let them scrimmage against the varsity?" We went down there to play, and after the first quarter we had them down. Branch told Lou, "Take those kids back upstairs." He didn't want us to embarrass the varsity.

Nancy started watching me play that year, and she watched me play all the time in all the years afterward. My goodness gracious, she was there all the way through the games at IU, the games when I was playing in the pro leagues, and all the games that I coached.

They didn't bring that many guys in, and not every guy went on to play for the varsity. Jim Schooley admitted that he took those steak knives, and then the issue kind of faded. Coach McCracken did not throw him off the team, but he didn't talk to us about being like Jim Schooley anymore. Schooley played on the varsity, but he didn't play much. He was one of those fan favorites who got into the game for a minute or two of a game when we were way ahead. Of course, they would cheer for him when he got a basket. They thought that was great.

We could have used Sammy Esposito after our sophomore year, but we were good anyway. Burke Scott moved into Sammy's spot and averaged 8.2 points a game.

Freshman year was pretty strange because we only played intra-squad games. It was all practice. But if you love the game, at least you had competition. You couldn't play varsity ball, and that was it. So you had to practice and play intra-squad games. That was all. That's the way it had been. I know you were chomping at the bit to be able to play. To compare it to now when freshmen do play varsity for us it was as if we all red-shirted.

One thing that was really worthwhile for us was playing together and against one another every day. That's how we got used to each other's moves. We were inseparable right from the beginning. Dick Farley and I were especially close. He married Marge Eckrich, Nancy's friend. Her family owned Eckrich Meat Packing. It changed his life. I was the best man at his wedding, and he was the best man at mine. But he died when he was only 37 years old.

Our senior year, Dick and I played in the Indiana-Kentucky All-Star game, and at that time we were invited to lunch at the Eckrich cottage. We thought we were going to a casual cookout and on the way we stopped and bought some hamburgers and potato chips. We rang the bell and were holding our grocery sacks when a butler opened the door. I wished we'd left those sacks in the car. Lunch was roast duck *foie gras*.

Although we may have only practiced together as freshmen, Lou Watson had played for Branch and he knew what kind of player Branch wanted. Lou helped teach us what we were going to have to know the next year with the varsity.

They were very close and if anything ever came up Lou would let Branch know what was going on. Branch always knew what was going on with his players anyway. He had informants, just like the time I got caught playing poker. Branch also had a license plate on his car that was 807. That was the whole plate. It was for his address at 807 South High Street. If you were downtown or someplace you shouldn't have been and you saw the car with that number parked somewhere, you knew you had to be careful. He had a Mercury, and most of the time you would recognize the car before the plate, but one of his old teammates, Jim Strickland, lived in Indianapolis and he had a Lincoln Mercury dealership. Sometimes he would get a new car from him.

It was a little bit of a change moving from Terre Haute to Bloomington. Terre Haute was a factory town, and Bloomington was a college town. Terre Haute was bigger, but I liked Bloomington. One thing that was interesting—and people still ask me this today—was being asked, "Are you from the South?" My mom being from Glasgow, Kentucky, I think gave me a kind of southern pitch in my voice.

Bloomington is also near Brown County. Brown County State Park is the biggest state park in Indiana. It's all country there, very pretty country. One of the big things that people do in the fall is come from all over to look at the fall foliage as the leaves change colors. It was always nice to go over there.

Just before my sophomore season started—we were finally going to get to play—Branch had us working out. One thing he did was make us do a four-mile run. We ran over the meadows where the football stadium and Assembly Hall now stand. It was all forest at the time. It was part of conditioning. We also had a free throw shooting contest that went on for a while. We shot 100 free throws a day and one of the managers, Bobby Howard, would rebound for us. He kept track of how many you made.

After a while they totaled up all of the free throws you made, and the top three guys got a reward. I was one of the top three, and Branch and his wife, Mary Jo, took us to the Nashville House in Brown County, which was famous for its chicken dinners. This was 1951 so of course it was pretty inexpensive compared to now. The dinners cost $1.75, and it was the big deal to order their chicken.

So we go over to Nashville. It is only about 20 miles or so away and we sit down for dinner at the Nashville House and Branch starts telling us about how great the chicken is, how famous it is, as they give us a menu. "This chicken dinner is superb," he said. (By the way, Nancy and I went back there a few years ago, and the restaurant was still there and they still had the chicken dinner, but it cost $18.)

While all of this was going on with Branch, I was looking at the menu. Branch was a bit of a tightwad. He didn't overdo it, but he didn't make that much money coaching at Indiana, certainly not like they make today. So we read the menu and Branch goes, "Go ahead and get yourselves a chicken dinner." The waitress came back to take our order and it went around the table and Branch and the other two guys from the team ordered the chicken dinner. It got around to being my turn and I pointed to the menu and I said, "I want that steak dinner." It cost $3.50. You should have seen the look on Branch's face. It was comical. It seems like I was always challenging him. That $3.50 seemed like an outrageous price at the time. But I got my steak dinner.

I was always a good free throw shooter. I was always good when the game was on the line, or if a steak dinner was on the line.

That was the year they changed the rule again to make freshmen eligible to play on the varsity. So the incoming group didn't have to practice upstairs in the old men's gym and miss out on a year of playing. We were sorry we had missed out on that, but it also benefited us. The reason they changed the rule that year was because of the Korean War.

The way it helped us was because Don Schlundt, Burke Scott, and Dick White were eligible to play right away as a freshman. Don was a great player, a great scorer, and he was a three-time All-American. He came out of Washington Clay High School in South Bend, and he was our big man. He was 6'9".

Don could score. He could score big-time, and he was just a heck of a shooter. He and I would go out and practice our shooting together on the big floor after regular practice. We'd play games of 21, taking all long shots from about where the three-point line is now. We took shots from about 20' and each basket was a point up to 21. It was a battle between him and me. He could shoot it from out there. That was pretty unusual for a big man at the time, and at 6'9" he was the center.

The change to make freshmen eligible in my sophomore year meant that we started all sophomores and freshmen in the 1951–52 season.

CHAPTER 5

VARSITY BREAKTHROUGH

While Nancy was worried that her boyfriend might not be good enough to make the Indiana University varsity basketball team, Bobby Leonard had no such concerns. When he returned to Bloomington after a summer in Terre Haute, it was quickly apparent that the former high school forward would be a starting guard for the Hoosiers.

Although Don Schlundt hadn't been practicing for a season with the group of freshmen that preceded him, there was no underestimating the immediate impact that he made on the team. The fact that he could play right away as a freshman was a huge advantage to the Hoosiers that season.

Schlundt was a freshman during the 1951–52 season, and he ended up being named an All-American in 1953, 1954, and 1955. He scored 2,192 points in his IU career, and that remained a school record for 32 years until Steve Alford broke it. Later, Calbert Cheaney set another new record with 2,613 points, which also remains the Big Ten mark.

When Schlundt won the Big Ten Most Valuable Player award in 1953, he became the first IU player to capture the award. Although Schlundt had the skill to shoot well from outside, he did most of his damage during games from inside and close to the basket. That first season with the varsity, when he was just getting to know his teammates, Schlundt averaged 17.1 points per game.

Branch McCracken won a very high percentage of his games at Indiana, and he coached several players who were famous in IU basketball lore, but the group that Bob Leonard came in with, plus the addition of Schlundt, showed him early on that it could accomplish great things.

McCracken had grown up on a small farm, and during his three years away from Indiana basketball during World War II, his hair turned prematurely white. McCracken had played for small Monrovia High School, and although he could be a stern taskmaster, he had a soft spot in his heart for boys like Leonard and Dick Farley who had known a certain amount of deprivation during their formative years.

It has often been said that stars do not often make good coaches because they can't identify with those less talented than they are, but McCracken, who was the star of his teams, seemed to have the knack. In *Mac's Boys*, a book focused on the Hurryin' Hoosiers, Dick White, one of Leonard's teammates, said, "He impressed us that in order to win anything one person can't do it. It has to be a team effort with all working together. Branch was a pretty big star himself, and I think that maybe he learned from that experience that you couldn't just concentrate on one or two players."

Schlundt was a tremendous offensive force, but his failings came on the defensive end. He was not as sharp as his teammates in denying ball possession and stopping his man from attacking the basket. McCracken liked to lean on experienced guards handling the ball, too, but on the 1951–52 team he was going to have to live and die with freshmen and sophomores who were better than his holdover players.

The first year they were all on the varsity together, McCracken made sure the freshmen and the sophomores knew his rules as well as the holdovers and that they got used to his habits. One aspect of pregame was the team meal where the entire Hoosiers team would gather a few hours before a contest. McCracken had very set-in-stone ideas about what the boys should eat—steak was part of the repast.

The championship Hurryin' Hoosiers were preceded on the varsity squad by Bill Garrett, who played for Indiana from 1949–51. Garrett was only the second African American to appear on a Big Ten roster and the first of star caliber. He was not always welcome at hotels when the Hoosiers went on the road, and it was generally conceded that McCracken had been pushed into his role as a barrier breaker when he allowed Garrett to come out for the team.

Anyone employing the jump shot as a weapon as far back as the late 1940s was still a rarity in basketball. Leonard was one of those rare ones. He could jump and shoot with accuracy, and he was not discouraged from doing so by his coach. McCracken was a disciple of this change in the game and didn't resist it the way some other coaches did who thought it was a reckless approach to offense. However, Leonard also used a two-hand set shot from greater distances such as 30'.

"Bob would practice shooting alone," Howard said. "He would count down the clock, '5, 4, 3, 2, 1' and then shoot from anywhere he was on the floor."

BOBBY LEONARD

When we moved into our sophomore years to play, we were the core of the team, but there were some leftover upperclassmen, juniors and seniors. There were a number of them, and they helped us along. We were young at that stage, and although we probably thought we knew it all, they still helped us.

We had Bobby Masters, who had been an Indiana Mr. Basketball in high school. There was Sammy Miranda from over in Illinois. And we had Tony Hill from Seymour. His real name was Sherman, but he went by Tony.

I don't know what Branch said to other teams, but early on he did tell us we could be good. I think he knew that we were a special group. He worked us very hard. The practices were brutal. You know, they talk about Bob Knight, who was an excellent coach, and tough, but Branch's practices and approaches were tougher than nails. We got better under him.

The Big Ten had been around for a long time, but it was changing around that time. The scheduling plan changed, I believe in 1953, where for the first time you played everybody else twice. There were 18 league games. That meant our schedule was pretty tough. Sophomore year was an important learning year. As freshmen we had only scrimmaged, and now we were playing a lot of the best teams in the country.

While I was in school Iowa was good, Minnesota was good, and Illinois was the big challenge. Those three teams were our biggest challenges in the Big Ten.

One reason Illinois was so good was because they had Johnny Kerr at center. Johnny and I became very good friends later when he was broadcasting for the Chicago Bulls and I was doing the Pacers. Johnny was about the same height as Don Schlundt, both around 6'9". Johnny was a great pro player and that year, our sophomore year, 1952, he led Illinois to the NCAA Final Four.

Our style was to feed the ball into the low post to Schlundt. Why not? The guy could really score. He had all kinds of inside moves, and we concentrated on getting the ball inside. Don could have played in the NBA, but he had an insurance business going while he was still in college. He was also already married and the insurance thing was doing real well, so he never chose to pursue pro ball. He definitely could have played. He was a scoring machine. You know, people ask me how good Don Schlundt was and I tell them, "Johnny Kerr played 12 years in the NBA, and Don outscored him every time we played them in college."

The older guys like Masters and Hill and Miranda educated us somewhat about what it was like to play at all of the locations they had visited already. They taught us the ropes. They had already been there.

Right now the Big Ten may be the best league in the country, and although college basketball is very different than it was, the Big Ten was still one of the best leagues back then, too. The thing that is so different is the importance placed on qualifying for the NCAA tournament. Now they take 68 teams with at-large teams, and there may be five or six teams in the tournament from the Big Ten. Not then. You had to win the Big Ten title to get invited to the NCAA tournament. They didn't take second-place teams, and they didn't take more than one team from a league.

I think expanding the tournament and having so many teams is great. March Madness is great. But when we played, you had to win the conference to even get in. That certainly made winning the league more important than it is now. If you didn't win the league, your season was over. Now you can be playing again the next weekend. I think Indiana made winning the Big Ten regular season a goal this year (2013). For us it was always a goal. There was no Big Ten tournament, either.

Some of the same teams that are strong now were strong then. The Southeastern Conference was always good. Kentucky, coached by Adolph Rupp, was always good. The SEC also had Louisiana State with Bob Pettit, who may be the greatest underrated player of all time. The best team in the Pac-10 at the time was the University of Washington. Kansas is good now and it was good then. They may be in the Big 12 now, but I don't remember what their league was called then. They've changed it a few times. Basically, the NCAA took champions from about 16 conferences and some independents. DePaul and Notre Dame were the top independent teams at the time.

In 1952, Kansas won it. The coach was the famous Phog Allen. That team had Clyde Lovellette on it. He could have been with us in Indiana, but if he was I'm pretty sure that we wouldn't have had Don Schlundt, too.

I got better every year that I played, but as a sophomore the scouting report on me would have been that I played good defense. That was the tennis helping me with the lateral movement, and the report would have said that I could shoot from pretty far outside. We played a lot of full-court pressure, so you're playing all over a guy all the time. I was a good defender because I was quick. I did the same things in college I did in high school, but I got better at doing all of them as I went along. Sophomore year I won the Balfour Award for being the Most Valuable Player on the IU team.

One thing I've always believed in as far as playing offense is that you have got to be a threat from the outside so they come out and cover you. Then you develop the medium game from 16', however you can get the shot off. And you've got to be able to take the ball strong to the hoop. And I could do all three of those things in college. A lot of times when I drove to the hoop and they dropped off on me, I fed the ball to Don.

It's funny that everybody thinks about the three-point line as being so far from the basket, but when I was playing I took a lot of 30-footers. Those weren't jump shots. They were set shots, mostly two-hand set shots. Way out there I was holding the ball with two hands to shoot.

We had some extremely tough games against Illinois. My sophomore year, when they went to the Final Four, they beat us 78–66 when they were ranked second in the country and 77–70 when they were ranked sixth. The next year we beat them 74–70 in two overtimes in Bloomington, and then we went to Champaign-Urbana to play them at the old Huff Gym.

It was a road game for the Big Ten championship. We could win the championship if we beat them because Illinois was a game behind us. Everybody made a huge contribution.

Johnny Kerr was the center. They had some good players like Irv Bemoras and Jimmy Bredar, and Harry Combes was the coach. Huff Gym was a tough place to play. The seating put the fans right down on top of you, and they were on me from the start of the game, yelling things at me. They knew that I could hurt them with my outside shot. They were on me from the opening tip, and then I missed my first shot. Boy, they were going wild then. But then I hit seven shots in a row. I shut them up. It might have been the greatest game we ever played. We beat Illinois over there 91–79, beat them by 12 on that floor. It was the best team game all the way around that we ever played while I was at Indiana.

I always admired Johnny Kerr's ability, and we became great friends later when we were both broadcasting in the NBA. One time a few years ago we were sitting at the same table in the press room at the United

Center, talking about old times. We played in the East-West College All-Star game together, and we talked about that and all the games between Illinois and Indiana, which were such great games, and life in the pros. I just had a feeling something was wrong with him, and he died a few days later. That was in 2009. Johnny was a special guy.

When I was in college, we got $65 a month from the school. That was for our room and board. Then you had to wait tables for a job. I did that at the fraternity house where I lived, and that got me $95 a month. We had a house father. His name was Lee Ford, and he was the greatest of guys. He made sure that we kept the house in top shape. All of the guys in the fraternity, especially the pledges, had to clean. Anyway, we used to have card games down in the basement. We played a game called Red Dog. Another name for that game is In Between. You get two cards. The best hand you could have is an ace and a deuce. You try to get in between your two cards. If you got a card that matched one of yours, you had to match the pot and some of those pots got pretty big.

One night I was really lucky, and I was winning. There was a young kid on a baseball scholarship from Peoria, Illinois, and he kept borrowing money from me. Pretty soon he owed me about $700 or $800, which was quite a bit at the time. When the game ended, Howard—that was his name—said, "I can't pay you all this at once, but I'll pay you." I said, "Howard, why don't you just forget about paying me at all. I'll tell you what I'll do. You work in the kitchen for the next two years, and I'll call the debt even." We were sophomores at the time. So I never had to work in the kitchen. I'd be in the dining room with the big boys, sitting down at the table at night with a coat and tie on, and Howard was waiting tables. That was wheeling and dealing.

From the time I started playing varsity in college, I believe I was a player who thought like a coach. Life was interesting. I had a serious girlfriend. I was playing for the Indiana Hoosiers. I was working toward a degree. And I was very much part of a good team, a winning team. Branch's team the year before we moved onto the varsity went 19–3. My sophomore year we finished 16–6, but we were all young and improving and we thought we had a lot of talent and could do something special at IU.

The old cliché is that the point guard is the extension of the coach on the floor. I was Branch's guy on the floor. Branch knew it. That's why I became captain as a junior. I was the floor leader. Branch and I had a great relationship.

Our home gym in those days was quite a bit different from Assembly Hall. The old IU Fieldhouse was where we played. It had an elevated floor. The court was above a dirt floor. The football team practiced in there when there was bad weather during the football season. They had batting cages up in there when it was baseball season. It was very much a fieldhouse. There weren't that many schools that had fieldhouses. Purdue had one. That's where we played our home games. We packed them in, standing room only. The official capacity was 8,000, but we got more than that—maybe near 11,000 at times.

Basketball was always big at IU, and the fans were always passionate. From 60 years ago to now, it's never changed. The tradition has always been there. The Hoosiers didn't win a championship when Branch played, but they won the first one with him coaching in 1940. He was a very young coach at that time, but after that the fans were always passionate. He had coached at Ball State. His wife, Mary Jo, was the daughter of the president of Ball State.

The first NCAA tournament was played in 1939, and IU won the second one. You know how they take five, six, or even seven teams from the Big Ten in the tournament now? Branch's IU teams finished second in the Big Ten many, many times, but they couldn't go to the tournament. I think if the tournament then had been like it is now, one of those ball clubs might have slipped in and won it all.

Basketball was always big in Indiana. The sport was invented in Springfield, Massachusetts, with Dr. James Naismith, and they started playing high school championships in Indiana in 1911. So Indiana basketball tradition goes way back. You know what's funny? As much as I loved basketball, there was a time when I knew the name of every single Indiana state basketball championship team. I couldn't do it today, though. I could go right down the line and name them. I can still name several of them from back then. I knew the history of Indiana high school basketball.

Some might say that IU tradition started in 1940 with that first NCAA championship, but I know they were playing before that because guys who had played before that 1940 title would come to our games.

IU won the NCAA title in 1940, but the Japanese bombed Pearl Harbor in 1941 and so many things changed. There was a stretch there of four or five years when so many guys went into the military that life became very different for people.

When I was in high school from 1946–50, basketball was just a way of life. It wasn't just me. Kids had dreams of playing for their high school team, of playing for IU, of playing college ball. That's why in the dead of winter you'd see them out in the alley, out in the barnyard, snow all over the place, or shoveling snow off the court so they could shoot hoops. That was Indiana.

There has always been a special relationship between basketball and Indiana, no question about it. When the rest of the country wasn't playing the game that much, they were playing it in Indiana. Branch helped make it special at IU. In the 25 years he coached, they were always in it. They were always in it with a chance to win the Big Ten title and even a national championship. We got us a couple. And then Bobby Knight came.

After Dr. Naismith worked at that YMCA in Massachusetts and invented basketball in 1891, he worked some other places, including coaching at Kansas. He founded the basketball team at Kansas. But one time during the 1930s, before he died at the end of the decade, he came to Indiana and watched the high school tournament. During his visit he said something like, "This is what I always had in mind. I may have invented the rules, but Indiana is the one that put everything into play."

53

CHAPTER 6

NATIONAL CHAMPS

The Indiana Hoosiers won their second NCAA basketball championship in 1953 with Branch McCracken as coach, junior Bob Leonard as captain, and Don Schlundt as leading scorer. The team finished 23–3 and defeated defending champion Kansas 69–68 in the title game.

One reason that the Hoosiers were able to win the national championship, according to Nancy Leonard, is that she wore her lucky pajamas. Superstition was definitely involved as Indiana worked its way to the title game.

"We won the national title because I sat on my bed in one spot and wore a certain pair of pajamas," Nancy said. Clearly, it was a team effort.

The Hoosiers were the best team in college basketball that year, and that's something that stays with players forever. For most NCAA champions it's a once-in-a-lifetime experience because so few teams repeat. After the passage of 60 years, the list of surviving members of the Hurryin' Hoosiers is also shrinking, with those still around in their eighties.

One member of that IU championship team is Paul Poff from New Albany, Indiana, who was a backup player as the Hoosiers swept to the crown.

"It was not only a thrill to be on a team that won it," Poff said, "but it's something you never forget. It is something that sticks with you. It does, believe me. It's a thrill even when you're not on the first five."

Poff said he remembers first encountering Bobby Leonard when they were playing Indiana high school ball, but they grew close as teammates.

Leonard was a team leader and key player and always came through with some kind of play to help IU win.

"He was not only a great player," Poff said, "but he was a great friend. He was a year or two older than me. We beat them in high school. With IU, Bob and Don Schlundt were such great scorers. Bob had the confidence regardless of who we were playing.... He always felt we were the better team. He's one of IU's best."

Poff always felt Leonard was generous with his knowledge, too, and he tried to help the backups improve and make them better players. It's something that Poff appreciated and has never forgotten.

"He always took the time to help you, even if you were just a sub," Poff said.

The Hoosiers of the 1952–53 season were particularly close. They were friends on and off the court, and many of them stayed close for years after the triumph. In the book *Mac's Boys*, one player, Ron Taylor, summarized that. "It's really teams that win," Taylor said, "and that team had great chemistry. There weren't any jealousies that I ever saw or that I ever heard of. We just wanted to play basketball and do well."

Burke Scott, one of those Hoosiers, confirmed the tight nature of the group, though Leonard was usually out front. "Bobby was an excellent leader," Scott said. "Everybody respected him. I think we respected each other right down the line, all of the players and coaches. It was a thrill to win, it and it still is. When we won the NCAA title, it seemed it was for the students and adults, but now everybody goes. Everyone just loves it now."

Much like Leonard, Scott was blown away by the public reception when the team got home after the championship. "It seemed as if there were 50,000 people out in the streets in Bloomington," he said. "They were hanging on telephone poles and monuments."

On their way to the title, as a necessary step to be invited to the NCAA tournament, the Hoosiers captured the Big Ten title. By the end of the regular season, they were also ranked No. 1 in the nation in the polls. The 6'9" Schlundt was a far superior player than he had been as a freshman star, averaging 25.4 points per game and earning his first All-American honors. Leonard also received All-American honors and was first-team All-Big Ten.

Howard remembers in a game against the University of Minnesota that was close, Leonard took charge with his outside shooting. "He took three dribbles and was across the center line and swish," Howard said. "It was the two-hand set shot. The crowd would boo, and it wouldn't matter."

Being on an NCAA championship team, especially one with a famous nickname like the Hurryin' Hoosiers, was something to be savored. The irony of IU winning the NCAA title that year was that the Hoosiers began the season 1–2. They lost to Notre Dame by one point, and they lost to Kansas State by two points. After that shaky start, Indiana went from December to March without losing again. The Hoosiers finished 17–1 in Big Ten play because of a March 7 loss by two points at Minnesota. All three defeats were determined by a basket or less.

At the time, the NCAA tournament consisted of a West bracket and an East bracket. IU was sent to the East side of the draw and met DePaul in its opening game. The Hoosiers prevailed 82–80 in Chicago, which is DePaul's home. Next, Indiana lined up against Notre Dame for a rematch. This time IU won 79–66.

That was enough to send the Hoosiers to the Final Four in Kansas City where their semifinal opponent was Louisiana State, featuring Bob Pettit. Indiana won 80–67. The Championship Game was played on March 18 against Kansas, and the contest came down to the last minute.

The score was tied 68–68, and it was Indiana's ball. Leonard made the pass-in to Schlundt, who passed it back to him. Leonard faked a shot on the perimeter and drove to the hoop. As he released the ball for a layup, Leonard was fouled, giving him two shots. The man guarding Leonard who fouled him was the captain of the Jayhawks and a player who would earn much greater fame later. Dean Smith was a guard for Kansas, but at one point he held the record for the most games won by an NCAA Division I basketball coach. While coaching North Carolina for 36 years, Smith won 879 games, lost 254, and won two NCAA titles.

There were 27 seconds left on the game clock when Leonard stepped to the foul line with a chance to win the national championship.

BOBBY LEONARD

My layup fell out, so I went to the free throw line. I knew how much time was left. I never spent a lot of time dribbling the ball or waiting at the free throw line. When the referee gave me the ball, I shot it pretty quickly. That was the way Branch wanted us to do it, too. I threw the first shot up and it didn't go. It fell out.

Kansas coach Phog Allen called time out. He was really trying to freeze me out. We came back out on the court, and I made the second one. So now we were up by a point with 27 seconds to play. That's plenty of time for a team to score. We put on the full-court pressure defensively. Dean Smith was out there, but I wasn't covering him. I can't think of who it was. We all matched up, and we sealed off their offense. They got off a desperation shot at the gun from the right-hand corner. A substitute took it because one of their starters had fouled out.

We had been beaten at the gun a few times that year by desperation shots, and when they took that shot I was afraid it was going to happen again. I just put my hands over my head. But the shot missed. I looked up and I saw that Dick White from Terre Haute, our sixth man, got the rebound and the game was over.

Branch talked to the press after we won and told them that he knew I was going to make the winning free throw because I had "ice water in my veins." Then the reporters came over to me and told me what he said. I said, "It sure felt awfully warm when it was running down my leg."

I was definitely relieved when that Kansas shot missed. That was a period of time when college basketball played four 10-minute quarters for a little while. At the end of the third quarter against Kansas, Burke

Scott got the ball to me and I went right across the midcourt line, took a shot, and made it. That put us up one going into the fourth quarter. It was a battle the rest of the way.

The clock was running down when I drove to the hoop and Smith fouled me. That ball hung on the rim. Had I made that baby, then the ball game's over because they didn't have the three-point shot them. But my free throw stood up, and we won.

It was great. That's what you play for, to play for championships, to win championships. We had a lot of fans out there, so there was a lot of jubilation in the stands. The Kansas City Municipal Auditorium was such a new building that the showers weren't ready to be used. So we didn't even get changed there. We went into the locker room, put on our sweat clothes over our uniforms. Everybody was hugging everyone and all of that kind of whooping-it-up stuff.

Our hotel was only a block from the auditorium and we were walking back. The streets were just jammed with people. They were drinking beer and yelling and celebrating. We walked back through the crowd to our hotel, and Branch had a dinner for us there after we got cleaned up.

Winning a championship is a wonderful feeling. As long as I've been around sports, junior high, high school, college, pro games, sportsmanship is taken for granted. That's a given. You should always be a good sport. But the only thing is the three-letter word, W-I-N. W-I-N, that's it. I believe that's what Vince Lombardi said, and that's the way it is. Sports are about winning.

You go out there to a Little League game and the parents are screaming for their kids to win. High school tournaments, college tournaments, playoffs in the pros...it's about winning. Winning is all there is. Losing is misery when you're playing a sport that you love.

So many times, too, there is such a thin margin between winning and losing. Look at our games in the early rounds of the NCAAs where we beat DePaul by two points and had to play Notre Dame again, a team that beat us early in the year. Those games were in Chicago, too. Chicago was DePaul's home, and Notre Dame is only 90 miles from Chicago. Both teams have huge followings there. Notre Dame got a lot of players from Chicago, so it was really like it was a home game for both of them. It was bedlam in Chicago Stadium.

They put 22,000 fans in there that night against Notre Dame, and it was wild. Don Schlundt scored 41 points on them. He had several of them, but that was one of Don's big ball games. Don just annihilated them. DePaul and Notre Dame had some very good players. One of Notre Dame's players was Dick Rosenthal, who became athletic director there. Dick's a good friend of mine. I don't think we played quite as well as we did against Illinois that time, but it was right there as one of our best games. We won the game by 13 to get to the Final Four.

We didn't play nearly as many games in a season in those days. We started the season with a game on December 1. Now they start playing in mid-November. They play those holiday tournaments around Thanksgiving and Christmas, too, with extra games. We played 26 games, counting four NCAA tournament games. A lot of teams now play 36 or even 40 games. Take away the NCAA games and that's 22. We played 18 Big Ten games, so we had only four non-conference games. We played Valparaiso, Notre Dame, and Kansas State to start the season, and we lost two of those games at the wire. We lost to Kansas State on a last-second shot from midcourt.

We also played Butler in the middle of the year and beat them 105–70. They had the Hoosier Classic back then with Indiana, Butler, Purdue, and Notre Dame. It went away for a while and they just brought it back within the last couple of years. The games were at Hinkle Fieldhouse, though that was before it was named for Butler coach Tony Hinkle. It was Butler Fieldhouse at the time since Hinkle was still coaching.

You couldn't get a ticket. You could not get a ticket to that thing. It's Friday and Saturday night and it is wild. All the Indiana kids were home from school for vacation for Christmas, and they had a ball.

We didn't play nearly as many non-conference games as teams do today, but the teams we played were good. Then we won our first 16 games in the Big Ten. We were 16–0 when we went to Minnesota and lost that game. Chuck Mencel beat us on a last-second shot, just like the other games we lost that year. It was probably the best thing that could have happened to us. That was our only league loss, and we finished 17–1 in the Big Ten, but more importantly, it woke us up. By then we thought we were pretty good. We were getting overconfident. The loss to Minnesota was shortly before the NCAA tournament.

When you get into March, when you get into the tournament, some crazy things happen. There are always upsets and that type of thing, so it's a tough row to hoe to win that baby.

You know what? On the night we won the championship, when we got back to the hotel in Kansas City, we got a phone call from Sammy Esposito to congratulate us. He was in the army and stationed in Washington. He called to talk to us. He knew he had missed out on something, but he did well for himself in his baseball career. He and I could have been the starting guards together. But he congratulated us, and that was nice.

We won the Big Ten championship that year and that was special, but there was nothing like winning the national championship. You're the best team in the country. We spent the night after the game in the hotel in Kansas City, and then we flew home. We stopped at Terre Haute, and there were a lot of people at the airport. I don't know how they knew that we were going to land there for a few minutes. Then we flew into Indianapolis and rode a bus to Bloomington. When the bus got as far as Martinsville, which is 18 miles from Bloomington, there were people lining the road with cars to honk at us and wave. It was 18 miles of cars all of the way into Bloomington. When we got to Bloomington, it was bedlam, just bedlam.

Later we had a banquet in Bloomington, and the Chicago sportscaster Jack Brickhouse was the speaker.

When you win the top championship available to you in your life, in any sport with a team, and especially something like the NCAA basketball championship, there is something about it that stays with you for a lifetime. It really is forever. It's very true. It's often said that if you walk through that tunnel to the arena accompanied by teammates with all of that pressure for a national championship game, there's a camaraderie that makes you friends for life. The Baltimore Ravens came out of that tunnel together and beat the San Francisco 49ers and they won the Super Bowl. They'll never forget each other. That's the way it is.

If we got out a list of NCAA champions right now, we would be able to find it right away—Indiana, 1953. It's a long time ago, but it's always there. It's history. It doesn't go away. It's still history. That is the pinnacle in college basketball.

I have stayed in touch with the other players over the years. Sometimes we talk on the phone or see each other at special events. We're aware of where we are, anyway. After this long, several of the players have passed away. Don Schlundt died young. He was only 52. And as I said, Dick Farley was only 37.

Dick and Marge had five children and were living in Fort Wayne. He got cancer and died. It just broke my heart. I still think about him all of the time.

I think about being part of that team a lot, too, but especially in March when the NCAA tournament is going on. It was a long time ago when my Indiana team won it all, but what I think about when I see March Madness on TV and what's going on in the tournament is that those players are going through the same thing we did. Indiana has also been great to us, great at remembering us. They've had us back and treated us special. They remember us and take note on special anniversaries.

It's hard to believe that it's been 60 years since we won that thing. The university totally goes out of its way for us. They make 80-year-olds feel like they can still play. The current coach, Tom Crean, is doing good things. When he came in, the program was in tough shape with all kinds of problems, losing players, losing games, and NCAA probation. It was in tough shape, and he has brought it all of the way back. I'd love to see him win an NCAA championship. He very well might.

I was back there for an anniversary event, and I spoke to Fred Glass, the athletic director. Before Nancy and I left I said to him, "You know, Fred, the university is just the way we left it. Great people, very caring. They loved us, and we loved them. They've got a different gym than we played in, but they do have the Branch McCracken Court in there."

CHAPTER 7

GOING FOR
TWO IN A ROW

Most of the key players from the NCAA championship team of 1953 returned for the 1953–54 season as seniors, although center Don Schlundt, at that point a two-time All-American, was still only a junior.

Schlundt averaged 24.3 points a game, and Bob Leonard continued to average around 15.5 points a game. One thing changed dramatically in scheduling. There were just 14 Big Ten games for the Hoosiers and a significantly larger amount of non-conference games on the schedule.

Indiana won its second straight Big Ten title with a 12–2 mark and finished its season with a 20–4 record. After the high of winning the 1953 championship, the Hoosiers felt they should be able to capture a second straight national crown. That was definitely the goal.

The more exotic schedule had the Hoosiers facing Cincinnati, Montana State, Oregon State, and Louisville in non-conference games as fresh faces, in addition to Butler, Kansas State, and Notre Dame in non–Big Ten play.

"We all thought that Indiana was going to win the NCAA championship again the next year, Bob's senior year," Nancy Leonard said, "but it didn't happen. They didn't do it."

The Hoosiers won their first six games before dropping an encounter with Oregon State. Then they ripped off another nine wins in a row. On their way to clinching the Big Ten championship, the Hoosiers lost games to Northwestern and Iowa but won the rest of their league games.

Winning the league title propelled IU into the NCAA tournament again. The Hoosiers were sent to Iowa City to meet Notre Dame in the opening round. This turned out to be another in the series of exceptionally close, tense games the two Indiana-based schools engaged in during that time period. This time the Fighting Irish scrambled to a 65–64 victory that was crushing to IU.

In those days even teams in regionals played consolation games, so IU's season wasn't over. Indiana played Louisiana State and won 73–62, but that win provided little consolation whatsoever.

Sometime later, after Burke Scott had served time in the army but hadn't yet finished his degree, he returned to campus and met with Branch McCracken about obtaining some scholarship money to complete school. During the course of the conversation, according to Scott, McCracken began talking about the missed opportunity in the NCAA tournament the year following the championship season. It was easy to tell he was still haunted by the one-point loss, and he second-guessed his own strategy in the loss to Notre Dame.

"He said that he should have moved Don Schlundt outside where they would have had to cover him," Scott said. "Don was just so smooth. He gave big men an awful time because he was a tremendous shooter. Branch thought he should have switched Don and Dick Farley and put Farley inside and that if he had we would have won. No one came up with that idea at the time. Branch thought the Notre Dame defense would have followed Don, and we would have had more room underneath."

BOBBY LEONARD

Our attitude going into my senior year, no question about it, was a mood of believing we could win the NCAA title again. Why not? We had just about everybody back. That was the thinking.

We did find out that being the defending national champion wasn't easy. Everybody's trying to knock you off. We got through the preseason undefeated, but once we got into the Big Ten season we had some great ball games. We won a lot of games, but we were definitely a target. There were some games that went down to the last shot with Michigan, Wisconsin, and Michigan State.

The Big Ten was always good competition, and even on the teams that weren't that good there was always a good player you had to watch out for and be prepared for.

Ohio State had a fellow by the name of Paul Ebert. He was an All-American and a very good baseball pitcher. He turned out to be one of the top surgeons in the country, and I saw a half-hour documentary on him. He was All-Big Ten, and he made some of the Chuck Taylor All-Star teams like I did. They had another guy named Robin Freeman, and he was very, very tough. Ebert set the Ohio State scoring record and then Freeman broke it.

You go over to Iowa and they had Deacon Davis, who later joined the Harlem Globetrotters, and Carl Cain, who won a gold medal as part of the United States Olympic basketball team in 1956. You get up to Minnesota, and they had Dick Garmaker, who I later played with on the Minneapolis Lakers, and he became an All-American, and Ed Kalafat. There were actually three guys on that Gophers team that I played with, Garmaker, Kalafat, and Chuck Mencel. Michigan State had a good player in Al Ferrari, who went on to the NBA. Northwestern had a kid by the name of Larry Dellafield. He was a good one.

Purdue wasn't very good in those years [9–13 in 1953–54]. We were the Hurryin' Hoosiers because we could put points on the board fast. Purdue came into Bloomington, but even if the Boilermakers weren't very good, it was still Purdue and the IU–Purdue rivalry was the same as it is today. We were playing them for the second time that season, and their coach was Ray Eddy. He had won an Indiana state high school championship at Madison in 1950. He let it be known the day before the game what he was thinking. He came out and said, "We're going to have to play zone because we can't play these guys man-to-man." So we came out onto the court that night and, sure enough, they put in the zone.

About five minutes into the game he called time out. We had them down 21–0. Eddy looks like he's going to have to go back to man-to-man because the zone just isn't working when you're down 21–0. There was a kid on the bench from Bedford, I can't remember his name, and he piped up and said, "Hey coach, does anybody ever get skunked in this game?"

Because Purdue was such a big rival in the state, if you played on varsity teams for three years that beat Purdue every game, twice a year, Branch gave you a present. That was six wins over your rival. If you did that, he gave you a new basketball. I've still got that basketball upstairs in my closet. We beat them six straight times while I was playing varsity basketball, and the ball says, "Indiana 6, Purdue 0."

Branch's teams were already known as the Hurryin' Hoosiers before I got there, but when we won the NCAA title, that sort of solidified it. That's because Branch was already playing that fast-paced game. But we became known as the Hurryin' Hoosiers all over the country. It fit the way we played. We put on the full-court pressure that caused a lot of turnovers. Branch pounded on rebounding like you can't believe. Defense and rebounding were his game. When you came off the board with the ball, those outlet passes were there and boom, we were gone. Of course we had to be smart enough that if we didn't have the fast break to pull the ball back and run the simple half-court offense.

It was to our advantage to play fast with the type of team we had and in the type of shape we were in. We were in great condition. Playing full-court pressure gets you into great condition, and we got a lot of turnovers out of that. I mean you had to be in great condition to play that way. Branch got us ready prior to October 15 when regular season practice on the big floor started. You don't hear about the Hurryin' Hoosiers so much when people talk about Indiana basketball. I'm a little disappointed to see that go away because for a lot of years that's how IU was identified.

The most points any Indiana team scored against Purdue was my junior year, the championship year, when we beat them 113–78. After 60 years, the record still stands. Had the three-point shot existed, we would have probably scored 130!

At the beginning of my senior year we were ready to win another Big Ten title and another national championship. We felt good and we thought we had all the pieces in place and that we should keep it up. We played that way with the good start before conference, and we won the Big Ten title again.

We're off to the regional in Iowa City. Notre Dame was there. Louisiana State with Bob Pettit was there. Penn State was there. And we got upset in the first game. Notre Dame beat us.

When I say that we should have won, I really mean it. We were down by one point with time running out, the clock ticking down to zero, and I stole the ball at half-court. I went in for the layup, and I put the ball up off the backboard. It's good. And that shot puts us up by one point at the very end. Dick Rosenthal, the forward, my Notre Dame friend, is trying to recover and catch up to me before I shot, but I made it.

There was a whistle and they somehow called a foul on me. The basket was good anyway, so we were ahead by one point with no time left, but Dick was sent to the free throw line for a one-and-one. He made the first shot to tie the ball game. And he made the second shot to give them the lead. That's how it ended with no time left. There was no time for a last shot.

I made the shot to win the game, and Dick made the shot to win the game. He and I still talk about it, and we laugh about it. As I said he's a good friend. I don't believe I fouled him. As I remember it he didn't get there in time to plant himself defensively. He did not get there fast enough. There was contact, but there are pictures of the play. I had him on the side of me, not in front of me. Of course, he fell down. He flopped. But he got the call. That probably cost us a national championship.

That was a heartbreaker. We were devastated. That's your whole life. To this day, you know, really, I haven't gotten over it. I feel like we should have gone into the books with two national championships. When the buzzer sounded, it was over. Just like that. That was the end of my career. The fact is that we were good enough to win two of them. It doesn't go away. Just like you remember forever when you won a championship, losing the chance at one doesn't ever go away, either.

This was the flip side of always remembering a championship. You're in the Super Bowl, and you lose. You're in the World Series. You're in the NBA championship series. Whatever it is the championship of, you've got to win. Winning, that's the thing. The San Francisco 49ers are going to remember losing to the Baltimore Ravens. The Detroit Tigers are going to remember losing to the San Francisco Giants.

I remember going back to the hotel after losing our game in Iowa City, and it was packed with IU fans. They wanted to console us, but we didn't feel too much like mingling. Dick Farley just couldn't take it. He ran up the stairs to his room, and he had tears in his eyes. He didn't want to hang out with the fans. He was heartbroken. We all were.

The funny part of how those games turned out was that Penn State beat Louisiana State the same night we lost, and the next night Penn State beat Notre Dame. Notre Dame had one game left in their system, and they saved it for us.

That was a hard ending to my IU basketball career. It was tough. But looking back at those four years, considering everything, the choice to go to Indiana and play for Branch McCracken, two Big Ten championships, a national championship, and I met my wife there—that alone made it unbelievable. Those were the four greatest years of my life.

Nancy and I have been together for more than 60 years—married for 59—and we have five children. Not too many people can say that. So many things during those four years were special. All of the people I met, all the good people, the stone cutters, Branch, the teammates, the fraternity brothers, and of course Nancy, what a wonderful time it was. I graduated with a major in physical education, and I could have coached high school basketball. I had that type of talent. I thought of my high school coach, and I thought that would be a pretty good life to help young kids, high school kids. In the end it wasn't my cup of tea, and I went in a different direction.

Of course, I didn't know what the rest of my life was going to be like. My teammate Charlie Kraak became a career military man, and he retired as a colonel. I could very well have had a military career. I could well have been a career soldier. I was a maverick, but I think you have to be a maverick to be a career soldier. Audie Murphy, the greatest American war hero, was a maverick. If you're a career soldier, at some point in your life you're going to be in a war. I just missed the Korean War while I was in school. I'm kind of a historian on the military. I love to talk about George Patton, Dwight Eisenhower, and Douglas MacArthur. Those are some great generals. And as I said, there will never be the *esprit de corps* this country had during World War II. The people sacrificed everything for each other.

If I had anything to say to kids who are coming out of high school and going to college, if they were going to IU, to Bloomington, or to any school, I'd say go down there and make your grades. Make your grades and enjoy college life because at some point in your life you're going to look back and say, "Those were four of the greatest years I had in my life."

As great as it was, my IU basketball career ended with disappointment. We won a consolation game, but that didn't matter. For all intents, my career ended with the loss to Notre Dame. When you think of the NCAA tournament today with 68 teams in it, it means that 67 of them are going to finish the season with a loss. A lot of those players are seniors, and their last college game is going to be a loss. Not all of them could have realistically believed they were going to win the title, but I bet quite a few teams felt that way.

We definitely believed we could have won two NCAA titles in a row—should have won two in a row.

CHAPTER 8

BEING DRAFTED
AND BEING DRAFTED

For four years, Bobby Leonard's life was on a pretty predictable path. He took classes advancing him toward a degree at Indiana University. He played basketball for the Hoosiers. He spent his free time with his girlfriend, Nancy.

But almost as soon as his senior basketball season ended, Leonard's life changed dramatically. He played in a major college All-Star game known as the East-West game. He played with a group of college All-Americans on a whirlwind tour against the Harlem Globetrotters. He graduated from college, and he and Nancy got married. Then he was drafted by the National Basketball Association's Baltimore Bullets and was also drafted by the United States Army. While Leonard was in the military for two years, the Bullets folded and the Minneapolis Lakers picked him up.

"We got married on June 15, 1954, the day after graduation," Nancy said. That date had not been set in stone, but the couple looked at the number 15 as pretty much a lucky number because that was how many points per game that Leonard averaged. A number of times Nancy said to Bob before an IU game, "Play well tonight and get your 15, or something like that," she said. "So we decided that maybe we ought to get married on the 15th."

Graduation took place in Bloomington on June 14, and the wedding took place at a church in South Bend the next day. The reception, which included about 150 friends and family members, was conducted at the Erskine Park Golf Club. "If you can, imagine your parents coming all the way to Bloomington for graduation and going back on that night for a rehearsal dinner," Nancy said. "Isn't that fun?"

When Bob was graduating, he was invited to play in a college All-Star basketball game. The East-West College All-Star Game began in 1949, and it featured players from around the country who were either going on to professional basketball or professional careers in other disciplines. Leonard was the Most Valuable Player in the game.

Once the issue of remaining an amateur and preserving eligibility was put aside following his four years with IU, Leonard was selected for a team of college All-Americans that went on a 21-game swing in 26 days, playing against the world-renowned Harlem Globetrotters. Although the Globetrotters continue traveling to this day as one of the most popular entertainment groups in the universe because of the way they combine basketball and comedy, in the early 1950s the Globetrotters also participated in "serious" basketball at times. The team sometimes faced the other best teams in the United States in games where the humorous parts of the script were left out in favor of competition.

At that time in the 1950s most young American men were expected to serve two years in the army. Leonard was completing the ROTC program at Indiana and as a result was going to be able to enter the army with a lieutenant's commission. Leonard ran into some problems when he took off on the college tour against the Globetrotters, and initial indications when he returned suggested that the army was going to delay his service until the next fall, either October or November. Leonard definitely wanted to give professional basketball a try. If he waited until the fall to begin his army service and he stayed in for two years, he figured that would cut him out of three seasons of pro ball.

Leonard decided that he would rather be a professional basketball player than just about anything else. So he gave up his officer's commission and entered the army as a private right after graduation so that he could finish his military commitment in two years and be available to play in the fall of 1956.

Bob was going into the army for two years with the first year mostly for basic training. Families were not allowed during the first nine months. Nancy was fortunate as she had received an offer from Bloomington High School, and she taught high school business classes, physical education, health, and she supervised the cheerleaders.

"I was surprised that they came to me and asked me if I was interested," Nancy said. "It was funny because I wasn't much older than the high school students. It was a little bit odd with the boys in health class because there were things you definitely didn't talk about with boys. I made some good friends at the school and stayed in contact with some of them over the years."

Nancy also worked to try to modernize the cheerleaders' look and move them away from an ultra-conservative approach.

"I had to fight with the school board because I wanted to get new cheerleader outfits," Nancy said. "They had these girls in long slacks, and I kept saying, 'Look, the cheerleaders really need to look like cheerleaders.'"

For the first year of their marriage, the Leonards had to be apart. But the second year was spent at Fort Leonard Wood where Bob completed his two-year commitment. After that stretch of time, they traveled and moved everywhere together across the United States before settling permanently in Indiana.

BOBBY LEONARD

One of the fun things the IU team did after we won the NCAA title was to go on *The Ed Sullivan Show* in New York. That was a pretty cool thing to do. People now can't really comprehend how big Ed Sullivan was in those days. The whole country practically stopped to watch his show on Sunday nights in the 1950s and 1960s.

He was ahead of *The Tonight Show*. Then came Steve Allen, Jack Paar,

Johnny Carson, and Jay Leno. Ed Sullivan had all of the biggest acts from all walks of life. He had Elvis Presley on TV first. He had the Beatles on when they came to the United States. That went on for years, and it was the same for athletes. It was a big thing to be invited because Sullivan usually only had champions on the show.

Actually, sometime later I got invited to a golf tournament in Las Vegas and Elvis was playing out there. Nancy came with me. I think Elvis had been out there for several years at the time. Nancy really wanted to go see him, and I said, "I don't want to go see Elvis Presley." Well, we ended up going, and he is the greatest entertainer I've ever seen. Unbelievable.

That was much later, but Elvis had what you would call his nationwide coming-out party on *The Ed Sullivan Show*. Sullivan would say, "Tonight we have a really big show." Only he would pronounce it "shoe." He would stand there with his arms folded in a certain way if he was asking a question.

Our college All-American team was in New York for the East-West All-Star game right before joining a tour with the Harlem Globetrotters for the World Series of Basketball. We practiced in the morning then later in the day we would go out and drink beer—we were 21 by then since we were at the end of college—and eat dinner. On this one particular day at about 3:30 in the afternoon, a bunch of us went over to Jack Dempsey's Restaurant. The waiters were in tuxedos and everything. We went in there and started drinking beer and instead of running a tab, this waiter wanted us to tip him every time he brought a beer. After a while Johnny Kerr got up and said to him, "Hey, we're gonna tip you when we get through." He got on the guy, and the guy got mad at him. Then Jack Dempsey walked in. The former heavyweight champion came over to our table and said, "What's wrong, fellows?" Johnny told him and Jack Dempsey said, "Anything you want is on the house. Whatever you want to drink or eat." Then he pulled that waiter aside and told him, "Anything." Jack Dempsey. That was a pretty good one.

I was named the Most Valuable Player in the East-West All-Star game, and I was pretty proud of that. I still have the trophy in the house. Dick Farley and Charlie Kraak from IU played with me. Johnny Kerr was in the game. Al Bianchi, Frank Ramsey, Cliff Hagan, Larry Costello, Bob Pettit, Richie Guerin all played at Madison Square Garden. My team won in overtime, 103–98.

The East-West game was held on March 27, 1954, and the very next day the All-Americans began playing a bunch of games against the Harlem Globetrotters. The Globetrotters were as tough as nails in those days. The first black players were just starting to go into the NBA, so the Globetrotters had all of the best black players in the country after college. I joined the college players in the spring. I got a telephone call from Abe Saperstein, the founder of the Globetrotters, who was based in Chicago. I was at the fraternity house, and when I got the call I thought someone was putting me on. He made me an offer. Now that my college eligibility was up, I could get paid.

That was back when the Globetrotters had Goose Tatum and Ermer Robinson and Clarence Wilson, and other guys who were really, really tough. My Notre Dame friend Dick Rosenthal was one of the other guys on the college team, and we played before more than 277,000 people in those 21 games. Some of the other players were Frank Ramsey, Cliff Hagan, Bob Pettit, and Frank Selvy. They were all college All-Americans.

In the early 1950s, the Minneapolis Lakers were the first great NBA dynasty with George Mikan at center, who was later commissioner of the American Basketball Association. They had Slater Martin as a guard, and Jim Pollard and Vern Mikkelsen were great forwards. But the Globetrotters were so good at playing serious basketball that they beat the Lakers in a game.

We got per diem as the tour went on—they didn't give you your check for playing until the tour was over. We flew around on chartered flights, flying in DC-3s. The last night in the series was a game at the Los Angeles Coliseum. They put a floor out in the middle of the stadium, and we played right out in the middle of that baby in front of 80,000 people. You needed a telescope to see the game from the upper levels. It was windy on the court that day, too.

The games were pretty much serious basketball. There was some clowning, but the Globetrotters did not use their full choreographed routine. They had their own referees, but we wanted no part of the comedy routines. We wanted to play straight up. When we did the games were all battles. Goose Tatum might run up in the stands and grab a fan's popcorn or something like that, but we weren't involved in the parts of the game that weren't serious. In the 21 games, the Globetrotters won 15 games and we won six.

We knew they had beaten the Lakers, so we knew how good they were. You didn't ever want to give them a lead because then they would go into one of their dribbling routines and kill the clock. There was no shot clock. They could dribble the game away.

This was different than when the Globetrotters traveled with their own opponent everywhere, the Washington Generals. We were temporary, they were permanent opponents. At that time if you were a good black player, you went to the Globetrotters. Then as the NBA opened up, all of the best black players came to the NBA.

There was a guy who played during that competition for the Globetrotters who did not go to college, but who attended Crispus Attucks High School in Indianapolis, and he was a great player. His name was "Wee" Willie Gardner. He was 6'9". To me the four greatest high school players in Indiana history are Oscar Robertson, Larry Bird, George McGinnis, and Wee Willie Gardner. Gardner was the Most Valuable Player of the tour. He spent a couple of years with the Globetrotters and then signed with the New York Knicks.

Gardner had a great training camp. He was scoring more than 25 points a game, and rebounding, but then they found out that he had a heart murmur and that was it. There is no question in my mind that if he could have played he would be in the Hall of Fame today. Thankfully, he is in the Indiana Basketball Hall of Fame.

The idea of going on that tour really appealed to me, but it took place before the end of school so I missed some classes. When I got back the ROTC captain had bad news for me. I was a cadet colonel, but because I missed too much class with unexcused absences, they were relieving me of duty. That was the end of me becoming an officer. But I also made the choice to put my name in early as an enlisted man to get going on my two-year obligation so that I could get out faster and get into pro ball faster.

I graduated from college in June 1954. Nancy and I got married the day after graduation. One day we were in Bloomington, and the next day we were in South Bend. Dick Farley, my Indiana teammate, was my best man. It was a big wedding. There were tons of people there.

By September I was in the army and Nancy stayed in Bloomington to teach high school. At that time they had only one high school there, Bloomington High. I put my army time in as a member of the 6th Armored Division at Fort Leonard Wood in Missouri, and I was in for two years. I had been through ROTC basic training at Fort Benning, Georgia, before that, but I had to do it all over again.

Basic training was 16 weeks, but it was peace time. The war in Korea had just ended. There are a lot of fundamental things that you do in the army that I don't think ever change. You get up early, you have your inspections, you shine your shoes—those are all normal. That's what the military is all about.

There was a post basketball team, and they held the All-Army tournament at Fort Leonard Wood. By that time I had been chosen by the Minneapolis Lakers, so I knew where I was headed, even if I had to wait two years to play. From 1949–54 the Lakers won five championships in six seasons. They were the best team for years.

One of the organizers of that team, and the biggest booster of pro basketball and sports in that city, was a guy named Sid Hartman. He was a sports columnist for the *Minneapolis Star-Tribune,* and he still writes for them sometimes even though he is in his nineties. But in the late 1940s for a while, he was the acting general manager, too.

Several years after that, when I was in the army and the Lakers took me, I got a call from Sid and he asked me to be on the lookout for talent in the All-Army tournament and if I saw anyone who was really good and could play, I should let him know.

One of the players who I played with was Ralph Beard. Beard was a great player from Kentucky, but he got caught up in the point-shaving scandals in the early 1950s and was banned from the NBA. I think Ralph was just about the greatest sub-6' player who ever played the game—he was 5'10". I think he got a raw deal in that scandal. Ralph and I became dear friends. I went to his funeral a couple of years ago [in 2007]. But because of the scandal the Lakers couldn't sign Ralph.

But there was another guy who struck my eye while I was in the army. It was Sam Jones, out of North Carolina. I called Sid Hartman, and I said, "Sid, you've got to get this kid. He is a player." Sam and I still talk about this. I don't know exactly how it worked out. I don't know if Sid made attempts to get him or not, but Sam ended up with the Boston Celtics. He is one of the greatest guards who ever played the game. He played on 10 NBA championship teams with the Celtics, and he was chosen for the Naismith Basketball Hall of Fame.

Oh boy, could that guy shoot. He made those perfect-form jump shots, and he banked them in off the glass. It's funny how things go. Sam has said to other guys, "You know what? I came so close to being with Bobby in the same backcourt." He was some kind of playoff player. He shot about 85 percent of those jumpers on bank shots, a lot of them in tough situations.

Sam loves golf and one time he called me and came to Indiana—he's got some relatives here—and we played golf out at Crooked Stick. He lives where the World Golf Hall of Fame is located.

It was fun to play in the All-Army tournament. At least I could still keep playing. Sam Jones and Ralph Beard were probably the best players I saw in it. Frank Ramsey went into the military, too. He did not give up his commission. One nice thing the NBA did for us was to give us credit for the two years we spent in the military on our pensions. I went into the army on September 21, 1954, and I got out of the army on September 20, 1956.

I always felt badly about Ralph Beard. The point-shaving scandal in the early 1950s was basically centered around New York City and Madison Square Garden, but not only there. The main thing gamblers tried to do was get players not to try 100 percent so they would win games by a smaller margin than the point spread. The gamblers would clean up, the team would still win, and the players would make some money.

But those were the guys in the middle of it. A lot of other players were approached who didn't do anything. And you know, there were always strangers around asking you questions about the team. They would ask how so-and-so was, was so-and-so healthy. You couldn't tell if they were just fans or gamblers. You didn't know them, and you didn't know what they wanted.

The guy behind the scandal was a player named Jack Molinas. He played for Columbia University, and he was a good player. He played in the East-West game, and he even played for a little while in the NBA with the Fort Wayne Pistons. He just went the wrong way. Some people have even said that he almost single-handedly destroyed college basketball. He went to prison, did some time, and later got murdered, and it was said that it was a mob hit.

Ralph told me that he never did anything wrong, but that some money kid sent by his daddy tried to get them to shave points. Kentucky was so good, and they were favored by so much all of the time.

If you went to Madison Square Garden to play, there were all of these guys standing around the outside of the court during warm-ups and they would talk to you. They didn't have security like they do now when they make people go to their seats and sit down and not hang out right at the edge of the court. There was nothing to prevent anyone from approaching you and asking you questions.

I was never offered money or asked to shave points. People did want some kind of tip. They wanted inside information, and they asked questions like, "What do you think tonight? How much do you think you're going to win by?" There were always people around doing the, "What do you think?" thing. Strangers yeah, but everybody. It might happen in other places, too, but it was always more common in New York. That was because they let all of those spectators come up to the floor.

That went on when I was in the pros and we were at Madison Square Garden to play the Knicks or to play in those doubleheaders. If someone was injured on our team, you could count on guys asking, "Is he going to play tonight?" This was long before everyone had a cell phone, of course, and the gamblers had to go place their bets with their bookies on regular telephones. Just when they started playing the National Anthem you would see these guys all run for the front lobby where they had a lot of pay phones. They were getting their bets down before the tip-off. I didn't see that in college, although I heard it happened.

Pro basketball was new right after World War II. When I was growing up in Terre Haute, there was no major league of pro basketball and nobody talked about it. There were barnstorming teams and the Harlem Globetrotters, and there were AAU teams where you maintained your amateur status but had a job working for a company. But there was nothing like the kind of pro league we saw later with the NBA.

The NBA was actually founded when I was starting high school in 1946. The original name was the Basketball Association of America. Another league called the National Basketball League also got going around that time. They merged in 1949, and that merger produced the National Basketball Association name.

So pro ball was out there when I was at Indiana, but I didn't know much about it. The very first time I saw a game, and the first time I ever thought about the idea of becoming a professional basketball player, was my sophomore year. Sammy Esposito hadn't left yet, and we hitchhiked to Indianapolis up Route 37 to the Butler Fieldhouse to watch a team called the Indianapolis Olympians.

The Olympians were founded in 1949 and only lasted through 1953. They were professional basketball forerunners to the Indiana Pacers. Some of the players on that Olympians team were Ralph Beard, Alex Groza, and Wallace "Wah Wah" Jones. Most of the players were former University of Kentucky players. They were packing them in for a while in Indianapolis.

Actually, it is incorrect to say that I was drafted by the Minneapolis Lakers. It didn't work exactly that way. I was drafted by the Baltimore Bullets while I was in the army. Their coach was Clair Bee, who was a famous coach and was also famous for writing sports books for boys. But those Baltimore Bullets folded, and Minneapolis picked up my rights.

A few things figured into me believing I could play pro ball. I had watched the Olympians play. Then I was MVP in the East-West game. And the NBA showed interest in me, two teams really. So it seemed as if it was a possibility. Some of the guys I had played against in college had not gone into the military and they were playing in the NBA, so the way I looked at it was, "If they can play, I can play." I knew them, and I knew I was as good as they were. I could compare what they had done and what I had done.

When I was discharged from the army in 1956, I knew exactly what I was going to do. I was the property of the Minneapolis Lakers of the NBA, and I was going to try pro basketball.

CHAPTER 9

GOING PRO

The Minneapolis Lakers were the NBA's first great team. Center George Mikan was the first dominating big man. Mikan, who played his college ball at DePaul, was 6'10" and a terrific shooter inside. The other teams couldn't stop him, and his supporting cast was also excellent.

However, Bob Leonard completely missed out on the Lakers dynasty because of his time spent in the army. He certainly knew of the Lakers' achievements when his opportunity came to join the NBA, but the peak years of the club had passed.

The Lakers still had a couple of holdovers from the championship years, but most of the roster was newer. Most of the roster, though, consisted of players that Leonard already knew. The center and team's leading scorer was his old friend Clyde Lovellette from Terre Haute. Other players on the team were guys he had run across in Big Ten play. Seeking to appeal to local fans, the Lakers had a few ex–University of Minnesota Gophers on the team in Dick Garmaker, Chuck Mencel, and Ed Kalafat.

This was the first time Lovellette and Leonard were on the same team.

"Bobby was really aggressive, and he was a good shooter," said Lovellette, who led the Lakers in scoring with 20.8 points per game during Leonard's rookie year. "He was a good shooter and a good playmaker."

During Leonard's first year in the army, Nancy was teaching school in Bloomington, Indiana. After the second year at Fort Leonard Wood she joined him to start a new life together in Minneapolis. Bob was ready to get going and play ball again at the start of the 1956–57 season.

In 1956 the Leonards became parents for the first time. Terry, the only daughter among their five children, was born that year, and she established a pattern in their lives. The birthplace of the children depended on where the family was living at the time, and where the family was living at the time depended on what team in what city Bob was playing for.

Terry was an infant during Leonard's first season in the pros. "It was a very interesting childhood," Terry Leonard Grembowicz said. "I attended a lot of elementary schools."

When asked if she was a basketball fan, she laughingly said, "Did I have a choice? Of course I was a basketball fan. It was what Dad did. We were always at the arenas, always. We frequently went to games, and we ran around on the floor. We have all been places and done things that other people could only dream of. Your team was your family wherever we were. My longstanding allegiance was to my father. We were very involved. Our parents involved all of us kids."

One of Bobby's teammates on the Minneapolis Lakers, who came along a year later, was "Hot Rod" Hundley, a guard who was famous for his showmanship on the floor, his colorful lifestyle off of it, and then his years of colorful commentary on the radio. Mothers didn't always want their daughters to be partying with Hundley, but the Leonards trusted him implicitly.

"Hot Rod Hundley was my babysitter," Terry said. "I'm sure he did spoil me. I don't know anything else about him off the court, but he was like a big kid with me."

Terry claimed family preeminence as a H-O-R-S-E player with a deadly outside set shot that could trump her brothers. "I always beat them at H-O-R-S-E," she said. "I was strictly a shooter."

Currently a third-grade teacher in South Bend, Indiana, Terry said her childhood was marked by several moves. She remembers spending third grade in Baltimore and grades four through eight in Kokomo.

"Our moving specialist was my mother," she said. "She was the CEO of the house. I didn't mind, until high school, and then we moved to Carmel."

The Leonards have lived in Carmel, Indiana, for more than 40 years, arriving just in time for Terry to start high school and to stay in one place through graduation. One thing that impressed Terry about her father during a trip back to his roots in Terre Haute was his memory.

"He has the most incredible memory of anyone I know," Terry said. "When we go to Terre Haute, it's like a riding tour. He can point out everything, saying things like, 'That alley used to have a basketball hoop.' He'll tick off the names of the players from Terre Haute. Sometimes he knows the weather on the day something happened."

Most of all Terry thinks of her father as a down-to-earth guy.

"There's nothing fancy-schmancy about him," she said. "He is who you see. As long as he has my mother, a piece of pie, a cup of black coffee, and a game on the TV, he's fine."

BOBBY LEONARD

I was discharged from the army, and I went directly to Minneapolis for the Lakers' training camp. The NBA did not get the nationwide attention it got later, but I knew there was a team in Fort Wayne, Indiana. That was the Fort Wayne Pistons, and after my rookie year they moved to Detroit. And I had followed the Lakers with George Mikan. I knew how good they were because they had won all those championships. They were a dynasty, the first NBA dynasty.

George Mikan changed the NBA. He was so good, and he was the first big man who was so good they had to widen the lane because of him. They also put the 24-second shot clock in because of him. Teams would hold the ball on the Lakers and bore the fans to death. People didn't want to watch games like that. The lowest-scoring game in NBA history was Fort Wayne 19, Minneapolis 18. That game took place in 1950, but it led to the invention of the shot clock a few years later.

Danny Biasone, who was the owner of the Syracuse Nationals, said, "We've got to do something about this." He developed the shot clock.

When I got out of the army, I reported to Minneapolis, and at first I was really disillusioned. I got there and they had this little Mickey Mouse office, with one gal as a secretary, and that was about all they had. It was very low budget. I said, "We're getting ready to go to training camp. What do we do about uniforms?" She said, "Go in there, in that back room." There were duffle bags filled with used uniforms. When you opened them up they had uniforms that had names on them. George Mikan, Slater Martin. They were leftovers, hand-me-downs. I was surprised.

We went up to St. Peter, Minnesota, where Gustavus Adolphus College is, and that's where we had our training camp. I was disappointed because what I had seen at Indiana compared to that was big-time. We had Spike Dixon, a great trainer in the training room, and Red Groh had all of the uniforms downstairs, the clean uniforms and socks. And the Lakers had these hand-me-downs. The Lakers! They were the best team. It just kind of showed you where pro basketball rated at the time.

I guess the glory years had left with Mikan. I missed the championships. I did not go into my time with the Lakers thinking I was going to be spending the rest of my life with pro basketball. It was pro basketball and it was professional sports, but the NBA was still a young league and it was struggling in a lot of ways.

After the Basketball Association of America and the National Basketball League merged, a lot of cities got squeezed out. One by one, a lot of teams folded. When I broke in there were only eight teams in the NBA. Each team had 10 players under contract. Now the active roster is 12 players, teams have 15 under contract, and there are 30 teams. Back then that meant there was room for only 80 players out of this country to play in the NBA. It was tough competition.

There were not too many of the small cities left. The whole league my rookie year was the Boston Celtics, New York Knicks, Syracuse Nationals, Philadelphia Warriors, St. Louis Hawks, Minneapolis Lakers, Fort Wayne

Pistons, and Rochester Royals. The Warriors moved to the San Francisco area, the Nationals became the Philadelphia 76ers, the Hawks moved to Atlanta, the Lakers moved to Los Angeles, the Pistons moved to Detroit, and the Rochester Royals moved to Cincinnati. Then they became the Kansas City–Omaha Kings and then the Sacramento Kings. That's all one franchise.

In Rochester they had Bob Davies at guard, a very good player. In Cincinnati they had Jack Twyman and Maurice Stokes. Maurice Stokes was a great player. He was 6'7". I always felt he was a lot like Elgin Baylor. Stokes could take it down the middle on the break. He was a heck of a player and a very tragic story. He fell during a game, got knocked unconscious, and then became paralyzed. Twyman and Stokes were teammates, and later Jack was his legal guardian. Then, of course, the Royals got Oscar Robertson. Jack was a good man. He just passed away last year.

Syracuse was always a very tough team. They had Johnny Kerr, but they also had Dolph Schayes, who was a Hall of Famer. Yardley, who was the first NBA player to score 2,000 points in a season, was mostly with the Pistons, but he also played with Syracuse for a little while. Then the Nationals had Larry Costello and Hal Greer in the backcourt. They had a heck of a ball club.

From there you go on over to Boston. That's where you run into the powerhouse. They had four guards who were Hall of Famers: Bob Cousy, Bill Sharman, Sam Jones, and K.C. Jones. Bill Russell and Tommy Heinsohn came into the league the same year I did. Heinsohn was the Rookie of the Year. Russell, who did not come in until December, was second, and I was third. Russ only got in a half season because he had played in the Olympics in Melbourne, Australia. That was the first year the Celtics won the title, the 1956–57 season.

Russell made the Celtics great, and they were lucky they got him. The St. Louis Hawks had the first pick in the draft and the Celtics traded Ed Macauley and Cliff Hagan for him. They were great players, but that trade has to go down as one of the greatest in history. They already had Cousy, who was a marquee player, and Sharman, who was a great athlete. Then you bring in Sam Jones and K.C. Jones off the bench. In the middle you had No. 6, Bill Russell. Unbelievable shot blocker and rebounder. Just unbelievable. I saw him block five or six shots on the same play before he tapped it back and got it. He just kept blocking it. The one thing about Bill was that he did not just go up and block a ball out of bounds. He'd catch it or tap it to one of his players. That's the kind of control he had.

Tommy Heinsohn was a great player, too. He could shoot from outside and was a great offensive rebounder. He had his hook shot, all kinds of stuff he could make. Jim Loscutoff was the first player, what they called the enforcer. Jungle Jim Loscutoff. The Celtics had it all. They never could win it all until Russell got there, but he made them unbeatable.

The Knicks weren't all that great at the time. They had Carl Braun, who was very good, and Richie Guerin. Richie was an excellent player. They got Willie Naulls from UCLA, and he was good. Kenny Sears was a forward from Santa Clara, but they weren't good enough.

Before they got Wilt Chamberlain, the Warriors weren't good enough. They had Paul Arizin, who was a star. Paul Arizin was special. Joe Fulks had retired. They also had Tom Gola, who had been the player of the year for LaSalle in college, and another big man, Neil Johnston, who scored more than 20 points a game. Fort Wayne was decent. They had Larry Foust and Gene Shue. That was the thing, though. With so few players in the league, everybody had someone who was a big scorer, who had been an All-American in college. There were only 80 players, and everyone was good.

The Lakers were going through changes when I got there. Slater Martin was still in the league, but he had gone to the Hawks. Mikan was retired. We had new guys coming in over my first few years. Hot Rod Hundley was one of them. Rudy LaRusso was a forward from Dartmouth. Hundley came from West Virginia, and he was a great scorer in college. Jim Krebs from Southern Methodist was a forward. Dick Garmaker, Chuck Mencel, and Ed Kalafat were guys I knew from

Minnesota playing at the same time in the Big Ten. But my roommate my rookie year was Jim Paxson.

Paxson played for the University of Dayton, and he was a 6'6" forward. He is the father of Jim Paxson Jr. and John Paxson who both played in the NBA. John won championships playing with Michael Jordan for the Chicago Bulls, and he is still an executive with the Bulls. For a while Jim Jr. was the general manager of the Cleveland Cavaliers.

Jim Sr. was a journeyman player who was only in the league for a couple of years. Then we had another guy come in named Steve Hamilton. Steve was from Morehead State, and he became better known as a major league pitcher. He only played with the Lakers for a couple of years, but he is one of only a very few people ever to play in the World Series and the NBA finals. He was in the big leagues for 12 years, but he played a power forward role for us. He died a few years back of cancer.

Steve was a really good guy, and he was a good pitcher. I knew a couple of pitchers over the years. I mentioned that Tommy John was from Terre Haute, but when I was in high school they used to allow some of the little kids in town to act as mascots for the basketball team. They were five years old or so, and they dribbled out onto the court in front of the team when we came out of the locker room. That was part of the deal. Our mascot at the time was Tommy John. He lives in New Jersey, but I see him every once in a while and we have lunch.

Tommy John had a great pro career. As crazy as it sounds, he is almost as famous for the surgery named after him that so many pitchers have had to extend their careers. Mostly when I see Tommy, we talk baseball.

Being the Minneapolis Lakers, when I first reported to St. Peter to training camp, I sensed that there was a little clique of Minnesota guys. The active Gopher players were there and Mikan was around the camp. St. Peter was a nice little town, but I didn't know anybody there and I wasn't part of the clique. Vern Mikkelsen was the elder statesmen from the championship team. They were all in their backyard in Minnesota, but it was all new to me.

BOOM, BABY!

During the exhibition season we took the bus everywhere. We went to different towns within a few hours ride of Minneapolis. I remember we played a game in Fargo, North Dakota. It would be a couple of hours on the bus, get off, play the game, and get back on the bus and go home. We never even stayed overnight in hotels in these towns. The bus was our hotel.

We spent plenty of time on the bus. One of the things we did to pass the time was play poker. There was always a poker game. I didn't usually sleep on the bus, though maybe sometimes I would on the way home. During that time period, with that kind of travel—trains, too—that was true not only of our team, but most of the teams had card games going to eat up the travel time.

The most memorable bus trip my rookie year was the last one. We were going from Minneapolis to North Dakota for the last exhibition game. The final roster cut was coming. We were going to have 10 guys, and we had 15 guys on the bus trip. The game was over and we were getting ready to go home with our bags packed for the bus. The coach, John Kundla, said, "If I call your name, get your player's bag and go and head out on the bus. If I don't call your name, the rest of you are cut." I have never seen anything like that, but it actually happened. This stuff doesn't exist now. Kundla cut five guys in the locker room, and then we had to ride home on the bus together. That's not how you do it.

It was the worst ride home in history. These were guys who were our teammates and our friends. They have families and suddenly they're off the team, out of a job. The worst circumstance for me was that I had played in the East-West game with Al Bianchi from Bowling Green, and I beat out Al for the job. I did well during the exhibition season, and I eventually became a starting guard. We were talking on the bus on the way back to Minneapolis and I said, "Al, you're good enough to play."

After we got back to Minneapolis, the team was going to be flying right out. I guess we were starting the season. He came with me to the airport, and we were sitting in the bar. I called up Johnny Kerr in Syracuse and asked if there was something going on where they needed a guard. He said he thought there might be an opening. He hung up the phone, called Danny Biasone, and we were waiting and waiting. Johnny called back and talked to Bianchi and said, "Al, come on up here." Al went up there and stayed 10 years. Actually it was something like seven years plus the Philadelphia 76ers when the Nationals moved there. That was just about his whole career.

I never did understand what Kundla did. First of all, you sit down with a guy one-on-one in your office. Secondly, why not wait until we got back to Minneapolis? "If I don't call your name, then you're cut." That's not the way to do it. He didn't play around.

The way it began I was not starting and then all of a sudden I was starting. When the regular season began I was a starter. I was confident when I joined the Lakers that I could play in the NBA. It may have been new to me, but I knew enough about the players and the game to believe I would make it. The season was 72 games long at the time, and I played in every game. I averaged 11 points a game, and I averaged just over three rebounds a game, too. I had a lot of assists, and I was third on the team. I had a good rookie year.

Another holdover from some of those good Laker teams was a guard named Whitey Skoog. Whitey was nearing the end of his career, and he only played in 23 games that year. One of our other players was Walter Dukes, the 7' center from Seton Hall. I once got trapped in the upper berth on a train with Walter Dukes. He was in the lower. He had a damned ritual where he sat down on the edge of those steel bumps on those old Pullman cars with some hot water and put sassafras in it. He'd mix it around and drink that and eat an apple. There was something that Walter had in his skin that gave off a sulphur odor. I was in that upper berth and I had that little fan up there you could turn on and I blew it all night. I didn't get any sleep at all. But old Walt was a pretty good player.

Clyde Lovellette was strong, and he was the center. Walter played forward next to him. Clyde was a big presence down low, but he could shoot from outside. Walter could run like crazy, and he was a good defender. Walter wasn't really a low-post player as big as he was. Clyde could play in or out.

It was kind of a strange season. All four teams in the Eastern Division had records of .500 or better, and all four teams in the Western Division had losing records. The Hawks, the Lakers, and Fort Wayne all had the same record at 34–38. We lost a one-game playoff with the Hawks to avoid playing a first-round series. They got us.

In the rest of the playoffs we beat the Pistons two straight in a best two-out-of-three series, and then we faced the Hawks. One of the players for the Hawks was Bob Pettit, who was a great, great player. I seemed to run into him all the time during college tournaments and pro playoffs. The Hawks beat us three straight games and went on to the finals against the Celtics. The Celtics won it all.

Pettit averaged about 25 points a game that season. In the last playoff game, St. Louis beat us 143–135 in double overtime, and I scored 42 points. That's the most points I scored in an NBA game and that was without the three-point line that didn't exist yet. I took a lot of shots back there. Pettit scored 35 points for the Hawks. I made 14 field goals, and I made all 14 of my free throws. It was a fun, high-scoring game. There were a lot of games like that back then. And we could score. We had five guys average in double figures for the season, but all teams scored more then, and all teams gave up more points on defense.

As a rookie I experienced a lot of things that were different from playing in college. It was a lot more games. The competition was tougher. I've often said the jump from high school to college is a pretty big jump, but the jump from college to the NBA, you can triple that or multiply it four times. It's the same way now. It's a much bigger jump from college to the NBA than it is from high school to college. That's why college stars don't always make it.

The most money I ever made in a season while playing in the NBA was $13,000, and I held out for that. My rookie year I made $6,500. The minimum salary for a rookie in the NBA during the 2012–13 season was $473,000, but for a guy with one year of experience it was $762,000. That's because the players now have a union, and they have a collective bargaining agreement with the owners.

The last guy on the bench does okay. It's a lot of money. I'll put it this way. I don't mind that if a guy comes out and plays every night. That's the way it is now, and I never thought the salaries would get this high. The players are flying in chartered planes, staying in top hotels, and getting plenty of per diem. It's a whole different ball game than it was for us in the 1950s.

The thing about those days was that hardly any player made enough money not to need a job in the summertime. Just about everybody except for the absolute top guys in the league had to get summer jobs. They needed the money to take care of their families.

CHAPTER 10

BECOMING SLICK

During Bob Leonard's first years in the pros, the NBA was a train league. Only eight cities had teams, and they were fairly close together. When a team went on a road trip, it could be a multi-day road trip. The Minneapolis Lakers were as far west as any team in the league. Many of the other teams were clustered together in cities only a couple of hours apart.

The Lakers could hit the road and play Rochester and Syracuse, which are located only 75 miles apart. They could go on to Philadelphia and then play the Knicks in New York, 100 miles away. Then Boston would be another 200 miles further along. Typically, the team would play a game and then go from the arena to the train station. That might be Pennsylvania Station in New York, 30th Street Station in Philadelphia, or North Station in Boston.

In the modern day NBA, every team owns its own airplane or has charter service to fly teams back home after night games. They are likely home in their own beds by 3:00 AM. They might take several-day road trips, but only to the West Coast. In part of Bob Leonard's era, the West consisted of Minneapolis and St. Louis.

By the time Leonard reached the NBA, his coach was a virtual legend. John Kundla took over the Lakers for the 1948–49 season and led them to five league championships. He was running the team when Leonard arrived and coached through the rest of the 1950s. He was briefly replaced by George Mikan, the best-known player during the league's first decade of existence and its best player during that time period.

There were many changes on the Lakers during the first few years of Leonard's NBA career. The last vestiges of the old dynasty were phased out and the Leonard family kept growing. In 1957, Bob's second child, and first boy, was born. This was Robert Roy, who is also known as Bob, but is not a junior.

Young Bob was interested in basketball from an early age, and although he was born when Leonard was playing in Minneapolis by the time he was of high school age, the family was again living in Indiana and Bob played for Carmel High. He also played for a year at Butler University as a 6' guard.

As a little kid, Young Bob recalled, the entire family went to games and he got to be a ball boy for the team. He was one of the kids who sat at the end of the floor under the basket and dashed out onto the court during time outs to wipe up sweat with a towel.

It was while Bob was playing for the Minneapolis Lakers that he picked up the nickname "Slick" that has stayed with him for the rest of his life. The younger Bob, especially as a kid, was sometimes called "Slick Jr." "Even to this day some of Dad's friends call me Slick Jr.," the younger Bob said.

Although it was fun being around pro basketball when his father was playing, and later coaching, Bob said, "We were normal kids. My mom and dad saw to it. We survived it."

His father traveled a lot because of his job, but he always included his kids in his activities the best he could when they were growing up. The younger Bob Leonard said there are a couple of character traits of his father's that stick with him.

"When it comes to Dad he is probably the most competitive person I've met in my life," he said. He remembers Bob rooting for the younger Bob's daughter in a golf match. "We're in a cart and one of the players she's going up against is putting and under his breath he goes, 'Miss it.'"

"But really, after all of these years, the thing about Dad that I am most proud of is the way he treats people. It's a good lesson for us."

One of the most frightening experiences of Bob Leonard's life occurred during his time with the Minneapolis Lakers, too. In what is very much a rarity for a professional sports franchise, Leonard and his teammates were passengers on a plane carrying them home after a road game that crashed in the snow. The accident happened on a wintry night in January 1960 and while it gained nationwide attention at the time, it has been largely forgotten—except by those who survived it—and those who were present that night on the ground when the plane hit.

Leonard was one of 22 people aboard the plane returning to Minneapolis from St. Louis. The weather was poor enough on the planned route home that take-off was delayed a couple of hours after the afternoon loss to the Hawks. But then the decision was made to fly and the team boarded. Out of 10 players on the active roster, nine were present. Forward Rudy LaRusso missed the road trip because he was ill.

Early on the entire electrical system fizzled out on the plane, including the heat. That was the reason the Laker party huddled under blankets for most of the rest of the night, and that was why they were wrapped up in them as the plane began its descent and ultimately crashed in a cornfield.

Usually the flight would have carried the DC-3 along at about 10,000 feet, but hoping to get above the weather and to avoid any other planes, the pilots brought the plane up to 17,000 feet at times. The clouds remained dense wherever they went. The place where the pilots determined it was best to try to make a landing as their fuel ran low was a farming community of about 7,000 people called Carroll, Iowa. Not that anyone on the plane knew that at the time.

Surveying the area to see if it would be acceptable for an emergency landing, the pilots circled the community sometime after midnight. They hoped the water tower would inform them where they were, but years later the co-pilot told a newspaper reporter that only two "LLs" were visible. He joked about that then, saying he thought they might be in hell.

The plane itself was in very good condition given the abrupt landing, and it was flown out by the pilot—and used by the team again that season. The players thanked the pilots with a cash present and a plaque presented at a game later in the year.

It's not something that Bob Leonard ever would have joked about, but he had to admit the pilots made a pretty slick maneuver to get them all out of trouble.

BOBBY LEONARD

John Kundla was a good coach, and I got along well with him. The only thing that disturbed me was the way he cut those players after the exhibition game my rookie year. Ordinarily, he was a laid-back guy, a very nice guy.

But there was one other problem. Back in those days our per diem was very low, about $2.50 or $3 a day. I remember Bob Cousy, who was just about the biggest star in the league for the Celtics, trying to get a 50-cents-a-day raise in the per diem and he got turned down. Cousy tried to help a lot of guys.

We would come into New York into the Pennsylvania Station by train, and you'd get all your bags together and go outside. We would pile into cabs for the ride to the old greasy Paramount Hotel. There were 10 guys on the team and John. We didn't have any assistant coaches, and nobody else traveled with us like a trainer—the home team supplied a trainer.

Four guys would get into one cab. Four guys would get into another cab, and John would get into a third cab with the other two players. If you were in John's cab, that was okay because he would pay. But John would be slow paying the other guys for reimbursement. You're in New York and you need the money for your per diem. So what happened was that when we got to the hotel, there would be a rat race to see who could get out of the cab first, get the hell out of there. You wanted to leave one guy in the cab who had to pick up the tab. You didn't want to be the last one getting out.

The ideal situation was that John had to pay for the cab because once you were at the hotel you had to get ahold of John to get your money back. One thing about John on the road is that he stayed in his room a lot. He smoked cigars like they were going out of style. When you walked in there, you knew he had been smoking. Johnny loved those cigars. You got reimbursed, but you had to fight for it. When I went to his room, I tried to sit by the door so there would be less cigar smoke—you didn't want to hang around.

My rookie year under John we finished 34–38. My second year, 1957–58, we finished 19–53 and were last in the West. John only coached part of that season going 10–23. George Mikan, who was the most famous player in team history, took over and under George we were 9–30. It was not a very good year for the team. Vern Mikkelsen led us in scoring with over 17 points a game. I averaged 11.2 points and led the club in assists. Clyde Lovellette went to the Cincinnati Royals, and he had been our leading scorer. Larry Foust, a very strong, 6'9" front-court man, came over to us and averaged almost 17 points a game.

It was George Mikan who gave me my nickname "Slick." It didn't have anything to do with basketball, at least not with me being on the court. We had drafted Rod Hundley and Rod was a great player who was so popular in West Virginia that we decided to schedule some exhibition games in the state during his rookie year. Rod was the first of three great West Virginia University guards to come along in a row. Rod was first, then Jerry West, then Rod Thorn.

We bussed down to Morgantown, where the university is, and played an exhibition game. Then we left right after for another town, it might have been Charleston, about 120 miles away. So we got on the bus, and most of the players fell asleep. I was still awake and so was George. We were sitting up front and we began playing Hollywood gin, a card game, under those two little peep lights. Those were the only lights on in the entire bus.

We got about halfway there up in the mountains and we saw a sign that read, "Truck Stop, 5 Miles." George said to me, "Bobby, do you think we ought to stop there and let the guys get a cup of coffee and a sandwich?" I said that I thought that would be a good idea. So we pulled into this truck stop. It was a really big one. The driver turned the lights on and all the guys were waking up.

I had blitzed George all of the way across West Virginia in that gin game and he said, "How about buying me a cup of coffee? You're too slick for me." Rod was sitting right behind us and he heard George say "slick." Right away he started calling me "Slick" and then everybody started calling me Slick. It started right then and there. I got a nickname from George Mikan, one of the all-time greats. After that we had guards named Slick and Hot Rod.

George was a great guy. He played for DePaul in college, but he was the biggest name in pro basketball when he came into the league. No one could stop him. He was 6'10" and that made him the first big star who was a big man. He averaged around 23 points and 13 rebounds a game. He was so popular when he was playing that they used to put his name above the team's name on the marquee at Madison Square Garden. It read, "George Mikan and the Minneapolis Lakers." He dominated and he was big in New York.

One time we were in New York on New Year's and he said, "Let's go out to dinner." There were a bunch of us, and this is New York City on New Year's Eve. He took us to where he always went, the famous Mamma Leone's Italian restaurant. We get there and there's a line two blocks long trying to get in. Mamma Leone's son, who was the *maitre d'hotel* at that time, saw George and said, "George! Come on in." We passed all those people in the lines, and he set up a table down in the basement, in the wine cellar.

He was a great guy. After he stopped playing George was an attorney, and he took the time off from his law practice to coach us that season because his company was involved with the Lakers. He wore No. 99, a great number, too.

Part of the time when I was playing for the Minneapolis Lakers, I roomed with Rod Hundley. Rod was always looking for the action and finding it. One time we were in New York on a trip and he had a friend who got us a table at the Copacabana. It happened to be the night Tony Bennett introduced the song, "I Left My Heart in San Francisco," to the critics in New York. Tony finishes the song and we're sitting nearby. They rolled out a cake with champagne for him. Rod goes right up to Tony Bennett and he said, "Mr. Bennett, I'm with the Lakers and we're in town to play the Knicks tomorrow night." And Tony said, "Why don't you just sit down and have some champagne and cake?" You know, Rod never did look over and invite me. I'm sitting there by myself.

It was a bad year going 19–53. We had some quality players but not great players. Clearly, the old days in Minneapolis were dead. But things started turning around very quickly. After that terrible year we had the No. 1 pick in the NBA draft and the Lakers chose Elgin Baylor.

Elgin Baylor is absolutely one of the greatest players in the history of the game. He's in the very top group, one of the few best players. We drafted him from Seattle University where he had led the team to the NCAA championship game. Elgin was the No. 1 overall pick in the draft, and he was fantastic from the beginning. As a rookie he averaged about 25 points a game, 15 rebounds, and 4 assists. He made moves that no one had ever seen before. He was 6'5", could rebound like a center, and handle the ball like a guard.

Baylor's high game as a rookie was 55 points. In his second year it was 64 points. And the next year it was 71 points.

I had never seen him play before he showed up to the Lakers, but I was very aware of him. I knew that Elgin played in Seattle and that he had taken that team to the Final Four. I had heard about him, but I didn't really know how good he was until I saw him. I was in the game when he scored 71 points. That was an NBA record at the time, though Wilt Chamberlain broke it not too much later with his 100-point game.

Elgin scored the 71 points at Madison Square Garden in a game against the Knicks on a road trip. Later, as a present, they gave everybody a pair of cufflinks with half a basketball on them and the No. 71.

I've still got those. I had never seen anybody score 71 points. The pre-Elgin record was 63 points by Joe Fulks in 1949, which Elgin had already broken with his 64-point game. We were playing the Boston Celtics in that game, and in the final minutes of it Boston coach Red Auerbach was doing everything he could to prevent Elgin from getting the record.

Elgin had the high-point game in each of his first three years in the league. Auerbach put two or three guys on him, fouling him and trying to prevent him from breaking the record. The next season he got 71 and that broke it again. When Elgin Baylor was starring and making the All-Star team every year, they didn't have many games on television and they didn't save films, so there isn't very much out there that people can see that shows how good he was.

A lot of people have said he was ahead of his time because he got off the floor so well and so high. He had a complete game. You had to get up on him because he'd hit the outside shot on you. Then if you got up on him, he had the quick step. He could put the ball on the floor and dribble past you. He could pull up and hit the jump shot or he could take it all the way to the hoop. He could jump. He was strong. He was just a great, great player. He averaged 25 points a game as a rookie and that was below his lifetime average, which was 27.4 points a game.

Elgin had moves that no one had seen at that particular time. Even today there have been so few who could do the same thing and it's almost 60 years later. Nobody could play better. He's as good as any of them that ever came down the pike. I heard somebody say that Elgin Baylor was Michael Jordan before Michael Jordan, and that's a good comment. That's fair. Elgin was just about in a class by himself.

Being on the court with him was something. He did unbelievable things on the court. He could take the ball down the middle on the fast break. He could pass in a sensational manner. Once you play with a guy for that many games, you don't think as much about it. You kind of expect the unusual.

After that terrible season and after all of the stars of those early Minneapolis teams left, we were not drawing many fans. Management was hurting and you had the sense that they hoped getting Elgin Baylor would turn things around and put people in the seats. John Kundla was back as our coach that year for the entire season.

Minneapolis was okay. The people were good to us. Nancy and I had never experienced winters like that. I would be on the road with the team and she was home shoveling snow off the walk and raising three kids. One of the things different in my early days playing in the NBA compared to the way things are now was that Nancy is the one who washed and ironed and folded my uniform. After a game I would bring my sweaty uniform home and it would get tossed in the washing machine with all of the family's laundry. Well, one day I was in the locker room getting dressed for a game and started to put on my jersey and shorts and a pair of my daughter Terry's pink panties fell out on the floor. You can imagine the guys were giving it to me. "Where did you get those?" is what they said.

My third year with Minneapolis is when we drafted Elgin, and he made an immediate difference. We finished 33–39, second in the West behind the St. Louis Hawks, but that was an improvement of 14 wins. A lot of our points came from up front with Baylor, Vern Mikkelsen, and Larry Foust scoring quite a bit. Dick Garmaker averaged more than 13 points. Hot Rod Hundley and I each averaged around 9 points a game and as a team we had a lot of assists. Baylor led us in assists, too.

We stunned people in the playoffs, though. We opened against the Detroit Pistons, and they had finished behind us. We beat them two out of three and moved into the West finals against the St. Louis Hawks. The Hawks were the defending champions. They beat the Celtics for the title the year before when Bill Russell sprained his ankle. We got killed in the first game of the series and lost by 34. We beat the Hawks the next game and it went back and forth. We won the series in six games and advanced to the NBA championships—with a losing record. But the Celtics swept us. That was the first one of what became a series of epic Lakers-Celtics playoff competitions for the NBA crown.

Getting Elgin in Minneapolis and making it to the finals didn't save the franchise for Minnesota. We were 25–50 that year. We got some new players, and they were good. Rudy LaRusso was a really tough forward, who was 6'7" and could score and Frank Selvy, who scored 100 points in a game at Furman University, were new with us, and Elgin got even better. His scoring average went up to 29.6 points a game.

Minneapolis was a great city, but you would have to live there for a while to get used to the cold and the snow. I like the warm weather, the nice weather, so I couldn't say that I was going to miss winter when the team moved to Los Angeles for the start of the 1960–61 season. John Kundla didn't come with us. That run to the championship series was the end of his time coaching the Lakers. He wanted to stay in Minnesota, and he got the job coaching the Gophers at the University of Minnesota, where he stayed for about nine years before he retired.

It wasn't a complete surprise that the Lakers moved from Minneapolis to Los Angeles. We had taken a few games out there to test things. The funny thing, something that no one ever really talks about, is how the nickname Lakers doesn't fit California. The name comes from Minnesota being the land of 10,000 lakes. I don't know how many lakes there are out in California, but it doesn't have anything to do with the basketball team.

The last season in Minneapolis was pretty bad. We didn't win much, and then it got worse. We were lucky that any Lakers got to go to Los Angeles to play basketball since the team was in a plane crash before the end of the 1960 season.

No professional sports team has ever had a plane crash that wiped out a team, although it has happened in college, and we were very fortunate on January 18, 1960, that it didn't happen to the Lakers. We had just played the St. Louis Hawks, and we boarded a DC-3 to return to Minneapolis. Bob Short, who later owned the Texas Rangers baseball team, was our owner and he got a plane. I don't know if he owned it or chartered it. The DC-3 was known as one of the most reliable planes of all. A lot of guys had parachuted out of it in World War II.

We took off and the route was carrying us over Iowa. We ran into a major blizzard and we lost all of our electrical equipment. We didn't know it right away, but we heard later that there was no radio. The pilots had no radio contact to try to get us to turn around or divert to another airport. So we just proceeded on. The snowstorm was very scary. The door to the cockpit was open, and we could hear and see the pilots. They talked about having flown in the South Pacific in World War II. They had to open the window and one of the pilots stuck his head out to scrape the ice off the windshield.

At one point during the flight we were flying pretty low and the pilots were trying to read the terrain in the snowstorm to see if there was anyplace we could land. We started following a car along a road hoping that it would lead us into a town. The car was going uphill and then all of a sudden, boy, the pilots pulled back on the throttle and the plane shot up in the air. I guess we were too low.

We kept flying low without the radio and with the pilots trying to judge the terrain in the dark and the snow. There was no moon out. We were up there for about two hours flying around because we didn't know where we were, so after a while the gas situation was getting short. I'll tell you, it was very quiet in the passenger area. It was pretty much the players and coach and a couple or three other people connected to the Lakers. Nobody else was on board.

It was so quiet back where we were that we could hear anything the pilots said. All of a sudden we heard one of them say, "That looks like a cornfield down there." We were in Iowa so they had plenty of cornfields and we found one when we needed it. They made a pass around this town—we didn't know what it was, but it turned out to be Carroll, Iowa. On the first pass they spotted some high tension wires so they knew they had to avoid that. We were flying so low that we must have been making noise enough for the people in the houses to hear us. We could see some lights start coming on one by one in the houses.

The plane made a second pass and when we came around we could see red lights. It wasn't a very big town, but those were police cars and an ambulance. Things started to get really scary as we began heading in for a landing. One of the pilots said, "We're going to have to take it in now. We have to clear those high tension wires. But we've got to take it in."

I was sitting up near the front of the plane so I heard a lot. We were all scared to death. One story people told afterwards, which I didn't see because I was sitting closer to the front, was that Elgin layed down in the aisle. He thought it would help him. When the plane landed he thought he would just slide down the aisle instead of being hurt if it hit hard and crashed. A lot of us were wrapped up in blankets and we decided that wasn't the time to look around while we were going down, so we didn't pull them off.

The pilots brought the plane down right in the cornfield and they hit the shucks standing up there. When they hit them we were still going pretty fast and it was like all hell broke loose. Everything was flying all over and then the plane tucked up on end. The plane tipped forward with the tail up and the nose down. It tipped forward, and then bang, it settled down. The plane stopped in a remarkably short distance and it didn't even break up. Those pilots did a fantastic job. We were lucky.

As soon as the plane settled into place, the co-pilot ran to the back door and opened it. He got the back door open in a hurry and had us clear out because you couldn't know if there was going to be a fire or anything from the crash. If you wanted to see a bunch of guys get out of an airplane fast, boy, you should have seen us. We were clambering out the back door of that plane as fast as we could.

It was snowing, and the snow had drifted. It was up to our chests and we were a basketball team, so we were pretty tall. We were so happy to be on the ground that we started throwing snow at each other. Nobody got hurt and we were only two blocks from the highway where there were all of these cars lined up and emergency vehicles watching us.

I rode into the town of Carroll, Iowa, in the back of a hearse. They had everything out there on that highway. A lot of people came out to help. The funny part of that night was that when we got into town, which wasn't very big, though I don't know what the population was at that time, but they brought us to a retirement home. A retirement hotel, of some kind, I guess. There were all of these older people there and they were coming downstairs to the lobby in their nightgowns and pajamas. They wanted to see what was going on. These older people had been in bed for several hours.

I'll never forget, they had a little bar there that would seat six or seven people. It was a little round bar and there was a liquor cabinet with a padlock on it. Larry Foust, one of our big guys, went right over to that padlock and twisted it off with his bare hands. He got himself a big glass, yanked a fifth of VO out of there, and filled up that glass and started drinking it.

We stayed overnight there in that building. They had some extra rooms, enough to accommodate us for the night. Not that we got much sleep. Everybody stayed pretty tense for a while. It's hard to get over a thing like that. On the plane I was sitting next to Tommy Hawkins, our forward out of Notre Dame. His knees were shaking he was so scared. We were all scared. I was thinking about Nancy and the kids. I thought to myself, *What a hell of a way to die*. Then Tommy Hawkins said to me, "Slick, do you think we're going to die?" I said, "Hell, no."

The next day they got a bus to take us from Carroll, Iowa, to Minneapolis. It was a couple of hours by bus. But right away when we set out we passed that cornfield with the plane sitting out there. It was eerie. It was an eerie sight, and it made me think how only a few hours earlier we'd been flying on that doggone thing. We could also see the situation in the light. If we had gone about another 50 yards, about half a football field, we would have dropped off down into a ravine and that probably would have taken care of everybody.

When we got into Minneapolis—luckily we didn't have a game scheduled—all of our families were there waiting for us. That was pretty good. Everyone knew by then. I started getting calls from my Indiana buddies, asking if I was okay and everything. The news spread very quickly.

BOOM, BABY!

Although the plane crash didn't have anything to do with the Lakers moving to Los Angeles, in a way it made it more welcoming. We were leaving behind the land of ice and snow for the sun. We were getting the hell out after the plane crash.

CHAPTER 11

GO WEST, YOUNG MEN

The Minneapolis NBA franchise gave up on Minnesota and moved to Los Angeles for the start of the 1960–61 season. They brought the name Lakers with them. They brought Elgin Baylor and some other players, including Bob Leonard, with them. They left behind brutal Midwest winters and former coach John Kundla, who was replaced by Fred Schaus after the 1958–59 season. John Castellani and Jim Pollard coached the team during its final season in Minneapolis.

Schaus was the first player at West Virginia to score 1,000 points during his college career and had some good moments in the NBA with the Fort Wayne Pistons and New York Knicks before returning home to coach the Mountaineers between 1954 and 1960. He had coached Rod Hundley in college, and even more importantly, he had coached Jerry West in college.

West was a top Lakers draft pick as the team moved to Los Angeles, and he began one of the greatest of NBA careers as the team made its debut in the sunshine.

California's population was booming. Pro football had long before made itself comfortable in Los Angeles and San Francisco. Major League Baseball's Dodgers had fled from Brooklyn and set up shop in Los Angeles, and the Giants had departed New York and now operated out of San Francisco. The Lakers were in the vanguard of pro basketball, taking up residence on the West Coast. Soon enough the Philadelphia Warriors would move to the San Francisco area, and the fledgling American Basketball League would take a shot in California, too.

The Lakers kept their nickname, even if it was out of place in Los Angeles, but they came to town with two of the biggest superstars in the sport, and over time they became one of the most beloved franchises in basketball, and one of the most successful. Going beyond Elgin Baylor and Jerry West, they would feature such other spectacular basketball figures as Wilt Chamberlain, Magic Johnson, Phil Jackson, Gail Goodrich, Kareem Abdul-Jabbar, James Worthy, Jamaal Wilkes, Shaquille O'Neal, and Kobe Bryant. In time almost no one would remember the Minneapolis Lakers, despite their five championships and glorious history.

Bobby and Nancy Leonard and their three oldest children made the move from Minnesota to California in May 1960. The second son in the family was William Ray. Bill was born in Minneapolis, and he doesn't remember the trip west because he was an infant.

As a kid, Bill related to his dad in ways other than basketball at first.

"He was always a jokester," Bill said. "He would jump out from behind the door and yell 'Boo!' My earliest memories of spending time with my dad have nothing to do with basketball. We had already left Los Angeles and he used to take me and my brother, Bob, fishing at a lake. Even there he was teasing us that the 'black hawk' was going to get us. He liked to give us a little scare now and then."

When Bill got to be a little bit older—although he was still a kid—he was thrilled, just as brother Bob was, to play the role of ball boy at NBA games.

"We went to all of the practices," he said. "I actually remember sitting underneath the baskets."

By the time the Lakers moved to Los Angeles, it was obvious that Elgin Baylor was one of the best players around. He averaged 34.8 points a game during the club's first season in California. The second leading scorer was rookie guard Jerry West, who was 6'4". West averaged 17.6 points a game and briefly, though only briefly, went through an adjustment period.

Although the team's 36–43 record was only good for second place in the West, the club was getting stronger and taking shape. It was also getting heavy on guards. Besides Leonard, the Lakers had West, Frank Selvy, and Rod Hundley. They all outscored him that year. Leonard only appeared in 55 games, and his average dropped to 3.5 points per game. He struggled with a shoulder injury all year long that limited his production and game action.

The health problems did not help Leonard make a good impression on the new fans at the Los Angeles Memorial Sports Arena and prevented him from showing what he could do.

BOBBY LEONARD

When the Lakers got to Los Angeles, the Sports Arena was brand new. It was right by the Los Angeles Coliseum. It had escalators and everything. It was nice. Professional basketball was new to Los Angeles and when they played the National Anthem and you looked up at the flag right there they had a view of the turnstiles rotating with the people coming in. With each person who entered the building it would click. You could see exactly how many people were in the place.

The first games we played the attendance was 3,500 or 4,000. But we had Elgin Baylor and Jerry West, and word spread. After the slow attendance start, it broke loose and it went up quickly. It went from 4,000 people to 8,000 and then to 12,000. The place was packed.

We had a pretty good ball club, but with Jerry and Elgin we had excitement. The fans out there had never seen Bill Russell or Wilt Chamberlain, Bob Cousy or Oscar Robertson. So pretty quickly it became a big attraction. The two top players I ever played with were Jerry West and Elgin Baylor. But it's a funny thing, I saw that Magic Johnson named his all-time Lakers team and Elgin wasn't even on it. It really is impossible to do that. Here's a guy who is near the top of the lists to this day. You can't have an all-time Lakers team without Elgin Baylor on it. It's automatic.

I don't think he really gets credit. They're always mentioning other people. I don't think he gets credit for what he achieved. He did stuff all of the time that was just unbelievable. I could see what he was doing every night. You stop and think about how many players were so good that they could completely dominate a game. There are not many of them. And he was only 6'5". You probably couldn't pick 20 of them going back to the start of the NBA.

That year in Los Angeles the Lakers had quite a bit of young talent. We had changed out a lot of the pieces and added several new guys. Elgin Baylor, Jerry West, Rudy LaRusso, Hot Rod Hundley, and Frank Selvy were all young and talented. That was not a great year for me, although I didn't miss the snow in Minnesota. I got hurt. I had a shoulder that I separated about five or six times. It got to the point where I couldn't lift up my left arm.

I shot right-handed, but the pain from that thing was terrible. I spent the whole year in and out of the lineup, missing games, getting treated. It was a miserable year for me. We got into the playoffs and faced the Detroit Pistons in the first round. We won that series and moved into the West finals against the St. Louis Hawks.

The Hawks series was a tough one. It went back and forth. They had good players like Bob Pettit and Cliff Hagan, and Lenny Wilkens was with them by then. We won the first game. They won the second game. We went ahead 3–2, and the sixth game was in Los Angeles. We were in great position. Then Pettit and Hagan ended up beating us. We lost the sixth game 114–113 in overtime, and we lost the seventh game 105–103. We were that far away from reaching the championship series.

One thing that was interesting during that time period was that teams scored more. Games in the 120s were routine, not like it is now. And we didn't even have the three-point shot. Most every team had a fast breaking ball club. It would be easy to say that the defense was poor, but it's not true. Right away when I first came into the league they said, "If you can't play defense, you can't make it."

Left: Bobby Leonard's parents, Raymond Albert and Hattie Mae Leonard. *(Photo courtesy Bobby Leonard)*

Below: Bobby Leonard and his date, Nancy Root, early in their courtship in 1951. They were married in June 1954. *(Photo courtesy of Bobby Leonard)*

Taking a jump shot for the Hoosiers, Bobby Leonard was a two-time All-American at Indiana. *(Photo courtesy Bobby Leonard)*

Indiana University starting players from the 1953 NCAA championship team. Left to right: Charlie Kraak, Dick Farley, Don Schlundt, Burke Scott, and Bobby Leonard. *(Photo courtesy of Bobby Leonard)*

Coach Branch McCracken is lifted up in a celebration on the court after the Hurryin' Hoosiers won the 1953 NCAA title. *(Photo courtesy of Bobby Leonard)*

The scene in Bloomington when the Indiana University basketball team returned to town after winning the 1953 NCAA championship. The players are riding in open cars or on the hoods of cars. *(Photo courtesy of Bobby Leonard)*

Bobby Leonard drives into the lane in an NBA game against the Boston Celtics as Bob Cousy (No. 14) watches on. *(Photo courtesy of Bobby Leonard)*

Bobby Leonard played for the Los Angeles Lakers during the 1960–61 season, the first year the team was on the West Coast after moving from Minneapolis, Minnesota. *(Photo courtesy Bobby Leonard)*

Bobby Leonard as a pro during the 1962–63 season with the former Chicago Zephyrs, which are now known as the Washington Wizards. *(Photo courtesy of Bobby Leonard)*

Bobby Leonard coached the Indiana Pacers to three American Basketball Association championships, and it sometimes seemed as if he stood up along the sideline the entire time during those years. *(Photo courtesy of Greg Kluesner)*

Nancy Leonard (holding microphone) along with other Indianapolis community officials helps orchestrate a "Save The Pacers" telethon aimed at signing up more season ticket holders in 1976. *(Photo courtesy Bobby Leonard)*

Bobby Leonard waves to Pacers fans during a courtside ceremony when the team acknowledged his contributions by raising a banner with "529" on it— the number of victories the team earned while he was its coach. *(Photo courtesy Bobby Leonard)*

Bobby Leonard's "529" banner hangs in Bankers Life Fieldhouse in honor of the 529 victories he accumulated as the Pacers' coach. *(Photo courtesy Frank McGrath)*

Bobby Leonard broadcasting a 2012–13 season Indiana Pacers game against the Detroit Pistons at Bankers Life Fieldhouse. *(Photo by Lew Freedman)*

Bobby and Nancy Leonard at the Great Wall of China in 2009 on an Indiana Pacers preseason exhibition swing. *(Photo courtesy of Jeff Foster)*

It was more of an up-tempo game in the half-court, too. We didn't mess around. There were no seven passes before a shot. If we had a big guy open in the middle, we came down the floor and got it into him. He tried to make his moves, and if it didn't work he came back outside with the ball and bingo! We didn't fool around.

I just loved Elgin Baylor's game, and we were pretty lucky to get Jerry West to go along with him. As a rookie the one thing West had to do was improve his ball-handling skills, which he did. After that all he did was get better and better every year until he got to the place where nobody could guard him. The big thing about Jerry was that he could jump. He got a lot of rebounds for a guard. If a kid ever wanted to look at how to shoot a jump shot, he had to look at Jerry West's form. Jerry had the classic jump shot. He squared up to the basket, and he had the right kind of release. He had the form, and he elevated straight up on his shots. He was a clutch player. You look at the list of top scorers in playoff history. He was one of the star players who never had an off night. Stars didn't have off nights. They did it every game.

Elgin Baylor and Jerry West are both among the top 10 players in NBA history. When somebody picks the top four guards, Jerry is always in there. But for whatever reason with Elgin, you don't hear as much about him, which is a joke. It's a joke. I really don't know what else is. He was a smaller forward at 6'5", but I don't think that has anything to do with it. They didn't have television covering the games when Elgin played, the way they do now, so a lot of people didn't really see what he was all about. They would maybe have a Saturday or a Sunday game on television, but the broadcast was pretty much on the radio.

Those radio guys brought a lot of personality to the broadcasts. The Celtics had Johnny Most. He was a great announcer. He was something else. Johnny was a special guy. There are so many of those guys. Buddy Blattner, the old infielder for the St. Louis Cardinals, did the St. Louis Hawks games. There were some good guys on the air back then.

The Lakers had Elgin Baylor and Jerry West, and we had depth in the backcourt. Rudy LaRusso was a good player and he was at forward next to Elgin, so we were in pretty good shape there. Ray Felix—Baby Ray—was the center. He wasn't bad at all. He won the Rookie of the Year Award in 1954 when he scored almost 18 points a game and averaged more than 13 rebounds. He did that with the Bullets. He was 6'11" and could score inside, though there were fewer opportunities for him with Baylor, West, and the backcourt around. Still, he scored about 11 points a game for his career. He couldn't match up with Bill Russell or Wilt Chamberlain, but of course nobody really could.

Jimmy Krebs was our top backup forward. He was 6'8" and he was also our backup at center. He had a premonition that he was going to die young, and he was particularly scared when the plane was going down in the cornfield in Iowa. Jim retired from basketball young, and he passed away at a young age. It was a freak accident. A tree fell on him. He was only 29.

Our No. 1 rival in the West was the Hawks. St. Louis was good, and they won a title in 1957. They kept making the finals and losing to the Celtics. To get to the finals, we had to get past the Hawks. The Celtics won 11 championships in 13 years. In the beginning those championships came at the expense of the Hawks. Then they seemed to get the Lakers every year, even long after I left the club.

They had some great series, but the Celtics always got the better of the Lakers back then. Elgin never won a ring. Jerry finally got one ring after the Lakers brought in Wilt Chamberlain. They set the record for winning 33 games in a row, too. Elgin and Jerry both got into management after that, Elgin with the Clippers and Jerry with the Lakers as general managers. Jerry pulled off some great stuff with the Lakers, getting Kobe Bryant right out of high school and the deal that brought Shaq to Los Angeles.

It was so hard to beat the Celtics then. They were the dominant team. Bill Russell was fantastic. Bob Cousy was the first great playmaking man. He was the marquee player in the league, and they had a great supporting cast. That backcourt with Cousy and Bill Sharman and Sam Jones and K.C. Jones, I can't get over that group. That was a heck of a backcourt. But Russell changed it all.

Wilt Chamberlain was not a secret when he came in, either. We knew about him from his time at Overbrook High School in Philadelphia. He played at Kansas and spent a year with the Harlem Globetrotters. He had a great reputation in terms of what he could do with his height, which was 7'1", and his strength. But when he came into the league for the 1959–60 season and averaged 37.6 points a game for the Warriors, he went way beyond the expectations that people had.

Look at the guy. I played against him. I know what he was all about. You were always dropping down low, sagging in on defense to help out your center. This guy was so strong that truthfully, you could grab hold of the ball and he would lift you off the floor. He was bench-pressing 400 lbs. No one had ever seen anything like it. Then he scored 100 points in a game in 1962 and averaged 50.4 points a game for a whole season. I was in a lot of games when he scored 50 points.

Philadelphia had a guy named Dave Zinkoff who was the public address announcer at the Warriors games, and he had a great, deep, booming voice, and when Chamberlain scored Dave would say something colorful like, "Dipper dunk." Or "tim-ber." He was great. The fans loved him.

Wilt was something else. Right now in the NBA we don't have a lot of centers. There aren't a lot of great big men around. We don't have any Bill Waltons. We don't have any Kareem Abdul-Jabbars. And we sure don't have any Chamberlains. If he was in the league today, he would dominate it again. I have no hesitation about that. I have been playing, coaching, and broadcasting with the NBA for 60 years, and I have seen everything that came down the pike. I have seen them all, one way or another—either played against them, coached against them, or broadcast games in which they played. Wilt was total dominance, absolutely total dominance.

He's not the only one. You look back at the greatest players and if they were in their prime and in the game now, my goodness gracious. Jerry West would be tearing it up. Elgin would be tearing it up. Oscar Robertson would be tearing it up. Wilt Chamberlain would be tearing it up. You just go down that list. I'm sitting here watching the NBA games every night now, and I know what those guys could do. It's just an enduring greatness. You know whenever they played, they would have been great.

There are always going to be people who say different things to suggest the players back then aren't as good as they are today. But those players had the 24-second clock, so it was the same game, and basically there is no team in the NBA now that has a fast break like the Celtics. The tempo of the game isn't as fast as it used to be. People want to say it's defense, but it's actually ball control, that six or seven passes around the perimeter. It's great for ball movement, but at some point in time a guy's got to take a shot and hit it. There are more good shooters today.

Years ago Bob Cousy and Red Auerbach from the Celtics and some other people went overseas to run basketball clinics. Most of it was about fundamentals. You know what they found? Those international players, most of them, could shoot the ball. They didn't really know the game of basketball, but they could shoot. As far back as then. They did a lot of those clinics, and it bears fruit. I've said it many times that the international players can shoot the ball. Look at Dirk Nowitzki with Dallas. He came from Germany. You can go right down the line. If you look at the international players, that's where it started, with us going over there and teaching them the fundamentals of shooting.

It seemed that one way or another, if you were a professional athlete in Los Angeles, you were running into celebrities of some kind. One time some of us were in a bar and Mickey Mantle was there. We got to know some of the Dodgers and Rams. Johnny Podres the pitcher, I remember well.

Once the fans in Los Angeles recognized what they had with two superstars in Elgin Baylor and Jerry West, they came around even though the team's record was only 36–43. But by playoff time a ticket was hard to come by. We were an exciting team. Freddy Schaus was the new coach, and he got things started in Los Angeles. Even back then the celebrities, the movie stars, started coming to the games. It was a murderers' row, just like it is today.

It seemed so funny to us, playing and looking up and seeing all of these Hollywood people you had seen in the movies watching you. People like Lauren Bacall, Doris Day, and Bing Crosby. They even had a Hollywood team, a show business team. Pat Boone played. Sometimes they played preliminary games with us. We'd walk through the next dressing room and they'd all be there.

The team was coming together a bit at the end of the year. We beat the Pistons in the playoffs and lost to the Hawks in the West finals, but the team was entrenched in Los Angeles. We made a good impression. It was my worst year because of the shoulder problems, and I picked the wrong time to have those problems. The Lakers may have become hugely popular in Los Angeles, but it wasn't because of me. That was my only year in Los Angeles.

The NBA was expanding, adding a team in Chicago, and the Lakers put me up for the expansion draft.

CHAPTER 12

OFF TO THE WINDY CITY

The NBA expanded from eight to nine teams for the 1961–62 season by adding the Chicago Packers. Chicago was one of the country's major cities, and to be a major professional league, the NBA felt it had to bring the game back to the Windy City. Chicago had previously been home to the Stags, but 11 years had passed without a franchise.

Chicago was awarded the No. 1 draft pick, and the Packers chose wisely when they selected center Walt Bellamy out of Indiana University, Bob Leonard's old school. Bellamy was 6'11", a tremendous scorer and rebounder. Bellamy averaged 31.6 points per game and was voted Rookie of the Year. Later he was inducted into the Naismith Memorial Basketball Hall of Fame.

Leonard bounced back from his frustrating year with the Lakers to average a career high 16.1 points a game and had a team-leading 378 assists. The Packers roster was stocked primarily with players made available by existing teams in the expansion draft and through the college draft. Six players in all averaged in double figures that year. The other four were Andy Johnson, Sihugo Green, Ralph Davis, and Woody Sauldsberry.

The Packers could score, but their defense was nothing special and their record was 18–62. While Leonard got considerably more playing time with Chicago than he received with Los Angeles, he had traded a good team for a weaker one. The coach was the former Minneapolis Lakers star forward Jim Pollard.

For its second season in Chicago, the team changed its name to the Zephyrs. Leonard played just 32 games, averaging 7.1 points a game. The club drafted Terry Dischinger from Purdue, and he scored 25.5 points a game and followed up Bellamy's achievement by being named Rookie of the Year. The season began with the wily Jack McMahon as coach, but partway through the season management fired him and named Leonard to replace him. This was the beginning of Leonard's second career in pro basketball. The Chicago franchise showed marginal improvement, finishing 25–55, a seven-win upgrade.

Although Bellamy and Dischinger were exciting players, the mediocre record was not enough to excite the populace, and after two years in Chicago the team relocated to Baltimore and became the Baltimore Bullets, assuming the name of an old defunct franchise. The team still exists in the NBA as the Washington Wizards.

Expansion teams always struggle, and the Packers were no exception. Leonard, Nancy, and their three young children, Terry, Bob, and Billy, made the shift from the West Coast back to the Midwest and then to the East Coast.

Bill Leonard was a kid when his father was the head coach of the Baltimore Bullets, but the thing he remembers best from the time period that the family lived in the area has nothing to do with basketball. President John F. Kennedy was assassinated on November 22, 1963. The country was in turmoil, everyone in the nation, it seemed, was glued to the television set all weekend after the president was killed. His accused assassin Lee Harvey Oswald was arrested, and then Jack Ruby gunned down Oswald.

On the Monday after the long weekend, Kennedy's funeral took place. "We went to the John F. Kennedy funeral procession," Bill said.

BOBBY LEONARD

Up until 1961 my only NBA team was the Lakers, first in Minneapolis and then in Los Angeles. Then I was taken by the Chicago Packers in the expansion draft. The Packers were named for the connection to the big, famous Chicago stockyards that housed the meat-packing plants.

After that they changed the name to the Zephyrs and moved into a renovated little coliseum on Wabash. The name was for the winds off the lake, the Windy City. So they put Zephyrs in there.

When I was put up for the expansion draft, I was thinking the No. 1 thing I had to do was get well from my shoulder injury. The Lakers had Jerry West, Frank Selvy, and Hot Rod Hundley at guard without me, so I could see that I was probably not going to get as many minutes as I wanted. Going to Chicago meant there was going to be an opportunity to play. It turned out okay.

I got healthy, and I had the best year of my career. We picked up a pretty nice player named Walt Bellamy. He was Rookie of the Year and had 1,500 rebounds that year. Walt was a talented guy. It makes a difference when you get healthy. It was the best year I had. Andy Johnson came to us from the Harlem Globetrotters. Si Green was a big scorer in college at Duquesne University. Ralph Davis played at Cincinnati. Ralph was a journeyman. Woody Sauldsberry was a tough player. Charlie Tyra was a big man from Louisville, a nice guy.

They pieced together an expansion team, and the expectations were not very high. We were not very good. I didn't have any options. If I wanted to play, it had to be with the Chicago Packers. You play, but it's like I've always said, losing is misery. It's no fun. Winning is all there is, and unfortunately we didn't have the players to get the job done.

We did accomplish a couple of things. We got the first pick and were able to choose Walt Bellamy who went on to have a great career in the NBA.

Then, because we finished last, we were able to get Terry Dischinger. He beat out everybody for Rookie of the Year for two in a row for Chicago. It was a good sign that we had the Rookie of the Year twice.

There was optimism in Chicago in the beginning, but being an expansion team it didn't take long for the optimism to wear off. We were the

Packers for one year and the Zephyrs after that. I had my best year with the Packers but didn't do as well with the Zephyrs. I hurt my shoulder again—it was the seventh time. That was my second year in Chicago, and it turned out to be my last year playing in the NBA.

Getting hurt changed my life. If they had the kind of modern medical equipment and know-how then as they do now, it probably could have been fixed permanently. I started taking cortisone shots to be able to play. When that cortisone wore off, the pain would take you right to your knees. They stick a really long needle in you. Guys today don't play injured as much as they used to because back then there weren't any no-cut contracts. You had to make the team every year. If you sat out too many games with injuries, then you knew you were going to be out of a job. So guys played with injuries the likes of which they don't play with today. We also only had 10 men, so we had a shorter bench, and if you lose a couple of guys to injuries, then it just makes it tougher to win.

Jack McMahon was coaching the Zephyrs, and we weren't getting anywhere. When I messed up my shoulder that season, I went from being a player to becoming a head coach. There was no break in between. Jack McMahon was out, and I was in. One minute I was a starting guard, and the next minute I was running the team.

That was the end of my NBA playing career. The shoulder took me out of basketball, at least at the playing end of it. I was 31 and wanted to keep playing. I lost two years to the military, and I would have played longer. My shoulder retired me. I did know I wanted to be a coach someday. That went back to when I played at IU. I had been the cadet colonel of the ROTC. That showed me that I could act with authority, and I felt I had the ability to be a coach.

I did not really have another ambition at the time. I felt I had two avenues. One was to be a coach, and one was to become a salesman. I could have been selling pharmaceuticals. I could have made a good living in selling and did so for a while later on. I wanted to stay in the game. I loved basketball.

The Zephyrs were struggling—they don't fire the coach if things are going well. We had a great 1-2 punch on offense with Walt Bellamy and Terry Dischinger. Walt averaged more than 27 points a game.

Walt was a big, strong guy. He could really run the floor. He could shoot from about 16' out. He was not just an inside guy. Because he could hit from that distance, you had to come out and play defense on him. Or he could put it on the floor and beat you. I saw him get 45 points off Bill Russell. For a young player to get 45 points off Russell, you knew he was pretty good.

Terry averaged more than 25 points a game that year. Terry had some of the greatest moves I've ever seen. He had all kinds of spin moves, and he could shoot the ball. Also, he could elevate. Terry could jump. There have only been a small number of guys who were ever All-State in Indiana in four sports. Terry was All-State in football, basketball, baseball, and track. He was an outstanding athlete.

Billy McGill was on that team. He had a tremendous career in college at Utah, but he was behind Walt Bellamy and only scored about seven points a game. He was known as Bill "The Hill" McGill. He led the country in scoring at Utah, averaging 38.8 points a game, but McGill never had the same kind of career in the pros that he did in college. Don Nelson came out of Iowa, and that was the beginning of his career in the NBA that lasted about 50 years. He was better known as a coach, but he was a solid player. Don averaged just under seven points a game that year. He was a hard-nosed player as a forward. Don was a journeyman as a player, and he'll admit that. He got on some good teams, though, and he was fortunate enough to win championships with the Celtics.

I did not want to retire from playing. I had mixed emotions. It's tough to give up playing, but when you can't do it anymore, coaching is the only alternative. I knew I couldn't keep playing because of my shoulder. It got so bad that it was career-ending. I still have trouble with it to this day. It kept separating. The seventh time that I separated my shoulder, it was the end of a ball game. I was so used to the feeling that when it happened I knew what it was right away.

There was a lot of contact in games under the basket, and there was a lot of contact trying to fight through screens and picks. The last time I separated the shoulder I ran into Clyde Lovellette. He was very good at setting picks, and he was a headhunter on picks. The contact didn't bother Lovellette at all. He probably had me by 40 lbs. For me, it was like running into a brick wall. He was the same kind of player who does well in today's game. He would run the pick, and if the guy didn't get through him he faded out and boom, they'd hit him with the pass, and he'd shoot from up to 20'.

Clyde was a high hitter. Your man would lead you right into Clyde, and it would drop you right to your knees. He was with the Celtics that year. Red Auerbach picked him up at the end of his career as a backup to Bill Russell. I knew I was hurt again right away. I didn't know what my future was going to be, but it just kept happening and I knew deep down that it had gotten to a point where I couldn't heal if I kept playing. The doctor took a look at it and didn't say I was through, but I was starting to feel that way.

A few days later Dave Trager, who was the big honcho of the Chicago Zephyrs and was big in the insurance industry there, called me on the phone. He asked me to meet him for lunch. I figured he wanted me to do something, but I didn't know for sure what it was. I thought he might be planning to hire a new coach and might ask me to become the assistant. At that time we had a general manager, Frank Lane, who had been a well-known baseball general manager. In fact, he had been general manager of the Chicago White Sox in town. He was known as "Trader" Lane because he kept swapping players wherever he went.

He would lather up in suntan lotion, which was probably more important in the sunshine in spring training. He sat in the bars and watched the ladies while he drank orange juice.

I met Dave Trager for lunch at a private club where he went. Seems to me the name was the Covenant Club, which has gone out of business. I went over to the table and he had been playing gin. The funny part was he was playing cards with Sid Luckman, the Chicago Bears Hall of Fame quarterback.

When I sat down, Dave made me an offer to coach the club. I was kind of surprised, but I thought it was great. He saw some things in me that he obviously wanted as a coach. He offered me the job, and I said I would take the job. Then he sat there and wrote out a check to Sid Luckman for how much he lost in the gin game that was more than he was going to pay me to be the head coach. I guess they used to play every day, and he was settling the payment. He wrote that check for $15,000. They were playing for keeps. That was a gin game to stay out of. I couldn't handle that. When I played gin, it was always for pennies. I'm sure that still goes on today in private clubs for even more money. The stakes can be pretty high.

We had this little meeting at the club and no one else knew besides me and Dave Trager. And Sid Luckman knew. Trager hadn't even told Frank Lane. I don't think Lane knew until after we made the deal. He may have, but it didn't appear that way. But he wasn't there at the club when I was offered the job.

After that Frank scheduled the press conference to let everyone know that I was going to be the new coach. I can't remember the name of the hotel we were at, but I went down there and Frank introduced me to the press, which knew all about me anyway because I've been playing. Right after he made the introduction Frank goes, "Coaches are hired to be fired." I always remembered that. I was thinking, "Boy, what the heck?" Frank played the game that way—he moved people in and out a lot. But you know, he was right. Coaches are hired to be fired. They don't usually mention it when they introduce a guy.

Of course, the first thing the sportswriters asked was, "How are you going to make them into winners?" Having Walt Bellamy and Terry Dischinger was a starting point that was going to make it more enjoyable than it would have been. I just felt like I'd take the guys and we'd work at it and see what we could come up with. There were a couple of other kids on the team who had potential. One was Johnny Cox. He had been a star at Kentucky and he averaged 7.8 points a game for us.

The big problem we had in Chicago at the time was that James Norris was never going to allow the basketball team to get into the Chicago Stadium, the big arena in town. Without that the Zephyrs were never going to draw as much as we could. It was a key issue.

One of the things I developed in Chicago was my style of coaching. I think it comes somewhat naturally to a person, depending on the kind of person he is. Today they call the coach who is up and around a lot a yeller and a screamer, and I don't like to use that terminology. I think of coaching more as teaching. But you can be a yeller and a screamer at the refs. I've always felt that you cannot sit down all of the time and coach a game. You've got to get up and get into it, just like you were acting when you were a player. I recognized that right away, so I was up off the bench. Some guys don't need a seat at all. I didn't sit very much.

We finished out the season and then the team got sold and we became the Baltimore Bullets for the 1963–64 season. I wasn't that attached to Chicago one way or another—I was more attached to the team—so I just felt like when you're in pro basketball you have to roll with the punches. That was it. So we moved to Baltimore and rolled with those punches, and I tried to do the best job I could.

The team finished 31–49. I had hoped we would do a little bit better, but I thought the team had a lot of potential. We made a pretty daring trade. I traded Terry Dischinger to the Detroit Pistons and got back about five or six players for him.

We also made a great draft pick. We took Gus Johnson in the second round out of Idaho, and he ended up in the Hall of Fame. I was tipped off about Gus Johnson being a great player and a great jumper. Scouting was not very sophisticated at the time, and college games with Idaho weren't on TV. There was a report that had the college statistics that came out once a month with the top rebounders and the top scorers, and I kept looking at this thing and saw Gus Johnson right at the top of the lists. Back in 1953 when we went to the Final Four of the NCAAs at Indiana, the University of Washington was there and they had a guy named Joe Cipriano. He had become the coach at Idaho, and I called him on the phone.

I said, "Hey, Joe, I've been looking for a good forward. Can this guy Gus Johnson play?" He said, "Hell, yes, he can play." That was enough right there. So we drafted Gus Johnson, and of course, that was a great move. Gus was 6'6", but he could jump out of the house. It was a shame he died young. So we had Walt Bellamy, Gus Johnson, Rod Thorn, Sihugo Green, and Terry Dischinger before the trade. It wasn't too bad of a lineup. Gene Shue was there, too, but it was the end of his career. Baltimore was his home, and if he was going to keep playing, he wanted it to be there.

We had another draft pick that we thought was going to turn out to be a good one. He was out of Utah State, where he had been a good player, All-League a few times, but after I drafted him I couldn't sign him. He wanted to play football. He hadn't even played football in college. He ended up with the Dallas Cowboys as a free agent and turned into a great defensive back. It was Cornell Green. I tried to sign him, and he said, "I really want to play football." Damn, he was a good football player.

On offense we were pretty good. We averaged more than 111 points a game. But we gave up a lot of points. We didn't stop anybody. That was a young team, very young. They were definitely getting better, and were going to get even better. At the same time Detroit had some players that I kind of liked that I thought could help us. They had a good scorer in the backcourt named Don Ohl. They had Kevin Loughery, who later coached in the NBA. They had a big kid by the name of Les Hunter out of Loyola who I got the rights to. And I got Bob Ferry, Bailey Howell, and Wally Jones. I gave up Dischinger, Rod Thorn, and Don Kojis. They were good players, but I got somebody who could replace them and more. You have to see what this trade was about. We got depth. It ended up being a hell of a trade for Baltimore.

I thought we were on our way to building something in Baltimore. The Bullets were trying to put down roots like the Orioles and the Colts. When the team went to Baltimore, we bought equipment from Brooks Robinson at his sporting goods store. I'd stop by Jim Parker's liquor store, and we sat outside and visited. Jim went to Ohio State and he was a Hall of Fame lineman with the Colts. What a nice guy. Gino Marchetti from the Colts was around, too. Oh, he was a tough player. He and Alan Ameche started hamburger joints that were very popular. Raymond Berry, another Colt in the Pro Football Hall of Fame, used to come to practices because he liked basketball.

Baltimore ended up having some great teams when they got Wes Unseld and Earl "The Pearl" Monroe. I made the trade and I never did get to coach them. It's like Frank Lane said, "Coaches are hired to be fired." Frank Lane was already gone when we went to Baltimore. He wasn't there. Paul Hoffman was the general manager then.

I definitely thought that team was on the rise, but we didn't win enough games and I got fired. I didn't see it coming because I thought we were going to be much better.

It was the first time I got fired, and it's a downer. But you have to take your life on from there and do something with it. We stayed in Baltimore that year, and Nancy taught school. I was very fortunate the way it ended up. If we hadn't been in Baltimore that year, the next phase of my life would not have come about.

CHAPTER 13

OUT OF THE GAME

By the end of the 1962–63 season, Bobby Leonard was a retired basketball player. The end of his career snuck up on him and caught him off guard. Injury did him in and he hated to admit that his body, at age 31, was not ever going to be as firmly muscled or as powerful as it was earlier in his career.

His playing days in high school at Terre Haute Gerstmeyer, in college at Indiana University, and in the pros with the Minneapolis and Los Angeles Lakers and the Chicago Packers and Zephyrs, were finished.

Leonard retired after seven pro seasons. His career concluded with 4,204 points, a 9.9 points per game average; 1,217 rebounds, a 2.9 average; and 1,427 assists, a 3.3 per game average.

A star in high school, an All-American in college, and a member of an NCAA champion, Leonard played on some good teams and not-so-good teams in the NBA. He had made a quick transition to a fresh basketball career as a coach, but that didn't last very long. Although he wanted to coach again, he was aware that with so few teams in the league—nine at the time of his departure—such jobs in the NBA were hard to come by.

So in 1964 he embarked on a new career, at least for the time being, as a salesman, a job that brought his family back to Indiana. They moved to Kokomo, Indiana, about an hour north of Indianapolis.

At the time Leonard did not know that his new career, selling high school class rings, would only be a temporary shift away from basketball. But it was the end of an era for him, and his time spent in the NBA was the end of an era for the league itself and the start of a bigger and better operation. In the 1950s the NBA was pretty much a provincial league. In the decades since, it has grown and expanded so much as to be almost unrecognizable to people like Leonard who saw the league in its comparative infancy.

BOBBY LEONARD

By the time I reached a year off after being fired by the Bullets following the 1963–64 season, the NBA was changing and it has continued to change.

This was still the old days of the NBA. It was growing, and wasn't as rough around the edges as when I broke in for the 1956–57 season. We took a lot of busses at first for exhibition games. Then we took trains. By my second year with the Lakers, we started flying commercial a lot. So I went through busses, trains, and to planes during a few years. Most of those were commercial flights, so the team was walking through airports with the so-called civilian passengers. Not everybody had charter planes like they do now. It's hard for me to believe the changes since those days.

The progress that I've seen that has been made in the NBA is unbelievable. We had a $3 per diem a day. You traveled by train. You didn't have no-cut contracts. Nobody had a long-term contract, and there were always these college All-Americans coming along every year, trying to take your job. When you went on a longer road trip you had a player's bag with your uniform and a clothes bag with a sport coat and slacks and you carried it all of the time. Now there's an equipment manager who handles the uniforms. When you get to the dressing room, they're all laid out for you. Sometimes on the road we went to a washateria, got some soap, and cleaned our uniform, or we threw it in the bathtub and hung it up in the room somewhere. It was kind of pitiful. Now the equipment managers do the washing for the visiting team. Or our equipment man washes our stuff.

There were a lot more fights in the sport in the 1950s and early 1960s. There were a lot of fights in training camp when players were after jobs. But there were also a lot of fights on the floor during games. There really were no penalties other than a small fine maybe. The refs just stepped into the middle of it and got the players to clear off. It was rougher back then than it is now.

You only had two officials, not three like they do now. You knew the referees pretty well. Some of them had a lot of personality and the fans knew who they were. Guys like Sid Borgia, Joe Gushue, Norm Drucker, Mendy Rudolph, Earl Strom, John Vanek—some of them went way back. They were all great officials. The fans knew them and called them by name, for better or worse.

Officials wouldn't put up with much guff. They would hit you with a technical, and you didn't want a technical because the other team shot a free throw on every one. There was no money involved from the league officially, but there was what we called a whispering fine of $15.

The shoot-around didn't exist for teams on the day of a game. Bill Sharman invented that when he was coaching the Lakers in the early 1970s, the year they won 33 straight games. And gradually every team began to do it. Teams got themselves to the arena, usually by piling into cabs. In a couple of places we walked. We usually walked to Madison Square Garden in New York and sometimes in Syracuse. Some fans would recognize you on the street, especially if you were carrying the team bags. They would recognize the big names, but not everybody. Not everybody is a fan of basketball.

Now teams ride busses from the hotel to the arena, and at the airport the busses take you right up to your chartered plane. The teams don't even go through the terminal. There are separate areas where they take care of chartered planes. They pick up your luggage at the hotel, and they take it to the airport. You've got more leg room on the planes. My goodness. I think that has something to do with how guys survive better and play more years now. They've got strength and conditioning programs. They've got dieticians. They've got everything if a guy really wants to work on it. The team has everything to make it easier for him.

Players don't need off-season jobs because they make so much money. They don't need the income. They need to be playing basketball in the off-season to try to improve their game. I'm not against the money. It's the entertainment business. I know the people on the street cannot identify with that and what they're making in basketball and baseball. It's tough for the small-market teams because they have to charge so much for tickets. But the money comes from television. Some of these multi-million-dollar contracts work out just fine. There are other ones where the team has signed a long-term contract and it doesn't turn out and they have to pay. I think that's when the fan resents it. I never thought I would see where it's reached with guys making $20 million a year.

The only area where I have a problem is that the guys who played in the late 1940s and the early 1950s, the guys that helped build the league—and there aren't too many of them still living—who get very small pensions. They could do more for them.

There have been player strikes and owner lockouts, but the fans today wouldn't believe how difficult it was for the players to even start a union where the owners would listen to them at all. Salaries were very low. A really big-deal salary for most good players, All-Stars even, was $20,000 in the early 1960s. Players fought for 50-cent increases in per diem to eat better on the road.

Bob Cousy was the first president of the Players Association because he was such a big name in the sport that he was protected. People knew that he wouldn't be cut by the Celtics. Tommy Heinsohn worked as president of the Players Association, too. He was an All-Star. One guy I remember trying to do a lot who was not as big a name was Gene Conley. Conley was Bill Russell's backup with the Celtics for a few years, and he also pitched in the majors at the same time, part of the time with the Red Sox. Conley is the only athlete who ever won a World Series—with the Milwaukee Braves—and an NBA championship ring. That was with the Celtics. Those guys helped bring things along, to make the league more major league.

Another thing about the NBA that is incredibly different now than it was when I was playing is the arenas. They were historic buildings, but they were old, not as fancy or as large as the ones teams play in now.

The Boston Garden was pretty big. The capacity was 13,909, but they didn't usually sell out. They did always have that parquet floor, though. The Syracuse War Memorial Auditorium was an old building. I played in the old Madison Square Garden, the one that was at Eighth Avenue and West 49th Street, not the one at Pennsylvania Station. The Philadelphia Convention Center is gone. I think just about all of the old buildings are gone. Some of the places, like St. Louis, don't even have teams.

Then there were the doubleheaders. For a while the NBA scheduled doubleheaders to get more fans because the home teams couldn't sell out. Four of the eight teams in the league would play on the same night in the same place. I've been in the 6:30 PM game, and I've been in the 9:00 PM game. That packed them in.

As I mentioned, one of the things that got our attention in New York was all of the gamblers ringing the outside of the court, waiting to put down their bets at the end of the warm-ups. I didn't notice it so much anyplace else, but at the old Garden if the game happened to go down to the wire and you happened to hit a shot—which I did one time—that changed the point spread, they liked to kill you. I had the fans run down to the court as I was walking off the floor at the end of the game and start calling me every name in the book because that shot cost them money.

Boston Garden was tradition. We came out to warm up, and we were running our layup lines. I can still see Cooz leading Boston out on the floor. A lot of tradition. You'd go over to the scorer's table and you've got the announcer, and Johnny Most, the radio guy. You've got Red Auerbach at the end of the game smoking his cigars if they won. In Boston the fans were tough on a visiting team, but it was a great place to play. We took the train into North Station. One place they had just outside the station was Joe & Nemo's hot dogs. That's where we ate a lot because we didn't have much money for our per diem. Luckily, they were good. That's where you had to eat. You didn't have enough money to buy anything but hot dogs.

Syracuse had a good ball club, but the fans were definitely tough up there at the War Memorial. There was a guy we called "The Strangler" who sat behind the visiting bench in Syracuse. He was a big guy, a horse if I remember, and boy, he was nasty. He'd call you every name in the book. You'd come over to the bench, and he was riding you like you wouldn't believe. It happened more than once that a player snapped and went after him. He did it to us, and he did it to other teams. I think they finally had to move him out of that seat. They either moved him to another place or out of the building.

The Hawks played in Kiel Auditorium. Ben Kerner was the owner. Remember I said that the home team supplied a trainer. At the least the guy they supplied was there to tape your ankles. The guy Kerner had was such a nice guy that you let him tape your ankles and then you went back to your locker room and took a pair of tape cutters and cut it off because he didn't know how to tape ankles. They were too tight. It would have cut off all of the circulation. But he was such a nice guy we always went in there. His wife even baked cookies and they had them in the training room. We didn't want to make him feel bad, so we let him do it and then cut off the tape.

The Convention Center was for the Warriors first, with Neil Johnston, Tom Gola, and Jack George, but it wasn't that big of a place. Neither were Syracuse or Rochester. They were places that held 7,000, 8,000, maybe 9,000 people. Philadelphia fans were typical East Coast fans. They were vociferous, but they knew the game. They knew the pro game. They were all over you. Let's face it, that's pretty much the way it was everywhere. It's somewhat like that today.

After the Royals went to Cincinnati they played in the Cincinnati Gardens. That was another place that wasn't very big. That was a good team. They had Oscar Robertson, the Big O, Jack Twyman, Bob Boozer, and Arlen Bockhorn. He was a guard for them and he's a friend of mine.

We were in the army together. He lives in Dayton. Our birthdays are close to one another's in July. We call each other on our birthday.

When you went into the Cincinnati Gardens, you knew you were going to play against one of the greatest guards who ever lived. I have guarded Oscar. He was so good and so strong. He was 6'5". He was a great passer. He could hit the jump shot on you in traffic. He was great. I also covered Bob Cousy, and after I went from the Lakers to Chicago I covered Jerry West.

When it came to those guys, the Big O, Jerry, Cousy, and Sam Jones, a lot of them had a little different twist in their game. You know their game, but they were all so good, they were monsters to guard. I never dreaded covering any of them, though. I looked at it as a challenge. I felt I was a big-time competitor. It's the way I knew how to play. They might get 25 points on me, but there might be something that happened in the game where I did something well and got a little victory out of it. The great ones would still get the shots off. You'd be right in their faces, but that's how good they were.

There were times when I held them below their averages, and there were times when I scored almost as much as they did. But those times were few and far between. They did it every night. I just tried to hold them to their average or below.

I had learned a lot coaching in the NBA, but I didn't know if I would be using it at all.

The big things I learned were what I call the intangibles of coaching. If you reach that level, all coaches know Xs and Os. It's the intangibles of your relationship with your players that is important. The level of the talent you have makes a difference, but it's also about your relationship with that talent. There are times when you've got to kick them in the butt, and there are times when you've got to hug them. And they've got to know that you're for real. If you try to fool players, you may fool them for a week, you may fool them for a month, but beyond that, they've figured you out. By that I mean that you have to be what you say you are.

Not being sincere, talking behind their backs, there are a number of things that you can't do in coaching. I picked up some of that stuff in the military. I can tell a phony a mile away. You can't be like that. You've got to be sincere and show the players that you care about them, that you care about their families, and that you care about their future. That's what I mean when I say coaching is all about the intangibles.

When I left the Baltimore Bullets, I think I was making $15,000 to coach. You didn't make much money in the NBA in those days.

After I got fired from the Bullets and we stayed in Baltimore that next season when Nancy was teaching, something happened that was lucky for me.

One day during the football season, the Green Bay Packers were in town to play the Baltimore Colts and I got a call from my old friend Bob Skoronski. We were at Indiana together, and he was playing tackle for the Packers. He told me about the business of selling school rings, and graduation announcements. Two of the biggest companies were Jostens and Herff Jones. One thing I always thought I could do was be a salesman.

That's what Bob did in the off-season. I found out that one of my old teammates from IU was in management with Herff Jones. One thing led to another and I ended up getting the Central Indiana territory for Herff Jones. That's when we moved back to Indiana and rented a house in Kokomo.

I got the region for nothing. I didn't have to pay to buy in, and my first year with Herff Jones I made more money than the Bullets paid me to coach. When I went to work for Herff Jones, it wasn't intended to be an interlude in my basketball coaching career—it was going to be my new career. I enjoyed it. I liked what I was doing. I didn't miss basketball. I was doing something new.

We were based in Kokomo for four years, from 1965–70, and I really enjoyed going into the high schools and talking to people and selling class rings. I got to know a lot of good people. After those years we moved to Carmel, where we have lived for more than 40 years.

I came back to basketball with the Indiana Pacers, but for several years I kept up my work with Herff Jones, too. I stayed with them until 1974, and when I left the company, they paid me for the territory even though I hadn't paid for it in the first place. Herff Jones was good to me, but it got to be too much trying to do both things at once.

I never missed basketball, and I could have stayed at Herff Jones a long time, but when I got another chance to work in basketball I was ready for that.

CHAPTER 14

CALL FROM THE
INDIANA PACERS

In 1967 the Indiana Pacers were in the process of being created to compete in the new American Basketball Association. The ABA was planning to do battle with the NBA in the growing realm of pro basketball, mostly taking the game to cities that were shut out of the NBA.

Indiana has always been one of the great strongholds of the game. The first Indiana state high school championship was contested in 1911. Indiana University was a national power and at the time had won two NCAA crowns. Purdue University had a long tradition and boasted among its alumni John Wooden, the UCLA coach who was at the time running off title after title in collegiate play. Butler University and its well-respected coach, Tony Hinkle, also had a fine program.

Indiana, and its capital city of Indianapolis, seemed like a logical place to start a franchise. When Bob Leonard was first approached to become involved with the team it was on an ad hoc basis. His first assignment, one he shared with old Terre Haute friend Clyde Lovellette, was supervising a tryout camp at the Indiana State Fairgrounds on behalf of the Pacers.

For its inaugural season, the Pacers already had a coach in Larry Staverman, who among other things in his basketball career had suited up for Bob Leonard with the Chicago Zephyrs during the 1962–63 season. Mike Storen was the Pacers' first general manager and also a vice-president of the club. It was Storen who reached out to Leonard in 1967 with a phone call asking for some help. Before becoming a top executive with a number of sports franchises following his involvement with the Pacers and eventually becoming the commissioner of the ABA, Storen was a ticket salesman for the Chicago Zephyrs.

Leonard and Lovellette helped the Pacers find talent for the first team they would put on the court. They were taken aback by the turnout at the tryout session at the Fairgrounds. The parade of players who showed up clearly proved that basketball was beloved in Indiana, but few seemed to realize what it took to play at the professional level.

"It was hilarious," Lovellette said much later. "It seemed like we had gobs of players to pick from in that group. They weren't very good, but they all gave it a heck of a try. They had a little bit more ego than talent. It was like a talent show. There were guys you had to wonder why they'd try out. It's like if you sing in the shower and then you get out on stage and you sing flat."

It wasn't terribly long before Bob Leonard was transformed from talent consultant to head coach.

One member of the Leonard family who was very happy that her father seemed prepared to remain in Indiana to work was daughter Terry. She was about to start high school and was glad it was in Indiana and not someplace fresh.

Just when Bob Leonard became involved in basketball again, his kids were starting to reach the age when they could have fun attending games, watching games, and appreciate interacting with the players. Bob believed in a family atmosphere around his team, and an offshoot of that was that his kids came to work with him and were as involved as they could possibly be with the team without interfering with his coaching.

"It was pretty normal for us," said the younger Bob Leonard, the oldest boy in the family. "It was a relaxed atmosphere. It wasn't ESPN-like. We hung out in practices. When I was a ball boy under the basket, I threw the ball to the players when they warmed up."

The kids knew the difference between how to interact properly with the players and when not be underfoot when it was time for serious business. The younger Bob knows he had a privileged lifestyle that his friends at school weren't privy to.

"When they went to playoff games, I rode the bus," he said. "I knew the players very well. They were just wonderful guys. The way they treated me was incredible. It was family." Yes, some of the players were among those, including his father's older friends, who sometimes called him Slick Junior. "I was very much into basketball," he said.

The entire Leonard family was connected, from Nancy, who attended every game and sat close to the court, to the kids, who attended all weekend games and some weeknight games on special occasions. Once dad became the coach, the Leonards were the biggest Pacer fans in the Hoosier state.

The Indiana Pacers took the court for the first time in the winter of 1967–68. Some of the notable players were guard Freddie Lewis, forwards Roger Brown and Bob Netolicky, and guards Jimmy Rayl and Jerry Harkness.

Lewis, who came out of Arizona State, was the leading scorer at 20.6 points per game. Brown had been unjustly accused of participating in the college basketball point-shaving scandal of several years earlier and had been banned from the NBA. Netolicky was a Pacers star for several years. Rayl was an Indiana legend as a high school star and two-time All-American at Indiana University, averaging 29.8 points per game as a junior. Harkness played for Loyola's 1963 NCAA championship team and with the Pacers that season Harkness made the longest shot in professional basketball history, a 92' heave to win a game over the Dallas Chaparrals with the clock running out.

"I took a dribble and let it go," Harkness said. "The ball hit the backboard and went in. It won the game. It was luck."

The Pacers finished 38–40 in their first season. After a 2–7 start to the 1968–69 season, Indiana made a change, replacing Staverman with Bob Leonard as head coach.

Leonard and Rayl were friendly. They were both living in Kokomo and played golf. "Neither of us were any good at golf," Rayl said. "We might shoot 79 or 80 on a good day. We weren't getting around in par. We had fun."

Rayl was stunned when Leonard cut him from the team, and while shocked that it happened, has not held it against Leonard personally.

"It's hard for me to say anything bad about him," Rayl said. "You can't help but like old Slick," Rayl said. "Slick's Slick. I started five days before I got cut. It was kind of a traumatic experience."

BOBBY LEONARD

One day I got a phone call from Mike Storen. I can't remember the exact date but I think maybe August. Training camp was going to start a few weeks later. He called me and said this new league was going to start, the American Basketball Association, and the Indiana Pacers was a new team that was going to be in it.

Mike came up with the idea of having an open tryout camp. There's some good reasoning in that, even if you don't find any players good enough. It lets people know who the Pacers are. It's free advertising. Mike approached Clyde Lovellette, too, and he asked us to run the camp. Well, Clyde and I got there and we're opening up the camp. Anybody could come and try out. But we got bushwhacked. They had 165 guys show up. I thought we'd be lucky if we got 50 guys.

This really was an anybody-can-come thing. Boy, anybody who ever played high school basketball in Indiana, anybody in the state of Indiana who had ever dribbled a basketball, showed up. They all had a dream. We had some former college players, but we had so many players that we had to sit down and figure out how we were going to handle all of them.

It was basically me and Clyde figuring this out. Mike Storen was there, but Clyde and I were organizing the tryouts. Finally, we organized them into groups, A, B, C, and D. This was supposed to be a one-day tryout thing, but because there were so many players it was clear that it was going to become a two-day tryout. We came up with ways to weed them out.

The first thing we did was give them a simple warm-up drill. We lined up the players to the midcourt line and had them drive to the basket. The rule was if you miss the layup you're done. That's pretty harsh, but it's pretty basic. If a guy can't make a layup, maybe he shouldn't be there. I didn't miss layups in warm-ups. I was always taught to lay that thing up against the glass solid. That was the situation. If you miss the layup, you were cut. We got rid of some of them with the layups.

Then we did passing drills, just basic fundamental basketball, defensive drills, rebounding. It was tough with that many people out there on the court, but when we got down to the end of that practice we said, "Okay, we're going to run." Everybody who has ever been in basketball knows one thing—you run at the end of practice. We were running from baseline to baseline, and we were going to run 15 of them. That's going to the free throw line, back, to the mid-line, back, to the other free throw line, back, and to the other end and back, 15 times.

If you come to a tryout like that you have to be in shape. This is what happened. Some of them ran two, some three, some four, some five, but it took a toll on them. The guys who really tried to make it and do all of them, they were over on the sides throwing up. They had been out on the court for a couple of hours.

One guy that I'll always remember came to this open tryout wearing a pair of cut-off bib overalls and a red sweatshirt. He had on tennis shoes and they looked as if he'd had 'em on out there shoveling manure. He was right from the farm, just a good guy. He tried everything, but the turning point was the 15 baselines. They were a monster for this guy. Nobody ran the 15 baselines.

At the end of that I got out there at midcourt and I said, "Now listen up. We're going to start practice at 8:00 in the morning. I'm going to tell you ahead of time, you tried to run 15 baselines today, but we're going to up it to 25 tomorrow." And I added, "The other thing is being on time. It's just as easy to be 10 minutes early as it is to be 10 minutes late."

The next morning seven guys showed up. We couldn't even scrim-mage full-court. Seven guys out of 165 guys that started the day before. There was nobody good enough to keep that could play on a pro ros-ter. Nobody made it. There were some who were decent players, good high school players, but they thought the Pacers tryout was going to be a joy ride and they found out differently. The odds were not good when it began that there would be a player good enough to keep.

Later on, at Bankers Life Fieldhouse, I've had this happen to me: A guy would come up to me and go, "Remember me?" I'd say, "No, not really." He said, "Well, I was at your tryout camp when the Pacers first came here. I was the last guy cut." Always it's they were the last guy cut. But there wasn't a last guy cut. There were seven last guys and 158 guys who cut themselves.

It would have been great if one guy had come out of it. Good public-ity for the team, too. You never know until you do it. Once in a while a guy makes it in the pros that you never expected would. He was a long-shot. A few of them have made it like that, but there have been a lot more where the expectations were high and they couldn't cut it. They were All-Americans. It happens all the time. People wonder about those guys, but it shows you the difference between high school and college ball and college and pro ball. Over the years a lot of All-Americans have been cut. Fans who don't understand that don't give the pro game enough credit for how good the players are. When it gets down to the nitty-gritty, see, sometimes a player doesn't want to pay the price.

It was like those players at the tryouts. When I said they were going to have to run 25 baselines, I might as well have opened the doors to the gym and let them run out. You might have thought that one of them would have said, "Slick, I'm not coming back." Nobody said anything.

They went home and they were hurting and they realized it was too hard for them. We wouldn't have been able to run a tryout like that today. We didn't have any doctors or anything out there when we did that. Some of them were overweight, and they could have been a heart attack waiting to happen. There were definitely guys there who were visibly out of shape. But at this camp everybody got a pop.

That's one of the big things in pro basketball. You have to have the quickness. You might be able to get the shot off in a college game, but you won't be able to get the shot off in the pro game. Defense is where it really gets you. Without quickness, it's a big-time liability on defense.

College basketball is great, and being a great college player is a great thing. The colleges do a terrific job in honoring their own players. It's tougher for a college kid going into the pros now because there are so many more international players coming in. A lot of Americans go play in Europe now, and a lot of international players are coming over to the United States. I think the breakthrough, the team that probably has done the best with international players, with finding them, is San Antonio and Gregg Popovich.

After I ran the tryout camp with Clyde, I did some scouting consulting for Mike Storen. I went on a few trips. I was still working for Herff Jones full time. I wanted to be able to sit down and talk about things with Mike, and it enabled me to be involved in the game. In fact, I recommended Larry Staverman to him for the coaching job. Larry was an assistant at Notre Dame. Larry was a good guy, and Mike mentioned him to me. He said, "What do you think about Larry Staverman?" And I said, "I think he would do okay." So Larry came in as the first coach of the Pacers.

They did not talk to me about the coaching job. I wasn't ready to go back to coaching. But I also didn't think the American Basketball Association would last. I didn't want to give up my job with Herff Jones.

To be perfectly honest, when I heard about the new league I thought, *This will never last.* They had the three-point line and the red, white, and blue basketball and I just didn't think they were going to make it. We were living in Kokomo and had just built a new house.

The Pacers did not start off the second season the way they hoped they would. They were 2–7. It wasn't happening. They weren't winning. They thought it was time to make a move. Mike Storen knew I had coached in the NBA, and after the scouting and conversations with me as a consultant, he thought I could do the job. I did not necessarily see Larry's firing coming. I knew their record, but I didn't have any idea if they wanted to make a change or not. I didn't really think about the situation.

To some degree I was surprised when Mike called and asked me to coach. That's when I mentioned the red, white, and blue ball and the three-point line to Nancy and said I didn't think the league was going to make it. I was happy in my other job with Herff Jones and the Pacers knew I was happy in my other job, so I wasn't really expecting the call. When Mike called, he said they needed an answer very quickly. I told Nancy, "You know what? I can go down there and coach for a year. I can do both." I hung up and talked it over with Nancy and called back pretty quickly.

No, I wasn't going to quit my other job. I didn't think the Pacers would be around for more than another year. I was very skeptical that they could make it. Most new professional sports leagues had come and gone, although the American Football League was still around and was merging with the NFL. To me, at first, the three-point shot and the red, white, and blue basketball were gimmicks. Later on they did not seem to be gimmicks.

One of the other gimmicks was the Miami Floridians ball girls wearing bikinis. They were ahead of the cheerleaders and dance teams at NBA games. The Floridians played some games in a converted airplane hangar. They had been the Minnesota Muskies but were losing money and moved. Because they were piling up debts, they sold Mel Daniels to Indiana—one of the greatest deals in Pacers history.

You know, one time in a game against the Floridians I made the referees call time out for something. Somebody got fouled and the referee was acting kind of cocky. He went to the foul line and just planted the ball there in a way so that the fans were going "Ooooh, oooh." He put the ball down and turned around staring right at me. While he did that, the ball rolled all of the way down to the other end of the court. That's how unlevel the floor was in that airplane hangar. He reached down to pick it up and the ball was gone. Boy, the crowd just bust out laughing.

So when the Pacers asked me to coach, I didn't think it offered much job security. I told Nancy, "I'll go down there for a year, just long enough to furnish the house." But it turned into a lot longer.

The toughest thing in the very beginning was going down to the arena to meet with the players. The players had heard about me. They heard how tough I was. That was my reputation. Word got around, I guess. And the players had liked Larry Staverman and they weren't all for the change. Mel Daniels is one of my best friends today, but at the time he made the comment, "If that guy comes in here and tries to pull off that tough stuff on us, I'll knock him out." Well, basically I went in and met with them and told them the way it was going to be and that was it. You have to have some toughness.

I wasn't trying to prove to them that I was tough. I told them that I didn't care what color they were—if they were black, white, or yellow, it didn't matter to me. If you can play, you will play. I said that straight off from the get-go. There will be no favorites. We're going to work hard. I want you to stick together. I'll do everything to help you win. It was all just basic stuff.

On offense, I changed a few things based on the personnel. I went to a running game. I went to a fast-break game somewhat like you see with the Miami Heat now. That was the old ABA game. I had a center in Mel Daniels who was our first option in the half-court. We went inside with him. Then it was fast-breaking and rebounding. Mel Daniels made the running game.

Mel and Bob Netolicky could jump out of the gym. Those two guys and Roger Brown up front worked a lot on how to fill the lanes on the break. They were good at not having two guys in one lane and when to release the ball. If you come across midcourt and you've got a three-on-one, you make a decision with the idea that a guy's got to go in or stop for a three-point shot. Or if there's a trailer, then it's ball movement to him. Boom, boom, you've got scores. We worked a lot on three-on-twos, but if it's three-on-three then you've got to pull back and run your half-court offense.

The last successful pro team in Indianapolis was the Indianapolis Olympians. Everybody thought that with Indiana's love for basketball that a pro team would be an easy success. But with big-time high school basketball, plus IU, Purdue, and Butler, everybody had allegiances, and it all took dollars to go to those games. I think that's why the Pacers were a hit-and-miss situation from Day 1. I didn't want to put a death sentence on it, but the way I felt in the beginning was that it was probably 25–75 that they would make it.

The owners were very enthusiastic about it, and they did a good job putting everything together. When I looked at the roster I thought, *You know, that's not bad personnel.* I thought we could do pretty well. What really made it go, though, after I took over as coach, we got pretty hot, played above .500, and got in the playoffs. We finished 44–34, beat Kentucky in the first round of the playoffs in seven games after coming back from being down 3–1, beat the Floridians in the next round, and then went to the championship against Oakland.

Coming back against Kentucky, which was our biggest rival, was huge. We were playing our home games at the Fairgrounds Coliseum in Indianapolis, and the seventh game was at home. For most of the game it was a nail-biter. We won 120–111, and the place went wild. It went wild! Thanks to people like Jerry Baker, who was a great radio announcer, our players' names became household names just like that. Mel Daniels, Roger Brown, Freddie Lewis, and Bob Netolicky were the big guns—and that all changed the franchise.

The series against Oakland didn't turn out our way, but it was fantastically high scoring, exciting basketball. Rick Barry got in a salary dispute with his NBA team, joined the Oakland Oaks, and led them to the ABA title in 1968–69 in five games over us. Barry averaged 34 points a game to lead the league during the regular season. And you know, that team was owned by Pat Boone.

Against Oakland we lost 123–114, won 150–122, lost 134–126 in overtime, lost 144–117, and lost 135–131 in overtime. We did not win the title, but we had reached the championship series in my first year, and we got the town excited about the Indiana Pacers.

After we made the deal to get Mel Daniels, I took one look at Roger Brown and said, "This guy is a player. This guy is a big-time player" and we had Freddie Lewis, I knew we could be good. We had some fill-ins that year and I hadn't known the league that well and what other teams had, but we finished up well and got to the championships. We went from there.

CHAPTER 15

PACERS BECOME CHAMPS

The 1969–70 season was Bob Leonard's first year as coach of the Pacers for the entire campaign, and he led Indiana to a 59–25 record and the American Basketball Association title.

A rookie on that team who enjoyed every minute of his transition from college at Purdue to the pros with Indiana was guard Billy Keller.

"To have the opportunity I did with a college career that ended in the championship game against UCLA and then to move in with the Pacers and go to the championship, that was a fun year," Keller said. "We won a lot of games. It was great for me. The Pacers were established, and the team was pretty well set, too.

"Slick is really a player's coach. He really knew how to bring young players along. He provided great leadership. He had been there as a player who had that advantage and took that background into coaching. Bob was able to take the player-coach relationship right up to the line. He could play cards with the players and have fun with the guys, but still you knew when practice started it was serious. For me, it was just a thrill to be part of a championship team. I had won a state championship with Washington, Indiana, in 1965, and you get a taste in your mouth. Each one builds for another one."

One of the cornerstone players of the best Pacers teams was Roger Brown. Selected for the Naismith Memorial Basketball Hall of Fame in 2013, Brown died at age 54 in 1997. He was a New York City high school legend but had been banned from the sport, accused of doing wrong in a point-shaving scandal. The ABA let him play, and Brown later won vindication in court.

Brown, a phenomenal, almost unstoppable scorer, and Leonard became good friends. In 2013, a documentary was made about his life called *Undefeated: The Roger Brown Story.*

"He was just a phenomenal player," Keller said, "and I didn't even have a chance to see him in his early days."

The raves about the 6'5", 205-lb. Brown's talent are lengthy and some were noted in the documentary. Julius "Dr. J." Erving faced Brown in the ABA. "He was the best player I'd ever played against," Erving said. "The Pacers were the class of the league, and Roger was the class of the class."

Brown was blackballed from the NBA, thrown off his Dayton University team, and banned from trying out for the Olympics. He worked at a General Motors plant in Dayton and played AAU ball until the Pacers signed him on the recommendation of the famous Oscar Robertson. Brown was the first player Indiana signed, for $15,000. Admirers called him "Ra-jah." He was a rajah on the court. Until the Pacers grabbed him, Brown had been a forgotten player.

"From 1961 until 1967, I was dead," Brown said.

Those who knew Brown best, playing next to him, or coaching him, were among the most impressed of his fans. "He rocked this city," star forward George McGinnis said. "Roger was 'The Man,'" Mel Daniels said. "Coach Leonard had a play in his arsenal called 7-Up. Roger was like the silent assassin," Leonard said. "Get out of the way and give him the ball."

A member of the ABA all-time team, Brown was a four-time All-Star, and, proving his popularity, he later served on the Indianapolis City Council. At Brown's funeral, Leonard was one of the speakers and, teary-eyed, he read a poem that he wrote about his former player.

That was all nearly 30 years in the future, though, when the Pacers blitzed the ABA in 1969–70. They swept Carolina in four straight in the first round of the playoffs. Then they handled the Kentucky Colonels in five games in the second round. The battle for the title came down to a showdown with Los Angeles, and the Pacers won the crown in six games, the last victory coming on the road in L.A.

"Guys were in the locker room pouring champagne over each other," Keller said. "We were able to celebrate, but not with the fans who were regulars at the game because we were on the road."

By the end of that season the original Leonard skeptic, Mel Daniels, had become a true believer. He also found out that Leonard could be tough.

"He was very demanding," Daniels said, "but he gained our respect because had gone through what we were going through as players. He was a very good coach. As a coach you have to have a feel for people, how far you can go and how far you can push them. Once he told me that if I took a 17' outside shot that he'd punch me in the nose. He made you accountable for your role."

At times the Pacers were so good that year that their wins came almost too easily. Leonard experimented with different playing combinations. He also found ways to keep the players humble.

"If we got too full of ourselves," Daniels said, "he took us to a children's hospital to visit with sick kids. If a guy was down and out, he'd take him out to eat."

Yet Leonard could make his players mad at him at times, too.

"He could be a tyrant in practice," Daniels said, "almost a taskmaster. But he had a heart of gold."

Winning the ABA title that year was special for the players who had suffered through a losing season, made adjustments to a new coach, and were playing in a league that some dismissed as not "real" pro basketball because it didn't have the NBA imprint. Bob Netolicky said he thinks the Pacers should have clinched the title in the playoffs two days earlier than they did—and that a big part of that failing was his own.

"I had a terrible game," Netolicky said. "Bob didn't know that I had been out water skiing on the day of the game. My arms were so sore that

I could hardly lift them above my shoulders. I must have missed about 10 shots that I should have made. We knew we were better than them."

Instead, Indiana took a 117–113 loss in overtime at home and had to travel to Los Angeles to clinch its first crown.

"That was a team that was very close, down to the last guy on the bench," Daniels said. "When we won the championship, my reaction was one of disbelief, one of elation. It took some time to sink in."

There was little doubt among the delirious fans who squeezed in tight at the Fairgrounds for home games and Hoosiers fans in general that Bob Leonard had ushered in a new era of Indiana Pacers basketball.

BOBBY LEONARD

The Pacers management wanted to change the coach, and the players didn't like that. So I had to prove myself to those players. But they had to prove themselves to me, too. When I say that, I mean they had to prove to me who deserved playing time. It was interesting.

It came out just the way we wanted it to come out since we rallied near the end of my first season and kept gaining momentum right into the next year. And our attendance picked up. The Fairgrounds held about 11,000 fans, and it was standing room only in there. Things were going so well that they decided to build Market Square Arena.

We were under .500 when I started, but we started to win our share. We got over .500 and we were in all our games. When we lost, we didn't lose by much. The Pacers came on strong enough that we won our division. That was key. It came down to that three-letter word—win. We won, and the crowds came. Then we started winning championships, so of course the crowds were even bigger.

The excitement level built when we made it to the finals my first year, and then we won the whole thing my first complete year. We got to be a better team, and the fans' expectations increased, too. We had some great core guys, guys who were all-time greats. That was sure a special group of players.

One thing I want people to know, to think about. I've been around the game for a long, long time. I've seen all kinds of great players come and go, but the front line players we had when they were in their primes, Mel Daniels, Roger Brown, and George McGinnis is as good as any front line I can think of in basketball. The one front line that everybody talks about—with all three of them in the Hall of Fame—is the great Boston Celtics group of Larry Bird, Kevin McHale, and Robert Parish. Robert Parish and Mel Daniels would really battle each other. But who would take Roger Brown and George McGinnis? And on the other side of the coin, who would take Larry Bird and Kevin McHale?

I can't think of another trio. It was Kareem Abdul-Jabbar and James Worthy with the Lakers, but the other forward was A.C. Green. It's hard to come up with a complete trio. It was Bill Walton and Maurice Lucas in Portland. What I am saying is there is usually an odd man out. The Pacers were as good as any of them and better than most. It takes three players and all three of mine could play. They all scored better than 50 points in a ball game more than once. You can't find front lines like that now. I think they all deserve to be in the Hall of Fame. Mel's in there now, and they just took Roger. I hope that I live long enough to see George in there, too.

Once we got going my first year when I replaced Larry Staverman, we did pretty well. We took care of Kentucky in the playoffs easily, and then beat Miami. We went to the championship, and that was pretty good since I didn't even start the year with the team and we had to make up for those early-season losses.

We met the Oakland Oaks, and they had Rick Barry. But they had some other good players like Doug Moe, Jim Eakins, and a kid who was very tough. At the time he was Warren Armstrong, but he changed his name to Warren Jabali. I had him later on.

The scores in those games were very high. We could score points. We got out and ran. We had that game where we scored 150 on them. The last game, when we lost 135–131 in overtime, was a killer. We had a play when we wanted to commit a foul. It was called "yellow." We had the lead. Yellow was the code name. They got the ball inbounds, and we didn't get to them fast enough to foul. Jabali hit a shot from almost half-court. That's a three-pointer, and it sent the game into overtime. We should have won the ball game without overtime. We should have won the other overtime when it was 134–126, too. Then we would have been up 2–1 in games.

We gave them a go, but they got us. They were favored mostly because of Rick Barry. They had won a lot of games. More than we did. But we came on strong at the end of the season. Winning that seventh game at the Fairgrounds against Kentucky really got it going.

That was a turning point for the franchise, and it helped carry us through the playoffs. Then after we reached the finals series, that helped propel us the next year when we won the championship.

When I say that we could score points, we really could score points. In early February of the first season when I took over, we beat the Los Angeles Stars 172–141. Bill Sharman was the coach of Los Angeles, the old Celtics guard. We got out ahead, and everything went right. We got a big lead in the ball game, and the guys on the bench came in and kept everything going. We were hitting almost every shot. At first, when the game ended, they said that we broke the professional record for most points in a game. That was during a stretch when we won 13 games in a row to get into the playoffs. But Sharman went right down to the scorer's table and told them that it was not right. He said, "No, that does not break the professional record. We scored 173 points." He was right. The Celtics had scored 173 in a game in 1959—against us, the Minneapolis Lakers.

Anyway, scoring 170-something points in a game is huge. But the next year late in the season, we beat the Pittsburgh Pipers, 177–135. That one broke the professional scoring record. Everybody has to have it going to score that many points.

We had guys who could put up points. Mel Daniels and Roger Brown scored better than 50 points in a game more than once. Bob Netolicky could put up points. Freddie Lewis could put up points. We had a lot of guys who could put points on the board. There was no Mickey Mousing around that game. We beat that 173. That was in a regulation-length game. There wasn't any overtime.

It was a perfect-storm type of day. Any time you jump on a ballclub like that and you keep hitting, there's a chance that they will start quitting. Going back to that day, I bet the bench scored the last 40 points. If you're the coach at a game like that, you just sit back and relax.

At the end of my first season we had a stretch where we scored 133, 131, 143, 128, 122, 125, 144, 143, 132, 140, and 134 points in consecutive games. The big thing at Indiana was that if we could control the backboards, we really controlled the game. If you've really worked where you had that fast break down to a system—and we did—you could score points fast. When I was at IU we were called the Hurryin' Hoosiers. With the Pacers we could have been the "Super Speed Pacers" or the "Supersonic Hoosiers."

We didn't have a lot of those 89–85 games that you see today. When I was a player, the best fast break I ever saw was the Boston Celtics. The Celtics put up points because of the break. That's what we had with the Pacers. We had the fast break going all of the time. We didn't get point totals like that by dilly-dallying down the floor. We were out there running. I had the same philosophy I always had. It was simple: defense, fast break, rebound to start the fast break, and score those points.

The ABA had a 30-second clock, which I liked. We didn't wait very long to shoot. Most teams didn't. The reason why I liked the 30-second clock was because if you had a lead, you could protect it a little bit better than with the 24-second clock in the NBA. The 30 was good. Actually, everything we had going in the ABA was good—the 30-second clock, the three-point line, and the red, white, and blue ball. The reason why the red, white, and blue ball was good was because you could see the ball spinning in the air. You can't see the brown ball doing that.

Even with all of that we had a tremendous scoring streak going into the playoffs. Late in the season we won 13 games in a row and we were ready to play when the playoffs started. When I came in we were under .500 and we finished 10 games over .500. By the time the playoffs started we had great confidence. We were the team that nobody wanted to play, and we got better and better.

By the spring, even though I had started the season late with them, a rapport had developed between me and the players. We had developed a family attitude by that point. They liked what we were doing on the floor. They liked my simple offense. We knew where our strong points were if we got into a critical stretch and it came down to the wire. And we gave it a good run to the finals.

The next year I was with the team from the start in training camp, and I had seen all of the players in the league so I had more knowledge. Once you come so close when the next season starts you're not just thinking about getting into the playoffs. We were thinking about winning the whole thing.

The standard had changed. We got into top-flight condition in training camp and came out strong. That second year we probably could have won 70 games. We were so far ahead in the division I started experimenting with things. Things went right from the start. We won five out of our first six games in October. Then we went 10–2 in November. Then we won 12-of-14 in December. By New Year's our record was 27–5.

We were so far ahead nobody was going to catch us. That's when we started making sure we gave the bench plenty of playing time to rest guys and keep them fresh for the playoffs. We could have won a lot more ball games.

Roger Brown scored 23 points a game for us that year. Neto scored 20.6. And Mel scored 18.8. Roger was 6'5" and he was strong, but really he was very quick. He could get a shot off any time he wanted. Talk about manufacturing a shot. Roger could fake people out and make his own shot any time he felt like it. He had moves with the ball, reverse dribbles, hesitation fakes, everything. He left guys standing still when he went by them. I even saw a guy trying to cover him fall on the floor. Roger faked him so bad the guy fell down. And he was a master at the pull-up jump shot from 15' or 16'. He could hit the three-pointer, too, so you had to play him out there.

He made 40 out of 120 attempts from three-point range that year, so once you had to play him out deep, that opened up the court for him because then he could drive on you. Roger could pass off, too. He just had a complete game. He was a great player. He just got into the Hall of Fame and oh my goodness, that was overdue. I think it took so long because he played his whole career in the ABA, and we were the upstart league.

I think NBA people always resisted giving the ABA credit. Once the players had a choice of two leagues they could go to, that upped the ante on salaries. That upped the price for every team, and the NBA was very, very bitter about it. It cost them a lot more money to do business. They had to pay more for things and even the referees came to the ABA for more money. Then we started signing players like Dan Issel, Artis Gilmore, Julius Erving, and George "The Iceman" Gervin. Everything started to change. Rick Barry jumped from the Warriors to Oakland.

All of a sudden the public started to realize that we were getting all of these star players and while we might not be there yet, we were headed in the right direction to become a very competitive league with the NBA. We had some of the best players on the planet on our teams and it seemed like we were catching up and were going to force a merger. The ABA was also the home for some players—great players—who were blackballed by the NBA because of the college scandals even though it was never proven that they did anything wrong.

Guys like Roger and Connie Hawkins and Doug Moe, that cost them five or six years of their careers and that's a long time. You can't do that. Thank god the ABA came along and Roger got the opportunity, and thank goodness for Oscar Robertson. He saw Roger play in an AAU tournament and he said, "Hey, this guy can play." Oscar gave the recommendation to Mike Storen, and Mike acted on it. The first player signed by the Indiana Pacers.

The thing about Roger was that he could take the ball down the middle on the fast break but—and I've never seen this by another guy to this day—he could end up taking a 16' jumper and still be at the rim to rebound by the time the ball got there. I'd hate to try to count two things, the number of game-winners that he had and the big plays where he tapped in that ball as it rolled off the rim because he hustled to get there.

Roger was kind of a laid-back guy, but he was only laid back until you got him mad. There were times I got him mad as a coach. I think it was the first year that I got on him pretty good because he wasn't going after it the way I thought he should. I left him home on a road trip, and that changed everything between us. He knew how serious I was after that.

I'm not sure if Roger used his circumstances for motivation, but I know he won a lawsuit. He told me once that it was $15,000 a year in payments for 20 years, something along those lines, but he could never get back the time he was blackballed. That's what he really lost. He would have been a great player in either league, the NBA or the ABA. It didn't matter.

Roger was the best when the game was on the line. He was at his best in the playoffs. For the biggest games he used to say, "When the money is on the line, I'll be there." And he was.

That second year, the championship year, the frontcourt was huge for us. They got a lot of points. But we had a good backcourt. Freddie Lewis was still there, and he scored 16.4 points a game. We had a new starter in the backcourt that year, too. We picked up John Barnhill. He was with the Baltimore Bullets in 1969 and signed with Indiana as a free agent before the 1969–70 season. He averaged 11.4 points a game and was a good addition.

Johnny still had a year or two left in him. He was still quick, and he had a lot of experience. I had told Mike Storen to keep an eye on the NBA on cut-down day and see who might get released. Mike did that and we sat down and talked about guys to see if it might be worth it for us to bring them in to the Pacers. That's how we got Johnny Barnhill. We thought we could use one more backcourt guy of his caliber, and he ended up starting a lot of games for us.

Freddie was the complete guard. He was a threat from three. He had a pull-up jumper from 15'. He could drive all the way to the hoop. He was an excellent defender. We didn't go with the division of responsibility the way they describe the positions now with a point guard and a shooting guard and a power forward and a shooting forward. Especially in the backcourt, I wanted two guards that can play basketball. None of this point guard stuff. I didn't need that.

We had Billy Keller in there as a rookie, and we still had Tom Thacker. Tom was a good ballplayer. He was a winner. He was an NCAA champion with the University of Cincinnati, and he got into 70 games for us. He didn't score much, but he got a fair amount of assists. Tom Thacker was a good passer and an excellent defensive player. He won an NBA ring, too, with the Celtics. He is the only player to win an NCAA championship, an ABA championship, and an NBA championship.

One of our best guys year in and year out, was Bob Netolicky. He was a 6'9" forward, and he was never better than in that championship year when he averaged more than 20 points a game. He could run the floor, and we needed that on the fast break. He could hit the jumper out to about 16', and he had an old-time hook shot of the kind you don't see much of anymore. He had the big, sweeping hook. There was only one guy that I saw who had a better hook than Netolicky and that was Kareem Abdul-Jabbar with his sky hook. Bobby had the same motion, and boy was he dangerous with it.

We worked to get him a mismatch down low, and he'd hit that sweeping hook.

And then we had Mel Daniels in the middle. Mel was a great rebounder, a big-time rebounder. He could score in a lot of ways. He had great inside moves.

That 1969–70 team was one of the best teams we had in Indiana.

One other important element that season was that the key players all stayed healthy and played in almost every game. That's helpful. I promoted the idea that you've got to play a little bit hurt sometimes, but we didn't have any major injuries to the starters.

We were ready for the playoffs long before they started. You could say we were ready for the playoffs from the moment that the finals series ended against Oakland the year before. We opened against the Carolina Cougars. They had Larry Miller out of North Carolina. He was their big player. They were coached by Bones McKinney. We took care of them in four straight.

In the next round we faced the Kentucky Colonels. They were our big rival from the first game in the league on. It was geographical. Indiana and Kentucky border one another, and the two states are always bragging about who has the best high school basketball. IU and Kentucky are big rivals, too, although non-conference. The Colonels had a lot of Kentucky guys on the team, guys from the University of Kentucky, Western Kentucky, Eastern Kentucky, Kentucky Wesleyan, and Louisville. Their big scorer was Louie Dampier. He was a guard who was a great shooter. They beat us in overtime in the first game, and then we won four straight to reach the finals. Louie was tough.

That put us up against the Los Angeles Stars. Mack Calvin was a good guard for them. He was a rookie. They also had Bill McGill and Wayne Hightower, who had come over from the NBA, and Bill Sharman was coaching them. One of their best players, who became one of the best players in the league, was a rookie big man named Willie Wise. They were trying to draw people head-to-head against the Lakers and that didn't work, so they moved to Salt Lake City and became the Utah Stars. They were still in Southern California at the time, though.

We were ahead 3–1 in games, and then we lost in overtime. We could have clinched it at home. We went to Los Angeles for the sixth game, and as long as we were out there, I invited my old teammates Elgin Baylor and Jerry West to visit with my team. They were still with the Lakers. They were big names, so I thought it would be kind of neat to introduce them in the dressing room. They said they would but to make sure that I didn't let the NBA know about it. They would look like traitors or something. I never did tell anybody and they came into the dressing room at the Los Angeles Sports Arena and said a few words to my team.

Then we went out and won the championship 111–107. You could say the Pacers were inspired by Elgin Baylor and Jerry West to beat a Los Angeles team. They got in and out unnoticed.

We won the ABA championship, and it was very satisfying. It was my second year but my first full year of coaching the Pacers. It was wonderful.

When we got back to Indianapolis, a lot of fans met us at the airport to celebrate. The airport was packed, and they had their cars all over the place. Then we had a big celebration at the Fairgrounds Coliseum. They packed the place for that. We had the trophy with us and held it up. It doesn't matter if you're a player or a coach, whether it's the World Series or another championship, it's great when you get to the end of the season and you can say, "We won it!"

You're elated, but you're also relieved. It was my first championship since winning the Big Ten with Indiana in 1954 and of course the NCAA championship in 1953. It was my first championship as a coach. I was at a different age. I was around 21 when we won the NCAA title, and I was in my late thirties when the Pacers won their first ABA championship. I still have to say to this day, though, that if I had a choice between winning a championship as a player and winning a championship as a coach, I would take being the player every time. That's because you can influence the outcome more as a player than as a coach.

Once you impart your philosophy to the players and you get across the intangibles that you want to teach and they are implanted and the players govern themselves, you've got a lot of your work done. After that I would say winning becomes probably 90 percent playing and maybe 10 percent coaching. I wonder if it's 10 percent. Once you get everybody to go along with the program, it becomes all about execution.

But it was absolutely, definitely wonderful to win that American Basketball Association championship for the Pacers. We made our mark on Indiana with that title.

CHAPTER 16

BIG WINNERS IN INDY

Bob Leonard had been the coach of the Indiana Pacers for less than two full seasons and he had already led the team to the American Basketball Association finals one year and to the ABA title the second year. But that was just the beginning. Indiana hoops fans were in for a treat. The Pacers were on a roll that extended for several more seasons.

Throughout the early 1970s, Indiana was the best team in the ABA and certainly one of the best teams in basketball with its core group of stars leading the Pacers to three championships in a short stretch and challenging for the title every year.

Leonard seemed to possess the magic combination for a coach to get the most out of his talent while keeping his players happy and getting them to follow his plan. At the same time he reached out to the Pacers as men and family men, and he embraced them as part of his extended family. Leonard's players and his family—which by 1971 had expanded to include five children—intermingled and shared experiences. Tommy was born in 1968, and Timmy was born in 1971.

The kids had the run of the arena, sometimes served as ballboys, sometimes visited dad in the locker room, sometimes made road trips, and sometimes hung out at dad's summer basketball camp where the players were instructors in the off-season. The team won all of the time, and everybody had fun.

"All of the guys hung around together and all of the wives hung out together, and we were there, too," Bob's daughter Terry said. "Your team was your family. We were very involved. The only thing was on game day you didn't want to bother Dad."

When the Leonards talk about the Pacers being extended family, that applies not only to players, assistant coaches, and trainers, but to the stat crew and the people they saw at the State Fairgrounds Coliseum and Market Square Arena year after year.

"It was just awesome when I was growing up," Bill Leonard said. "The basketball atmosphere was just what you grew up into. I've always followed the Pacers. I remember taking bus rides to Kentucky for the games against the Colonels and what a big rivalry that was. The stat crews were part of our family, and they still are today.

"I remember when one guy [Bill York] turned 40 and as a birthday party joke they had a wake for him at our house. There were caskets because he was getting so old it was like he died."

During the summers Bob Leonard ran a basketball camp in Bainbridge, Indiana, called Bob Leonard's All-American Sports Camp. His kids and his players went. There was basketball instruction, but also fishing and horseback riding. Mel Daniels, Roger Brown, and Bob Netolicky were some of the big horse riders, and Daniels owns horses to this day. The Leonards lived in a trailer on the premises. Bill can remember a pickup truck, its bed loaded down with Chuck Taylor basketball shoes, shorts, and T-shirts.

"The kids didn't want to take them off," Bill said. "How fortunate it was to live that lifestyle when he was coaching. It was growing up in basketball, but sometimes in school it wasn't too much fun if the Pacers weren't going good. Then other kids would say, 'Your dad's a bad coach.' I didn't always react in the proper manner. Of course, I stuck up for my dad."

For all that basketball intertwined with their lives, Tom Leonard said most of the time Bob was a regular dad and a lot of what they did in their childhood were the same things other kids did.

"He seemed as normal as any other dad out there," Tom said. "He would say, 'Let's go kids, we're getting in the car and we're going fishing,' or, 'We're going to King's Island Amusement Park.'"

The Pacers were a dominant team, if not a perfect one, for several years in a row, beginning with the 1968–69 late-season run that thrust them into the championship series against the Oaks.

"We were all in our prime, and it was the perfect time," said forward Bob Netolicky, who remains a close friend of Leonard's and lives near him in Indiana. "We had this young core. For six or seven years we were really the best. We had this attitude, 'Who's gonna beat us?' A few little tweaks and we could have won five titles in a row. Nobody knows how good we were. In the 1970 season we were as good as anyone ever was. We clinched the division in early February. We could have won 65 or 70 games if we hadn't started platooning."

Once in a while Leonard would really show his teeth to the players if he felt they were getting complacent or losing focus.

"You'd lose a few games and we'd always know if he was mad at us," Netolicky said. "He'd sit us down and he'd get this look on his face and start lecturing us. We might have lost three games in a row and he would go, 'We have lost our way. We've got to be more of a family.'"

In professional sports it's important for the coach to remember that the players are adults, not teenagers as they may be on college teams, and they wish to be treated like men. Pro coaches who have a lot of rules don't usually last. One rule that is fairly common, though, is that the coach gets dibs on the hotel bar so he doesn't have to go out and the players are usually not allowed to drink where he does. It saves on potentially embarrassing situations if anyone was to drink too much. Leonard never had that rule. He would drink at the hotel, but he invited the players to drink with him.

"Slick would come into the bar at the hotel and be with the players," Netolicky said. "One time there were a couple of us, and a waitress came over to take our order. Slick orders two beers and the waitress starts to leave. He goes, 'Whoa, whoa, these guys haven't ordered.' He was definitely a player's coach."

However, the players never forgot that Leonard was in charge because he never let them forget it, even if he could share fun with them. One thing that impressed center Mel Daniels about Leonard was his ability to change the game plan on the fly if things weren't going well.

"This is what kind of coach Bob was," Daniels said. "If the offense was not working, he would put in five or six new plays right in the huddle. Tell me another coach who can do that. They weren't brand new plays, they were variations."

BOBBY LEONARD

As a coach I developed a Bob Leonard philosophy of what I wanted from my Pacers players and what they could expect from me. To start with, to play for me, I'd go back to the fact that I promoted togetherness in the dressing room.

One thing I did to promote togetherness was say that after every road game we were going to get together in my room for 20 minutes. So they came to my hotel room. Some guys stayed a few minutes longer. After that they were on their own and could go out to have dinner or go out with friends. But we had that meeting together. I think that developed a camaraderie and it still exists today with Bob Netolicky, Mel Daniels, Billy Keller, George McGinnis, and other guys who have been Pacers. That's because we cared about the player, but we cared about the family, too. So we made it a family situation and I was the dad. That also meant that I might kick their hind ends sometimes.

It was developing a philosophy in a big picture where you develop an atmosphere of caring for each other and caring for each other's families, and if handled properly you could jump all over a guy one night for his performance and hug him the next night and it's forgotten. That's the way I did it.

Every coach has a system, but I didn't believe in putting everything in during training camp and sticking with it. We had basic plays that I did keep, but that wasn't all. One time Nick the Greek said, "Be careful about betting on a team that Slick Leonard coaches because he will change his offense at halftime." But remember I had a simple offense. The players understood where the shots were coming from, who was setting the picks, and I could change things at halftime in the time when the team was in the dressing room getting ready for the second half. I would say, "Here's what they're doing. Let's come out and give them an entirely different look." With all of our players, we got to the place where we could do that and it didn't bother us one iota.

The principle was always the same. And it's the same as it is in the NBA now, night in and night out. You can have nights when you can't shoot it into the ocean, but if you're defending and rebounding, it'll keep you in the ball game. And if you're defending and rebounding and get out on the fast break, you'll get some easy ones. That will help keep you in the ball game, even if you're shooting the ball terribly. Defense and rebounding will always be the keys to winning.

There are professional sports teams that don't get along that have won championships. The New York Yankees had their problems. The Oakland Athletics did, too. Not every winning team is a happy team, but I think it helps. Above all, you've got to have talent. In the pros, that's the big-time thing—talent. You also have got to have the kind of guys who realize if they work together and pay the price, then they can win, they can be the best. If you look back at the ABA, for about seven years we were the best. We either won it or got to the championship round or the conference finals. We won a lot of playoff games.

Part of the coach's job is to create the atmosphere where the players believe they can win. You've got to do it. I did it in a number of different ways. One time in Utah before a playoff game I told Davey Craig, our trainer, to go get a bunch of $20 bills. Then I had the ball boys tape them under the chairs in the locker room.

It was a tight game, and we were down a point or two at halftime. I said very little, but then I said, "Lift up your chairs." They raised them up and saw the $20 bills. Then I gave them a little talk. I said, "Now, I want you to understand that out on the floor there are $20 bills 6' deep. That's the playoff money. Either you take the playoff money, or they take the playoff money. Now which one is it going to be?" We went out and won the ball game. There are little things you can do along the way, but whatever they are they should always be positive. You have to always be thinking and promoting the idea of the only thing in the game: W-I-N.

I had had experience coaching in Chicago with an expansion team, and I had been around the Lakers when they were good. But that wasn't coaching. Coaching in Chicago with the talent I had there and coaching in Indianapolis with the talent I had was two different things. I always repeat the saying, "You never see a jockey carry a horse across the finish line in the Kentucky Derby. The horse carries the jockey across the line." And that's the way it is.

Coaching in Chicago when I was younger, I did learn things. It was part of my coaching education, and I took things with me to Indiana. Maturity alone was important. The Chicago job was my first coaching job, and when you are more mature you sometimes see things a little bit differently. I generally had the same approach all the way through, but it was a different talent level. When we got to Baltimore and had Walt Bellamy and Terry Dischinger and then got Gus Johnson, that would have been different. We were just so young. Bellamy had that game where he scored 41 points on Bill Russell. They didn't blow us out, but we weren't quite good enough yet to beat them.

You may feel you are a good coach, but the rest of the world is waiting for results. It's all based on championships. In college basketball they have a preseason, a stretch of games before conference, and they play teams that they are going to beat up on. Then they get into the real crux of the schedule. All coaches try to schedule to win 20 games to keep their jobs. But to me it's not how many games you win in the regular season, it's what you do in March in the conference tournament and the NCAA tournament. That's the name of the game. It's the same way in the pros. What you do in the playoffs is what counts. The regular season is for getting into the playoffs.

People look at you and talk about you differently when you win a title, and I went up against some pretty good coaches like Alex Hannum, Bill Sharman, Larry Brown, and Joe Mullaney. There were a number of good coaches in the ABA. Larry Brown's first coaching job was with Carolina. Another time he was with Denver, and we beat them in the seventh game of a series. They had a heck of a ballclub, and they won over 60 games. He had David Thompson. It was highly competitive, and as we progressed through the ABA seasons, it got tougher and tougher.

Johnny Kerr was vice president of the Virginia Squires. He was the one who found George Gervin. "The Iceman" was playing in a pick-up league in Michigan, and he ended up in the Hall of Fame.

After we won the championship in 1969–70, the owners decided to give the guys a trip to the Bahamas as a reward. But at the time my old college coach Branch McCracken was in the Indiana Medical Center. He was dying. I didn't go to the Bahamas. I went to visit Branch. He was in bad shape, and he had hoses coming out of him and everything. He called me over to his bed and here's his exact words—and it really surprised me. He said, "Bobby, don't you ever take that coaching job at IU as long as that Michigan Man is down there." He was talking about the athletic director, Bill Orwig. There was such a strong conflict between them. Branch was so popular on that campus, and Orwig was a Michigan Man. They didn't get along. He tried every way to get Branch fired, I guess, and he eventually succeeded. So that's why Branch said that.

After I left Branch, I told Nancy and I said, "Why would he say something like that to me? I just won an ABA championship. I'm not even thinking about college basketball." Well, a few days later, not even a week, I got a phone call at the house from Bill Orwig and he said, "Bobby, how would you like to take this coaching job?" Nancy recorded the call. This was in June 1970. I said, "What are you saying to me, Bill?"

He said, "If you want the coaching job at IU, it's yours." I said, "I had a wonderful time down there for four years, Bill, but I don't think so. I really like the pro game. I don't think I'd be interested."

For us with the Pacers, the plan was to win it again in the 1970–71 season. I didn't hear from Bill Orwig again until February 1971. He said, "Will you meet me at the Indianapolis Athletic Club? I want to visit with you." I didn't want to say no, I'm not coming down there, so I met with him and he offered me the job again. Jerry Oliver had been the coach for one year as acting head coach in 1970, and Lou Watson was the coach in 1971. At the time the Pacers were leading our division by about 15 games and trying to win our second championship. Orwig wanted to offer me the job face to face. I turned it down again. Soon after that they hired Bobby Knight.

I have often thought back and wondered what kind of college coach I would have been. I still think about it to this day. Could I have gone in there and worried about the kids going to class and all of those NCAA rules? Had I gone into college coaching, I would have patterned myself after Branch McCracken because he was a great one. No question about it.

One thing about the college game is the handshake line that they have afterwards that they say is sportsmanship. You don't see that in the pros. It's a joke because none of them want to do it. The losers don't even want to get near those guys. That's a bunch of baloney. I'm totally against it. You're not going to see that in the pros. It's just something that's not really necessary. It's like rubbing salt in the wound. Your heart has just been broken and you have to shake hands when all you want to do is just throw up or lie down on the floor and hide your face.

Branch won two titles in 25 years—and should have had a third in 1954 with us—and Knight won three titles in 29 years. Those were two terrific eras during 54 years. IU built a lot of tradition under Branch McCracken. We were the Hurryin' Hoosiers. We thought our red satin warm-ups were very classy. They have those red-and-white striped pants. Anyway, IU wasn't hurrying anymore.

Our regular season record was really good again at 58–26. That was the year we had six guys average in double figures, and the team averaged 119.1 points a game. Mel led us in scoring with 21 points a game, and Roger Brown was right behind him. Freddie Lewis, Bob Netolicky, and Billy Keller all averaged in double figures, and so did Warren Jabali. That was the year we picked him up.

Warren was a different type of guy. He had trouble getting along with everybody. But I knew he had ability, big-time ability, and he was a very physical guard, stronger than a bear, and he could really jump. Warren was a good player. We brought him in after the season started, and he played 62 games. Warren could play defense. He became available, and Mike Storen grabbed him.

Billy became a great three-point shooter, and he took playing time away from John Barnhill, who was winding down his career. We also had Rick Mount. Rick was one of the most famous high school players in Indiana history from Lebanon and then he was a superstar in college with Purdue, a two-time All-American and a phenomenal scorer. He and Billy Keller were teammates in college. Rick had a lot of pressure on him. He always had a lot of pressure on him. The people of Lebanon who followed him knew that he had been a great college player. He had done just about everything in college. His senior year he averaged more than 35 points a game.

He was a good kid. He worked hard in practice, but he had trouble getting his shot off in the pro game. Everybody was looking forward to having him on the Pacers. He was the Pacers' and the league's No. 1 draft pick. He was from Lebanon, a half hour away from Indianapolis, he'd been a high school star, and he was a college star at Purdue, an hour away. We scouted him, and we knew what he could do. There was nothing we wanted more than for Rick Mount to make good.

In his second year with us Rick scored more than 14 points a game and averaged almost three assists. Down the road we traded him to Kentucky and he played about the same for the Colonels as he did for the

Pacers. He averaged 15 points a game for Kentucky. His last year in the league with the Memphis Sounds, Rick averaged about 17 points a game. He could shoot. He was a great pure shooter. But that year he dislocated his shoulder and that ended his season.

Given their roles at Purdue, it was a little bit ironic with how things turned out for Rick Mount and Billy Keller with the Pacers.

A few years later, Rick wasn't playing and Billy came up to me before training camp at Rose Hulman and asked me if it was okay if Rick gave it another try at camp. I said sure he could. So Rick came to training camp for a few days, and he was working hard and looked okay. Then one night he didn't say a word to anybody and he just packed up and went home. That was the end of his comeback.

At the end of the 1970–71 season we were defending our ABA title when the playoffs began. We were playing the Memphis Pros, who changed their name to the Memphis Tams a couple years later and then to the Sounds. They were owned by the baseball man, Charlie Finley, who was winning all of those World Series with the Oakland A's around that time. We beat them in four straight games and moved on to the Western Division finals against the Utah Stars.

The Stars had moved from Los Angeles. Bill Sharman was still the coach, and they won 57 games. They still had Willie Wise and George Stone, but the big addition to the Stars was Zelmo Beaty. He had left the NBA Hawks to come to the ABA. That series went to seven games, and we lost in the seventh game, 108–101. That was a blow. We were expecting to win. A guard by the name of Glen Combs shot the lights out on us. That was a tough loss for us. We thought we should have won that one, and the Stars went on and won the title.

CHAPTER 17

THE WINS KEEP ON COMING

The Pacers reported to training camp for the 1971–72 season with a feeling that they should have been two-time defending ABA champions. Mel Daniels, Roger Brown, Freddie Lewis, Bob Netolicky, Rick Mount, and Billy Keller were all still there, but there were also two notable additions to the roster.

George McGinnis, the powerful 6'8" forward who was one of the greatest high school players in Indiana history, had spent two years at Indiana University, one of them during his freshman season when he couldn't play varsity, and the other turning in one of the most fabulous seasons ever compiled by a Hoosiers player. McGinnis averaged 29.9 points and 14.7 rebounds a game in an All-American performance.

It was not nearly as common for undergraduate players to leave school early for professional basketball in those days, and the NBA did not welcome such players. But McGinnis had the opportunity to make money and support his family while staying at home to play for the Pacers, so he made the jump. He averaged 16.9 points a game as a rookie and eventually had his No. 30 jersey retired by the Pacers.

The other key addition was Darnell Hillman. Hillman was a 6'9" forward out of San Jose State whose nickname was "Dr. Dunk." Hillman is still employed by the Pacers in marketing. As a rookie Hillman averaged 7.0 points a game on a high-scoring team that finished 47–37 during the regular season and once again excited Indianapolis with a tremendous playoff run.

177

As a native of the area, McGinnis was well aware of Bob Leonard, his new coach, before turning pro.

"The Pacers were already good when I got there," said McGinnis, who operates a business in Indianapolis. "I knew a lot about Slick. The stories were legendary. I talked to Lou Watson [Indiana University coach], and he talked a lot about Slick. I knew he wanted me there, and I wanted to be there."

McGinnis had just turned 21 years old and was joining a team of veterans, older men, who made him feel welcome. As dominating a player as he had been, this group of Pacers players did not need him to be the top gun so he could ease into the pros. McGinnis appeared in 73 games that season but started just 46 of them.

"Those guys were pretty good," he said. "It was a well-coached team, and it was as close a team as I have ever been on. It was a true family. There was always something going on where you would be with the guys. That's what made it so special. I think being in there against the NBA was one thing that made the togetherness. We were trying to prove a point about how good we were."

Consistent with Leonard's kick-'em-in-the-butt and then give-'em-a-hug philosophy, McGinnis felt he was the recipient of both extremes of Leonard's moods based on his play as a rookie.

"He was a coach and he was a father figure," McGinnis said. "One time he got on me, and I'm telling you my eyes were as big as two Susan B. Anthony dollars. He calmed down and I said, 'I'm sorry. What did I do?'"

To the players and to the public for the most part, in McGinnis' mind, Leonard was the franchise.

"He begged the corporate folks for sponsors," McGinnis said. "He is synonymous with the club. He was a very impressive coach. He was so amazing at playoff basketball. I remember a seventh game against Kentucky where they were pressing and he had me bring the ball up court. They didn't know what to do. He changed the complete offense for the seventh game in a series. That would throw a little bit of a wrench into what they had been seeing."

Hillman was a rookie addition to the team, and from the start he liked the atmosphere Leonard created and the way he instructed players on the nuances of the sport.

"He was an excellent teacher of the game," Hillman said. "Every night he had something. Bob made the team a family. I don't think you see it anymore. It's very unique, rare, once in a lifetime. He wanted to understand what you were like as a person as an extension of the player. He would ask, 'Are you feeling bad?' If you were on his team, you were a member of the family. It was part of Slick's character. You could tell right away, 'This guy has got my back.'"

Leonard's leadership mixed with the players' talents to produce first-class results for Indiana, and Hillman said Leonard's ability to meld together all the parts was huge.

"Having all of that talent and making it work was his challenge," Hillman said. "That was big for us. We had such chemistry, and it worked for us. It was gratifying because we knew everyone was going to get his chance to shine. To this day I have people come up to me and talk about those teams from the 1970s and say, 'It looked like you guys were having fun every night.'"

Sometimes fatherly Bob could get into trouble making his case to referees. Forward Bob Netolicky remembers one occasion when an official really got Leonard steamed.

"There were three bad calls in a row," Bob Netolicky said. "I want to say it was against the Minnesota Pipers. Slick was just getting furious. He yelled to a referee, 'If you make one more bad call, I'll sock you in the mouth.' Sure enough, there was another whistle, and he went after the ref. He took a swing at him and missed as two players grabbed him. Of course, he got ejected."

At the time of the incident, George Mikan, Leonard's old friend and the famous player who had bestowed the nickname Slick on him, was the commissioner of the American Basketball Association. The way Netolicky heard the story was that Leonard was called into Mikan's office for disciplinary action. He was not about to fight the penalty, so he said, "How much is the fine? Let's go get a beer."

Leonard, said Netolicky, made the Pacers into winners and champions by the way he handled the players.

"Slick taught us to believe in ourselves," Netolicky said. "And he taught us to believe in each other."

That 1971–72 team brought another championship back to Indiana with a mix of old faces and new faces. Netolicky was part of that group, and he still thinks Indiana should have won the year before and again, a fifth time in their run. That season, though, they were working on a second title.

The Pacers met the Denver Rockets in the first round, which was not an easy series, but the team advanced by a 4–3 margin. Then they had a rematch with the defending champion Utah Stars. This time they beat them in seven games after falling behind 2–0 in games.

The championship series pitted the Pacers against the New York Nets. At that point Rick Barry was the leading scorer with that bunch, and they were coached by long-time St. John's coach Lou Carnesecca. Indiana prevailed in six games and earned another parade in downtown Indianapolis.

BOBBY LEONARD

I did not make a trip to Bloomington to see George McGinnis at Indiana, but I was very aware of him. One reason I was so aware of him was because George led the Big Ten in scoring and rebounding when he was only a sophomore. Some of the founding owners of the Pacers and other guys who had been instrumental in bringing the Pacers to town were the ones who worked on signing George. He never went into the pro draft.

The ABA had a rule, which the NBA observed before, that if a guy was in your area, a big star, and it would be good for the team and the league, you could get him with a territorial draft pick. Part of it was about helping attendance. That's why when they first started out that the Kentucky Colonels had so many players from Kentucky. The George McGinnis deal was handled for us by upper management.

George wanted to take care of his mother in Indianapolis. This was an opportunity for him to make some money. He wanted to go pro after spending two years at IU. He was with us by training camp, and it was no surprise to me what we were getting.

We held our training camp out at Indiana Central, which is now the University of Indianapolis. They had a nice facility. One of the first interesting things that happened was an argument between the new guys about who was faster, George Mcginnis or Darnell Hillman. Darnell had been a track man at San Jose State, and they were very good in track. He ran the quarter mile. There was a track right outside the door, so I stopped the argument by saying that the only way to solve things was to go outside and have a race.

Well, Davey Craig, the trainer, got one of those starting guns and we're going to run a 100-yard dash. Davey shot the gun, and it sounded like a thundering herd coming down that track. George ended up beating Darnell by a yard, a yard-and-a-half. In basketball shoes he ran the 100-yard dash in 10.4. That shows you the kind of speed the guy had. Darnell ran a heck of a race, too, but he thought he was going to beat him.

George was a natural athlete. He never lifted weights or anything. He just had that powerful body that was unbelievable. I often thought, and he was a heck of a high school football player, if they put him on the Colts at tight end with his speed and his hands that he would have been great. In high school George just dominated everything and he had a teammate named Steve Downing, who was 6'8", at George Washington High School in Indianapolis. Downing went to IU, too, and played a couple of years in the pros. Can you imagine how tough it was to play against that high school team?

As soon as I saw George on TV in his IU games, I knew he was going to be a great player. He just had it all. He could dominate a game. He had size, strength, speed, good hands. He was one of a few Indiana players who could take over a game, along with Larry Bird and Oscar Robertson.

During that first training camp, which is the time when you really have to get into condition for the season, I have the players run baselines, or suicides as some people call them, just like the ones I had the players do during the tryouts. The Pacers who were coming back knew that the suicides at the end of practice were not to be treated in a Mickey Mouse fashion. I wanted them to run, to be in shape. They were not for punishment. They were a conditioning drill.

They all knew that they had to run hard. I had the players running 10 of them. Well, George had never run 10 of them down at IU, so about four or five baselines into it, he stopped. He just stopped. I blew the whistle and the guys were all over him saying, "George, keep running, or he'll just keep us out here." See, they knew the story. Anyway, I went over to George and he was just exhausted. He said, "Slick, you're gonna kill somebody. I think I'm gonna be the first one to go." I said, "George, I'm gonna have Davey Craig take you in there to the shower room and turn cold water on you. Then you're going to come out here and finish those baselines." He didn't like it, but we were fine from there. Oh, I got on George once in a while, but George and I became great friends.

George is a great guy. He'd do anything for anybody. He's just one of those guys who have a great personality. He never talks about himself. He never brags. He was such a natural athlete that I think it hurt him later as he got older because he hadn't had to train as hard. That first year I wanted to break him into the thing so he didn't start every game. But he got a lot of points and rebounds. His shooting percentage was 46 percent or so, which was pretty good. One thing he didn't do was shoot threes. He tried 38 and made six.

I've seen every player at IU for more than 60 years, and in my mind

George is the greatest. He had only one varsity season but averaged about 30 points a game and led the Big Ten in scoring and rebounding.

That was a pretty good club. Adding George and Darnell gave us more depth, and we had a lot of guys who could score. We had a lot of flexibility with that team. We had six guys average between 14.3 and 19.1 points a game. That's pretty strong. The seventh guy was Keller at 9.7. Look at teams. You never find six who are averaging those kinds of numbers.

Darnell had been a good player in college and then he went into the military before he came to the Pacers. A friend of mine called me and told me how good he was. He had seen Darnell in an army tournament. That's how we found Darnell, and he gave us another good forward. He could jump out of the gym and run. With his track background he could run the floor, and he was in good condition. We had quality depth, and that's what you're looking for as a coach.

Rick Mount was still there, too. In his second year, and he upped his scoring average and his shooting percentage increased from 37 to 44 percent.

One of the other key additions to the Pacers back during that time period was Davey Craig, the trainer. My first year the trainer was Bernie LaRue but he left for the Chicago Bears. Pinky Newell, the trainer at Purdue, called me and said he had this kid who was the best student trainer he had ever had.

Davey came to Indianapolis for an interview when the Pacers' offices were on 38th Street, and we walked across the street to a pub. Davey began to tell me about himself and give me his presentation and I had sized him up pretty quickly and knew I was going to hire him. I said, "Ah, forget it. You're hired." He stayed with the Pacers for 35 years.

That year we got back into the playoffs, and in the first round we met Denver. That was a very tough series, and it went back and forth. We won the first game but lost the second game by a point. Then we won the third game by two points in overtime. That's how it went, every other game. Alex Hannum was coaching Denver, and it came down to a seventh game. We won it 91–89.

In the second round we had our rematch against Utah. They always gave us trouble. Besides Zelmo Beaty in the middle, they had a lot of good shooters. They went 60–24 in the regular season. Beaty averaged 23.6 and 13.2 rebounds again. Willie Wise averaged 23.2 points and 10.6 rebounds. Jimmy Jones averaged 15.5, and Ron Boone averaged 13 a game in the backcourt. Utah was tough.

We lost the first two games against them in Salt Lake City. And then we won two in a row at home. During that series the Fairgrounds Coliseum was booked for something and we took one of our home games to Indiana State University in Terre Haute. They had a Tartan floor there, like you would have for track and field.

In one of the games in Salt Lake City, I kicked the ball out of the court. I was mad at the referees, and the ball was the first thing I saw. There was a time out and the referees lay the ball down on the free throw line I just ran out there and kicked it up into the stands. Way up into the stands. It livened up the joint. They'd never seen anything like that. If that happened today you'd be in the locker room before the ball landed, and they would fine you, too. I didn't get fined. All I got was a technical foul. I didn't have to leave the game. I'll tell you, I think it was about a 50-yard field goal.

Dealing with the referees was a constant battle for me. But I learned how to do it. I could call them something, and by the time they looked over at me I'd be walking down to the end of the bench with my back to them. You know how they have a rack of balls that the players use to warm up with before the game and after halftime? One time I threw a whole rack of balls out on the floor. There were all of those red, white, and blue balls bouncing all over the place. The balls were bouncing everywhere. One time—and they don't do this anymore—when the referees were still wearing the whistles around their neck on the ropes, I grabbed the chain and just yanked it off a referee's neck. That was definitely a technical. I got kicked out of the game for that one. I got kicked out of several games during my coaching career. Many, I would say.

One time Paul Furimsky, the guy in Indianapolis who ran the clock for the stat crew, escorted the referees to their dressing room. Then he came back to me and said, "You know what one of the refs said? 'I wonder what that crazy SOB is going to pull tonight?'" So I had a reputation. I wasn't as animated in Chicago. I did a little bit more in Baltimore. I used to throw a towel now and then, and the refs would say, "You're not going to throw a towel on me." I'd just throw it out on the floor. It was wherever it landed. But I always picked spots in the ball game where I was not going to get a T that would hurt the ball club. The trouble was, every time I got fined for a technical, Nancy felt she could spend the same amount of money to buy a new pair of shoes as payback to me for wasting money.

Some of what I did was premeditated to get the team fired up and some of it was my temper reacting to what the refs called or didn't call. It was a combination. You hoped if you said something that it would be in the back of their minds the next time a call came around. You had to pick your spots based on how the game was going. Yelling like that can motivate the team and let the referees know that they've made a bad call. I was a battler, and I wanted my team to battle. Some of it was definitely spontaneous. It was not all premeditated. If a referee makes a bad call at an atrocious time, you're gonna react, but you've got to be careful. You've got to look up there at that scoreboard and see how the flow of the game is going. There are a lot of things involved before you go off your rocker. I look back at that now and think I had to be half nuts to do some of the stuff I did.

I might have seemed out of control to the refs and to the fans, but I wasn't. By the time I walked out of that dressing room, I was back to being Bob. Nancy rode the officials from her seat worse than me. She knew them all, and they knew her. She was right there in a seat near the court, and she was on them all the time. I told her several times not to, but she's still doing that. Now I say, "Nancy, I wouldn't even go down there and sit by you at a ball game now." Because she's gonna get on those referees. She could be funny about it.

185

For me, when I walked out of the dressing room, it was over. When you walk out of the arena, you either won or you lost. That's what you're taking out of there. The good thing about the pro game is that you don't have to wait a week to play another game. You're right back at it. I don't know how my stomach would be if I was a football coach and had to wait a whole week until another game. That's tough stuff. I think it would be an especially tough loss, knowing that you had Monday off and had to go to practice for a week.

The person I was closest to in pro football was Bob Skoronski, who tipped me off about the Herff Jones business. We were roommates at IU one year when I was a senior and he was a sophomore. We were in the same fraternity. If we happened to be in the same city with our teams over the years, we would call and have dinner. One time he called and said we should get together for a late dinner. He brought Ray Nitschke, the Hall of Fame linebacker. Ray was a great guy. He died at a young age. It was at a restaurant in Baltimore that was famous for rack of lamb. Bobby's a good boy. I think he made more money with Josten's selling class rings and graduation things than he did for the Packers.

We had tough work getting past Denver and Utah, and then we had the Nets with Rick Barry, Billy Paultz, and John Roche. There again we had a problem with the Coliseum being booked and we went down to IU's Assembly Hall to play a game down there. It was 2–2 in the series, and we came back to the Fairgrounds for the next game. That thing was a barnburner. I can still see it.

We won 100–99. We were down by five points with like 30 seconds to go or something like that. Freddie Lewis stole the ball, goes in for a layup, gets fouled, and that was a three-point play. The Nets come down the floor and throw the ball away, a bad pass, so we got it back. We go down the court again, and Freddie makes a three-point shot so we were up one with five seconds to play. The Nets took the ball inbounds at half-court. They ran a double pick with Rick Barry coming off the baseline. We didn't have a defender within 10' of him. They got picked off. Rick shot the ball before he caught it and it slipped through his hands and went out of bounds. That was how it ended. That was huge. What a ball game.

Then we went to New York and we won the series. That was another close game. We won 108–105, beat them in the sixth game in the Nassau County Coliseum on Long Island. We went seven, seven, and six to win the championship, 20 playoff games. That gave us our second championship. That was very satisfying. Winning two sevens and a six, that's tough. That's real pressure.

We got nice championship rings. Nancy wears one of them that was cut down to her size. I had five rings, three for the Pacers championships, one for IU, and one for the IU Hall of Fame. The kids have the other ones. I don't wear any because I'm not a jewelry guy. I don't even wear a watch. I wear a wedding ring when I go to church or out to dinner or some other event.

Those series were tougher than nails. Close games, long series, they would wear you out. Those were character series. When the games are that close, you've got to come up with the plays. You've got to come up with them when you go down to the wire. I remember those series how tough they were as long ago as they were.

CHAPTER 18

INDIANAPOLIS
TITLE TOWN

In the rapidly changing sports world it's almost impossible for a team's roster to remain stable, even if it is a championship team. There is constant pressure to adapt because retirements happen, injuries happen, aging interferes, and fresh faces come along. At the same time the other teams in the league are trying to catch up and they are adjusting and adapting, too.

The Indiana Pacers entered the 1972–73 American Basketball Association season as the defending champions and very much anxious to win another crown. The Pacers finished 51–33 that year, a solid regular season that guaranteed a return berth to the playoffs. But it was not precisely the same Pacers team that had won it all the year before.

All-Star forward Roger Brown had some back problems, and although he played in 72 games, he started only 38 of them. Old reliables Mel Daniels, Freddie Lewis, and Billy Keller were still playing. Darnell Hillman was in his second year, and George McGinnis blossomed into a superstar, averaging 27.6 points a game. Two important new backcourt players appeared, too, Don Buse, a rookie out of Evansville, and Donnie Freeman, a five-year ABA veteran out of the University of Illinois.

Bob Netolicky was gone to the Dallas Chaparrals that year, though he was reacquired after that and back with the Pacers where he belonged.

This time period, when the Pacers were perennial contenders and three-time ABA champions, was the heyday of the franchise and also the good times that Bob Leonard's children remember. This segment of their youth was totally wrapped up with the Pacers. They went to the games and practices, treated the home arena as if it was their own house, and reveled in the big victories along with their father the coach and the rest of the Indiana community.

"I remember the excitement of being at the games," the younger Bob Leonard said. "I'd throw the balls to the players when they were warming up. I remember Roger Brown making plays I couldn't believe he made. The real difference between myself and my brothers with the Pacers was that all of the time I was growing up, until at least my junior year in high school, they were really good."

While Bob was more of a student of the game at the time as he was playing high school ball in Carmel, his younger brother, Tommy, was just a kid on the loose at Pacers games. To him it was a big playground.

"I was three, four, five years old, and I ran around as if I had a free pass," Tommy Leonard said. "I was all over the locker room and the hallways." His father may have been a basketball coach, but Tommy said he was as down to earth as his friends' dads. "To me, the example he set for his own children and other people is what stands out. His work ethic. He let us know nothing came free in life, that there were no handouts and that you had to work. He was the same person who walked out of Terre Haute and went to IU. He never put on airs. He says, 'All I ever did was throw a ball in a hoop.'"

Although he was too young to watch his father play professionally, Tommy Leonard didn't need to be told that Bob Leonard was one competitive man when he was involved in a sport.

"Whatever he's doing, he wants to win," Tommy Leonard said. "If he's playing golf or if he was taking us fishing. He'd say, 'I'm going to catch more fish than you do.'"

Brother Tim also regards Market Square Arena as his old playground, but he understands why the kids were always there with free rein. It was one way for his father to stay in closer touch with them.

"I enjoyed being up close with these great players like Roger and George in the locker room," Tim Leonard said. "We pretty much went to every home game, as long as it wasn't a school night. I kind of grew up at Market Square Arena. When you go to the arena now everything is regimented and you can't roam around. It was just completely different when I was a kid. You could do whatever you wanted to do. It was so family oriented. It's all business now. My dad spent as much time with us as he could. My dad never, never lost sight of his family. We were always No. 1."

Being No. 1 on the court was important to Bob Leonard, as well as the fans and players. Guard Don Buse was a rookie in the 1972–73 season, and after coming out of NCAA Division II Evansville he was happy somebody noticed him and wanted him to play pro ball.

"I was just wanting to play basketball somewhere," Buse said. "Slick was an ex-player, and he related to the ball players. Everyone knew he knew what he was talking about. He was a competitor, but he'd go out and have a beer with you. I can also remember him at halftime, chin to chin with you to get a point across."

McGinnis was unstoppable that season and Mel Daniels did his thing at center, scoring 18.5 points a game. Lewis, Freeman, Keller, and Brown also averaged in double figures, while Hillman scored at a 9.5 clip.

After a solid regular season the Pacers met the Denver Rockets in the first round of the playoffs and took just five games to knock them out. Once again Utah was in the way, the puzzle to be solved to advance or be sent home. The Pacers won 4–2. That set up a finals series against Kentucky. Indiana won that series in seven games, with the last game a low-scoring 88–81. For the third time Indiana won a championship, and for the third time the Pacers won the last game on the road, this time in Kentucky.

"We won them all on the road," guard Billy Keller said. "That was the only thing I would have changed. It was a great time in my life. It was fun. We had the Pacer family and community."

And by the end of the 1972–73 season, they had three championship rings.

Bobby Leonard

Roger Brown had some back problems that year and that could have really hurt us. But George was fantastic for us, and we got a few new faces.

Donnie Freeman was only about 6'3" or maybe a half-inch bigger, but he was a great scorer. He actually was a bigger scorer for other teams than he was for us, but that's because we had so many guys who could score. What an addition he was. He could manufacture a shot like you couldn't believe. He came into the game and had all kinds of footwork, and you would be watching his feet and he would get off a 15-footer on you. That was our backcourt: Freddie Lewis, Donnie Freeman, and Billy Keller.

Plus we had Don Buse. The Virginia Squires drafted him, but they didn't have room on the roster for him. Al Bianchi was the coach, and those many years earlier I helped keep him in the NBA. Al and I were friends. Al called me up and said, "We've got this good, hard-nosed kid that can defend and he's from Evansville, Indiana." I said, "I'll take him." That was a good choice. Later, Don became an All-Star.

In the beginning Don was known more for his defense. He played defense, could steal the ball and run it. That's what we did. He was the kind of guy that you'd put on Michael Jordan or Jerry West. He was as good a defensive guard as I've seen. When I used him with Freddie, boy, you had two guys who could play lock-down defense. And Donnie Freeman scored 14 points a game. He didn't take threes, but he could get where he wanted to go to get a shot off. He was a very good mid-range jump shooter inside 17'.

That team had about as good a depth as any group I had. That was one of our best teams. I also brought Gus Johnson back, I had him in Baltimore. Gus played 50 games for us as a backup at forward. He was near the end of his career, had a bad knee. Phoenix put him on waivers, and I picked him up. I didn't know how much Gus could play, but there was a personal feeling between me and Gus, and if he joined me in Indiana and he couldn't play a lick, that was something I still wanted to do. Wouldn't you know that when we got into the seventh game of the last series against Kentucky—and they had big men like Artis Gilmore and Dan Issel—Mel Daniels got into foul trouble. Gus was only about 6'6", and those guys were much taller, but Gus was strong. I put Gus in that game on Gilmore, who was 7' tall.

What Gus was able to do because of his strength when he was covering Gilmore was move him away from the basket. Kentucky would run its offense, move the ball around, but by the time they were ready to throw it inside, Gus would have moved Gilmore probably 15' out on the floor. He would just put his back into him, and it really took Artis out of his game. I got Gus at the end of his career, but he got a championship ring. It was the only championship ring he ever got. Gus was only 48 when he died of brain cancer. I talked with him the week he was dying. He didn't get into the Hall of Fame until after he died.

That was a great year for us, with a great mix of talent. I would have loved to have had Gus with that group when he was a younger player. Nobody would have touched us. We might have finished something like 70–10. That was right up there with the best we ever were.

We were lucky we had the depth we did that year because Roger was not his usual self. He had a lot of injuries. That was kind of different for us when he wasn't able to start. That year was George McGinnis' second year, and he fully blossomed. Not only did he score almost 28 points a game, but it seemed as if he got almost every rebound. George could have hot streaks like that. Of course, Mel was still our top rebounder, but George got all of the ones that were left over it seemed.

There were two other guys who were pretty good players who I just couldn't get into the games all the time because we had so much talent. One of them was Bill Newton. They called him "Fig" Newton. He was an Indiana high school basketball star and played with Pete Maravich at Louisiana State. Fig averaged about 18 points and 10 rebounds a game, though, after Maravich graduated. He played some pro ball in Italy, too, which was before most Americans went to Europe.

Fig just couldn't get into that many games, but he was a great guy to have. We still get together to this day. Bob Arnzen, who was out of Notre Dame, was another guy like that. I didn't get those guys into more than 20 or so games, but they never complained. They were good teammates, just good guys. They played in almost the same amount of games and they played almost the same amount of minutes. When you were ahead you put them in, and when they were behind you put them in.

The more I think about it, that was our best Pacers team.

We took out Denver in five games, and then we came up against Utah again. That was a tough series, as it always was against the Stars. We matched up well. But they were talented. Zelmo Beaty was one of the best big men in the league. Willie Wise could really play defense. They put him on Roger Brown, and those match-ups were very good. Willie was an excellent player.

Utah had guys like Willie Wise and Red Robbins, and we had Roger Brown—and fans across the country didn't know that much about them because they were never on TV. All of the TV coverage was focused on the NBA. That was a shame. Even Louie Dampier, he probably got more TV attention when he was playing for the University of Kentucky than when he played for the Colonels. Guys like this could play anywhere. They just didn't get the ink or exposure the way the NBA players did. For a while if you were a basketball fan, you really had to work hard to find out who the best guys were in the league, although that started to change in the mid-1970s. You know who started in the ABA in the early 1970s? Caldwell Jones. He was one of four brothers who played pro ball after going to Albany State in Georgia. I had his brother, Wil. There was Caldwell, Major, Charles, and Wil.

Caldwell Jones played for about 17 years until he was almost 40, and that was very unusual to have such a long career at the time. Back then the guys didn't play as long. We didn't have the training facilities, the weight training, the strength coaches, the medical specialists, or the nutrition programs. There was one team doctor, but now you have a doctor for orthopedics, a doctor for this, a doctor for that. In the arenas they serve nutritional meals for the players, the whole thing.

Teams have gyms that are open for them to practice when they want to. Almost all of the arenas have practice facilities that let them play. The guys just didn't play as long as they do now. It used to be in my day that if a guy became a 10-year player, it was a helluva career. Now it's up to 15 years and some guys are playing beyond that. Not too many, but you are looking at careers that last three, four, or five more years and that's a bunch, especially with the kind of money they're making.

I worked in construction in the off-season sometimes, not on getting my game better. I didn't have time. I needed the money. You always wonder how much better guys from that era would have been if they had all of these advantages. No question about it.

When I was playing, guys were looking for any kind of job for the off-season, in insurance, investments, construction. Nancy's mom and dad owned a small roofing and tiling company, and her father was the head of the Building Trades Union in South Bend. That's what I did in the off-season, work for the roofing company. We did some jobs at Notre Dame in South Bend. We put the original roof on the library that has Touchdown Jesus on the front of the building. I was pulling gravel in buckets, pulling gravel all summer. That was physical work.

I would have been a better basketball player if I had played all summer instead of doing that. There wasn't really anyone to play against in South Bend at the time.

We got past Utah in that series again and played Kentucky for the title. These two teams were pretty familiar with one another. The core of our team was the same, and the core of their team was the same. This year they had Rick Mount instead of us, but their main guys were Artis Gilmore, Dan Issel, and Louie Dampier. They were a good team.

We had played in our share of very high-scoring games in the ABA, during the regular season and in the playoffs, though defense was always a little bit tighter in the playoffs. You're playing against better teams, and the rebounding difference is closer. You can't really kick a good team to death on the boards and get out and run on them. You have to grind it out more. A lot of the games in the Kentucky series were much lower scoring. We lost 92–88. We won 90–86. We won 89–86. And we won the last game 88–81, the game where Gus Johnson made a difference.

That series with Kentucky is a pretty good memory. It went seven games, and we were really going after each other at both ends of the floor. There were big crowds and a lot of pressure. There was that Indiana-Kentucky thing going, too. Any time it goes seven games, it's a monster. It's down to the one game for the whole ball of wax.

Winning that third championship felt pretty good. We were the premier team in the American Basketball Association. Somebody came out and said that we were the Boston Celtics of the ABA. It sounded good, but I didn't think of it that way at all. The Celtics won 11 championships in 13 years.

At the same time, the ABA was getting better and better across the board. There was no question it was better by 1973 than it had been five years earlier. The depth was getting stronger, and the talent level as a whole was better. There had always been stars, but now the talent level was running deeper. Up until then I never thought about whether there would be a merger with the NBA. I was just doing my job. I never thought anything about it except if I heard people talk about it.

We were fortunate that we had a lot of the same guys, very talented people who were the foundation of those championship teams. But we kept adding talent, with one guy at a time that could help. We won three of those babies and we could have won four straight. I always think about the one that got away in 1971 when we lost the Western Division finals to Utah. We lost the last game by seven points, and they shot 60 percent.

But if you look at it we worked to get stronger. We had Mel Daniels, Roger Brown, Billy Keller, Freddie Lewis, and Bob Netolicky for most of it, but we added George McGinnis, Darnell Hillman, Donnie Freeman, and Don Buse. We had a good run with the key guys. At that particular point we had gone to the championship series four times, and we won three of them.

As I said, I didn't think much about a merger with the NBA except during the exhibition season. After the 1970–71 season there was an NBA-ABA All-Star Game, which the NBA won 125–120. The gap was clearly shrinking in talent. The first exhibition games were played between the ABA teams and the NBA starting in 1971. Most of them were played in ABA arenas, too. I think the merger talks began heating up when the ABA began kicking their butts in exhibition games.

We had an exhibition game in there in 1971 against the New York Knicks. The Knicks won the NBA title in 1970 and 1973, and we won three ABA titles in there. They still say the Knicks of 1973 is the greatest Knicks team of all time. They had Willis Reed, Bill Bradley, Dave DeBusschere, Walt Frazier, and Dick Barnett. They came to Indianapolis, and they had that New York swagger.

Before the game I talked to the guys and said, "Here's a real opportunity for you." This was after the Knicks beat the Lakers on national TV, and Reed limped out to play when no one thought he was healthy enough to be in the game, all of that drama. I had the sense that the match-up was supposed to be them coming out of the big city to embarrass the little boys. That's why I talked to my players and said, "Hey, you guys are every bit as good as they are. We won a championship. They just get more attention. So the big thing now is to go out and kick their butts."

My guys believed that anyway. It was two champions going head to head. The whole of Indianapolis was out there. They wanted to see this. We wanted to be noticed by somebody and have them say, "They've got an awful lot of good players over there, and we need some more good players."

There was a luncheon, and the thing I remember about that luncheon was that Bill Bradley got up and made some remarks about cornfields in Indiana and that teed off our guys.

Roger Brown said, "Let me have him." That night Roger tore him up, and Bill Bradley's in the Hall of Fame. You know if you play in New York you get all this ink and this, that, and the other thing. Roger was a lot better player than Bill Bradley. Probably people will say that I'm biased, but if they saw that game they wouldn't think so. We had them down after the third quarter. It was a two-point game at the end. If we had stayed with what we had in there, we could have kicked them pretty good.

That was the first year there were exhibition games, and it kept building after that. They became commonplace. If you go back and look at it, the ABA won more games than it lost. In 1973, the ABA won 15 games to the NBA's 10. In 1974, it was 16–7. And it 1975, it was 31–17. No wonder they were very seriously discussing a merger by then.

CHAPTER 19

CHASING A
FOURTH CROWN

After the Indiana Pacers won their third American Basketball Association title, the drive was on for another one. The team was hungry for a fourth championship, and management demonstrated how hungry it was by adopting the motto, "4 in '74."

Winning had made the Pacers popular in Indianapolis and throughout Indiana, which is usually the case in professional sports. In the case of the ABA that was particularly important because the league was founded by team owners whose long-term ambition was to merge with the NBA, and to merge with the NBA it had to prove that it was financially viable.

The ABA took its inspiration from the American Football League, which had parlayed a good television contract and the nation's seemingly insatiable desire for more football into a merger with the established National Football League.

The ABA made the NBA uncomfortable fairly quickly. By 1967 when the upstart league began, there were only 12 NBA teams and the ABA mostly moved into markets where there was no other professional basketball. As early as 1970 the first discussions were held about the topic of becoming one league. That's why teams were playing an inter-league All-Star Game and inter-league exhibitions as early as 1971.

Players liked having two leagues because it gave them more employment choices, and more jobs. So when the NBA and ABA first announced that it was moving toward a merger, the NBA Players Association filed an anti-trust lawsuit. It became known as the Oscar Robertson suit. It also took until February 1976 for the case to be settled, and that delayed the merger.

This was all background as the 1973–74 season and the Pacers' quest for a fourth title began. The team looked about as strong as ever with forward George McGinnis assuming the role of go-to guy with his 25.9 points a game, but he was still backed by Mel Daniels, Donnie Freeman, Roger Brown, Freddie Lewis, Billy Keller, Don Buse, and Darnell Hillman. Plus, Bob Netolicky had returned after playing one year in Dallas.

Netolicky and Bob Leonard had a memorable run-in after a game when the coach did not think his 6'9" forward had been hustling enough. Netolicky recalled the occasion happening in Duluth, Minnesota, where a game was played against the Muskies or Pipers, depending on what they were called at the time. But the Pacers were definitely borrowing a hockey locker room.

"I was dogging it, I guess," Netolicky said. "He picked up a hockey stick and said, 'I'm gonna beat you with this.' He didn't actually hit me, but he was tremendously angry. I wasn't sure he wasn't going to hit me. My teammates hung a hockey stick in my locker every day for a month after that. They broke the mold when they made Slick."

Bob Leonard put the 1972–73 season to bed with a third championship and went into the next year optimistic that what was probably the best team he had ever coached could win another title. Playing that tight exhibition game against the Knicks also vindicated the Pacers' talent in his mind—they were as good as anybody if they were even with the NBA champs.

But the 1973–74 season did not play out quite as smoothly. The Pacers finished 46–38. Good enough to make the playoffs, but not good enough to stamp Indiana as a dominant team. Except for McGinnis, almost all of the old standbys posted seasons where their scoring averages were a little bit lower than what had come to be expected. Indeed, while Brown played in 82 games, he started just 46 and his scoring average dipped to 11.6 points per game. Daniels, Freeman, and Lewis were all in their final years with the Pacers.

Indiana opened the Western Division playoffs against the San Antonio Spurs, which had been the Dallas Chaparrals. Indiana prevailed in a seven-game series and then moved on to face Utah. This was an epic encounter. After a slow start, the Pacers lost the first three games in a row and then won three in a row. The seventh game was in Utah and the Stars won it, 109–87.

The Pacers came closer to winning their fourth title during the 1974–75 season when the playoffs brought them face-to-face with San Antonio, Denver, and Kentucky in the finals.

BOBBY LEONARD

One of our founders and owners was Chuck DeVoe who was a great tennis player. He was involved in a little match at one of the local tennis clubs, and he'd gotten these T-shirts that read, "4 in '74." We were going to win our fourth championship in 1974. Well, it didn't happen.

Our record wasn't as good during the regular season, and we might have felt more vulnerable going into the playoffs. We had some injuries that year.

Once during that season, we played the New York Nets in Terre Haute. Sometimes the Fairgrounds Coliseum was booked so we'd go over to Terre Haute and play at Indiana State. I had a lot of friends there so it was always kind of neat. A lot of old friends came out. Still, we lost that game 124–117 in double overtime. I was never all that sentimental, but it was still good to go there. When I was with the Lakers and Clyde Lovellette and I were teammates, we played an exhibition game there.

Bob Netolicky rejoined the Pacers in the middle of the season. Bob was really a big part of the Pacers' glory years. When he was a young player, he sometimes seemed a little bit spoiled to me. He came out of Drake University, and his father was one of the top surgeons in the state.

Sometimes I had to get on him. He was kind of my whipping boy. I remember we were in New York one time [versus Netolicky's memory of Minnesota] and he was doing nothing in the first half. At halftime we were in a big dressing room where the hockey team dressed, but they were out of town. This was against the Nets, so it would have been the New York Islanders hockey team.

I got on him real bad at halftime, and when I got mad at him I grabbed a hockey stick off the wall and I went after him. He ran into the men's room and locked the door, and I broke that hockey stick over that door. He came out and scored 24 points in the second half. I woke him up. No, I didn't get a two-minute penalty for high sticking, but I did get on him more than once if he didn't go hard the whole time.

Another time we were in the playoffs and it was very warm, probably late May. He went into the game and took about a 16' shot and it traveled about 4' or 5'. And I thought, *What in the world is wrong with this guy?* That was the time that he went out water skiing. He had no strength in his arms. And we're in the playoffs!

There were a lot of good coaches in the ABA, but one of the most entertaining was Babe McCarthy. Babe was a great guy. He was in the league from the start and coached a few teams, but in the 1973–74 season he was coaching the Kentucky Colonels, our rivals, and he won Coach of the Year. They called Babe "Magnolia Mouth." He sure could talk.

Babe had that southern drawl, and he always carried a flask of whiskey in his travel bag. He might take a nip at halftime or whatever. He was just one of those people everybody liked. Boy, if you got him talking he would just talk, talk, talk, but he was a very good basketball coach, and he was funny. Babe was a special guy. He liked that Kentucky bourbon. He died young, though, from cancer at only 51 in 1975.

The way that year ended was a disappointment. There was definitely a lot of regrouping. Roger Brown was only able to play 10 games and then he retired. He couldn't play anymore. He had a lot of back problems. Roger at his best, boy, was something else. There was one playoff series early on in his career when he scored 45, 43, and 54 points. I was very glad to see him chosen for the Hall of Fame in 2013.

We were quite a different team in the 1974–75 season. We finished 45–39, but the personnel was changing. Billy Knight was our biggest addition. Knight was a 6'6" forward out of the University of Pittsburgh who averaged 17.1 points a game as a rookie. Some people missed Billy in the draft, and we got him. Nancy and I used to own a restaurant in Carmel, Indiana, called Bobby Leonard's All American Scoreboard Restaurant. It was just down the road from where we live, and we only had it for a couple of years. But Billy Knight and his mother came in, and I signed Billy for the Pacers in that restaurant.

Also, Kevin Joyce, who had been mostly a backup the year before when he scored 7.3 points a game, scored almost 15 points a game. Kevin was 6'3" and came out of the University of South Carolina.

We also got Len Elmore out of Maryland and our front-court was George, Billy Knight, and Lenny Elmore. Bob Netolicky was a backup. Billy Keller was still there, but he only started like 13 games. I usually brought in Billy off the bench because he would give you some quick offense. Don Buse was still there. He wasn't a big scorer, but I always put him on the other team's best guard. Later with the Phoenix Suns, he made an NBA All-Star team.

Don covered Jimmy Silas from San Antonio. Nobody will ever know how good Jimmy Silas was. Until his knees went bad, he was some kind of player. George Gervin was a great scorer and won the NBA scoring championship. He was so good we used to have to double-team him at the top of the key. That's the kind of player I put Buse on.

There was a little shake-up after the 1973–74 season. Freddie Lewis went to St. Louis. Mel Daniels went to the Memphis Sounds, and he played part of one other year but he was winding it up.

It's not easy to deal with changes like that. Those guys were with me for a long time. The one thing I never did like about coaching was when you had kids come in, good college players, but you can only carry so many and at some point in time before the season you've got to cut players. I hated to cut players because you have to bring them in, sit them down, and go over why they didn't make the team. It wasn't easy for me. It was one of the worst parts of coaching. Cutting players, or trading them for that matter, I didn't like it. It was way worse when it was a guy who had been there for a long time and done great things for me.

But this was really George McGinnis' team. I don't know if anyone ever had a better season than George did that year. He put the whole ballclub on his back and carried us to the championship series. He averaged 29.8 points a game with 1,126 rebounds and 495 assists. That's a huge number of assists for a forward. He was fantastic. That had to be the greatest season he had as a pro and he was even better in the playoffs when we needed him to be.

At that point, before that season started, we had lost a number of players that we had won championships with. It was also the first year of Market Square Arena, which had been built because of the fan demand based on what we had accomplished while playing at the Fairgrounds Coliseum. We were only 45–39 during the regular season and San Antonio and Denver had better records than we did. We were the underdogs.

San Antonio was 51–33, and one of their players was George "The Iceman" Gervin, who later won four NBA scoring championships. The first two games were at the HemisFair Arena, and we won both of them. The first game we won 122–119 in overtime. In that game there were two plays that occurred back to back that were almost identical. On the first one, Gervin missed a jump shot, and we got the rebound. George McGinnis filled the outside land on the fast-break, Don Buse filled the middle, and Billy Knight was in the other lane. The Spurs had George Karl back on defense. Karl is now an NBA coach and came out of North Carolina. Well, George McGinnis gets called for an offensive foul, and he goes berserk. I ran out on the floor because I was afraid he was going to get thrown out of the game.

A minute or so later, we had the same scenario. Gervin missed a shot, we got the rebound, and we had McGinnis, Buse, and Knight on the fast-break and Karl was back on defense again. The ball got thrown out of bounds, but George hit Karl so hard he knocked him into the basket stanchion. Then George goes, "Now that's an offensive foul."

We won the next game 98–93 and brought the series back to Indianapolis. We won again 113–103, and it shocked the Spurs that we were ahead 3–0.

The fans loved it. It was wild. They called that series the Hang 'Em High series. I'm not sure why. Maybe because they were from Texas since the Clint Eastwood movie had already been out for a while. They came up with a theme song for the playoffs, too. I think it was called, "So You Think You Can Dance," or something like that. We just packed them in, and the place was going crazy the whole time. I think it was because we were the underdogs who went down to San Antonio, and a lot of people thought they were going to blitz us. When we won the two straight, everybody said that was a fluke. Then we came back to Indianapolis and beat them again.

They won two games and then we closed them out 4–2. I was talking around the offense and saying, "We've got to get these people, the fans, frenzied up." Sandy Knapp was vice president of marketing, and she went out and hired the guy who called himself Dancing Harry. He was all dressed up, and he put a hex on the Spurs. All the fans were wiggling their fingers at the Spurs like they were putting a hex on them, too.

Denver—in their first season with the name Nuggets—at that time was a pretty good team. They had diversified scoring, a lot of guys in double figures, rather than one big superstar leader. Their top scorer was a guard named Ralph Simpson—not Ralph Sampson, the big center from Virginia. Simpson averaged almost 19 points a game. Most of that was a high scoring series. We opened with a 131–128 loss in Denver but came out with a split after beating them, 131–124. It went back and forth until we beat them in a seventh game in Denver, 104–96.

BOOM, BABY!

One thing that happened during that series was very ironic considering what happened to me later in life. During one game in that series, a close game, we were running an out-of-bounds play where we wanted to pass in to George McGinnis. Since he was our high scorer, it wasn't hard for Denver to figure out what we wanted to do. We passed the ball in to George, but when we did, all five Denver players came at him and surrounded him. George jumped in the air and hit Billy Keller in the far corner where he was open. Billy rose up in the air for a jumper. I don't know if it was a buzzer shot or if it was just that the shot clock was going off, but he hit a buzzer shot for a three-pointer. I was on the bench and I yelled, "Boom, Baby!"

That was the first time that I ever said, "Boom, Baby!" during a game, which became my trademark radio call later. I didn't start doing it all of the time, but that was the first time I did it. It came back to me later when I was doing radio. "Boom, Baby!" came from Billy Keller. It was a great three.

You know, Larry Brown was coaching that Denver team and he's still coaching. Larry will die on the bench. I've got a couple of artificial hips, and the same doctor who did mine did Larry's. Larry was one of those guys who ran. He was a fanatic on running to stay in shape. I remember once when we had a league meeting in San Diego, they had a running course set up near us from a race. It was a 10-kilometer course, 6.2 miles.

Anyway, Larry said to me, "Hey, Slick, you want to run with me?" I said that yeah, I would. I didn't really want to, but I didn't want him to think I was a wuss or something. So we went outside and ran, and we ran the whole doggone thing. We ran it together and when we got to the end he said, "You know, I didn't really get a good workout. Let's run it again." I wasn't going to let him know how I really felt, and being the competitor that I was, I wasn't going to say that I wasn't up to it, so I ran it again. I ran it again with him, and about the last 200 or 300 yards I was seeing spots. I mean it was a killer for me. But Larry and I ran that thing twice—almost 13 miles.

Back during the playoffs, we beat that Denver team, and in a season when people didn't think we could make it, we were back in the finals. Kentucky, our old rival, was waiting for us. Kentucky was a very powerful team that year. They still had their best guys, including Artis Gilmore, who scored more than 23 points a game, Dan Issel, and Louie Dampier, but they also had some others who averaged in double figures with Wil Jones and Bird Averitt. They also had a guy named Ted McClain, who only scored 8.6 points a game, but he was a terrific defensive player and averaged more than five assists a game. He was like Don Buse. The Colonels finished 58–26 that year. Hubie Brown was the coach.

That year Kentucky got us. They beat us four out of five in the finals. Without Mel Daniels we just didn't have anyone who could contend with Artis Gilmore, who also went on to the Hall of Fame.

At this point it was clear that the ABA was an artistic success. We knew there were good teams, and we knew that we had a lot of great players. There wasn't as much talk about merging with the NBA as there had been a few years earlier. The big problem was that the ABA was starting to go bust financially. Some teams were starting to come apart. That made a big difference when it came time for the merger. If the merger had come about a little bit earlier, the ABA would have been a little bit stronger.

The period between the end of the 1974–75 season and the 1975–76 season was kind of a turning point for a lot of teams. The Pacers were one of the healthiest teams for a while because we had good fan support, but we were starting to run into problems, too. I didn't know it when we lost in the finals to Kentucky, but we had some bigger problems on the horizon. We needed a big television contract, and we didn't have one.

What we did have was loyal fans. When the team got started for the 1967–68 season, the average home attendance was 5,167. Two years later it was 7,787. In the 1975–76 season we drew 325,000 fans, which was an average again of 7,739, but the next year we went up to 432,726 and averaged 10,551.

The Fairgrounds Coliseum was good to us. Standing room only was 10,000-plus, but we were popular enough that we needed a bigger place and Market Square Arena could hold around 17,000 fans. We had a lot of success, and it was terrific to move into a new building like that.

The landscape of downtown Indianapolis changed once a big arena was built down there. They had the Indianapolis Racers hockey team, too. I don't know if they were thinking of trying to get an NHL franchise. That team was in the World Hockey Association, and that's where Wayne Gretzky played as a rookie. The land the arena was on was owned by the family of Richard Lugar, later the United States senator, who was the mayor at that time and friends with all of our owners. His mother owned the land.

Indianapolis turned itself into a sports town, developing sports as an industry and attracting the NCAA headquarters and all of these events, but Market Square Arena for the Pacers was really the first thing the city did. Now we've got Lucas Oil Stadium, Bankers Life Fieldhouse, and all of these restaurants and hotels that didn't exist back then in that area. A lot of people feel that the Indiana Pacers were the start of the renovation of downtown Indianapolis. That's what followed.

The city started getting college league cross-country and swim meets, and then they had the Pan American Games, and they've gone from that to the Super Bowl. The Pacers were the beginning of Indianapolis as a sports city. It was a 40-year process from the time I was consulting with the Pacers. The Pacers are still part of downtown, and downtown has just grown spectacularly from those beginnings.

Conseco Fieldhouse, now called Bankers Life, replaced Market Square Arena and it is one of the finest arenas in the country. Many years ago when my friend Bob Skoronski was playing for the Green Bay Packers and I was with Chicago, we played an exhibition game in Green Bay. While I was there he took me into the Packers' dressing room and the thing I remembered was what they did for the players. They had nice stalls for them, and they had carpeting on the floors. At the Fairgrounds Coliseum the dressing room was nasty. They had one showerhead and a bunch of old tin lockers that had been around forever. The floors were all beat up and everything. The first thing I did was have them come in there and install lockers so that each player had his own place. I had them put in a half-dozen showerheads, and I carpeted the floors in the dressing area.

When we went to Market Square, it was like that from the start. It was state of the art with everything. It was way ahead of the Fairgrounds. Now, Bankers Life is better than Market Square Arena. It's got all of the amenities.

Market Square was great for the fans, too, but by then the team was starting to have financial problems. The Pacers couldn't keep up with the salaries.

CHAPTER 20

ON TO THE **NBA**

When the changing Indiana Pacers pushed through to the American Basketball Association finals against Kentucky at the end of the 1974–75 season, it turned out to be an ending more than a beginning for the franchise. This was the last time that the Pacers would play for the ABA championship, and the ABA itself was about to undergo major alterations.

The Pacers were starting to hurt for money and had trouble holding on to their top players. The biggest loss going into the 1975–76 season was the departure of star forward George McGinnis to the Philadelphia 76ers of the NBA. McGinnis was offered a great sum of money for the times (and still a great sum of money outside of the realm of professional sports) and left for a new club.

Younger players who took on a greater role were Billy Knight, who averaged a phenomenal 28.1 points a game, and Len Elmore, who scored 14.6 points per game. Holdovers from the glory era included Billy Keller, Darnell Hillman, and Don Buse, but Bob Netolicky played in just four games.

One of the things Netolicky did before he became an ex-Pacer (the two developments were not related) was play a practical joke on coach Bob Leonard that he did not tell Bob about for years.

Netolicky had a friend who did a very accurate Bob Leonard imitation, and they were talking one day as they became aware of the local March of Dimes Telethon. It so happened that the Pacers were playing

211

the Utah Stars that day, and Netolicky and his friend called in to the television station. Netolicky's friend identified himself as Leonard, and made a pledge to the telethon of $100 for every point the Pacers won by that day. They figured Indiana would win the game, but it would be close because just about all games against Utah were close.

"In the first quarter the Pacers got ahead by a little bit," Netolicky said. "Then in the middle of the game the public address announcer told the fans that Bob had made this pledge. You should have seen the look on his face when they made the announcement since of course it was news to him. Well, the Pacers' lead kept getting bigger and bigger, and the PA guy reminds the fans and they give him a standing ovation.

"Wouldn't you know it, we beat them by 27 points. That's $2,700. The story made the front page of *USA Today*. I don't know what Bob said to the Pacers management, but the team paid it. I didn't tell him what we did for 35 years. He started laughing."

Some newcomers who made a mark were Bo Lamar (15.6 points a game), Dave Robisch (13.4), Travis Grant (9.7), and Dan Roundfield (5.1) who was regarded as having tremendous potential.

However, the ABA itself was living on the edge. The Memphis Sounds moved to Baltimore and were renamed the Claws but the team folded by the end of 1975. The San Diego Sails folded, and so did the Utah Stars. From its inception, the ABA wanted to gain strength each season and eventually force a merger with the NBA. Instead, with a merger on the horizon, the ABA was weakening.

The ABA had fought a good fight—proving in many instances that large American cities previously without pro basketball teams were enthusiastic about the game and wanted representation. But creation of a professional sports expansion league is always a risk, and after signing top players, introducing innovative rules, and playing in an entertaining style, the league was almost tapped out.

After winning three championships and reaching the finals two other times, the Bob Leonard–coached Pacers had their first losing record, a mark of 39–45 during the 1975–76 season. They still made the playoffs, but lost two out of three to the Kentucky Colonels to end the season.

Talk of a merger heated up as the litigation filed by the Players Association wound to a conclusion. Just what form it would take was unknown, but ABA owners had one eye on the NBA and one eye on survival. It was like a game of musical chairs. When the music stopped and the NBA beckoned, the ABA owners still wanted their teams to be bouncing those red, white, and blue balls, not be left on the sidelines.

By the 1976–77 season the Pacers were members of the National Basketball Association and the ABA was no more. But the ABA teams did not enter the NBA merger from a position of strength, nor were the final merger talks based on viewing the ABA as an equal partner. The final deal was almost punitive and seemed designed to hold down the new NBA franchises based on demanding take-it-or-leave-it terms.

The Virginia Squires had once been a proud ABA franchise that featured Julius Erving. But the team was hemorrhaging money at the end and went out of business in May 1976. That left six ABA teams in existence: the Pacers, the Denver Rockets/Nuggets, the Kentucky Colonels, the San Antonio Spurs, the New York Nets, and the St. Louis Spirits. A month after the Squires folded, the leagues met to hash out a deal to merge.

Although the Kentucky team had been one of the most successful ABA clubs and had a supportive fan base, owner John Y. Brown was selling off its stars at the time. The Chicago Bulls desperately wanted Artis Gilmore but didn't want to pay for him. The Bulls held Gilmore's NBA rights and they fought the inclusion of the Colonels in the merger. Brown gave up and took $3 million from the other ABA teams to bow out. Then, as NBA owners insisted they would only take four teams, the Spirits became the odd team out.

Spirits team owners Ozzie and Dan Silna made a different kind of deal to close up their shop. They folded the St. Louis team in exchange for a share of future television rights. What at the time was of minimal value has in the intervening years gained stupendously in value—and the deal was for a share of those rights forever. The owners have received more than $250 million over the decades for not playing basketball. It is one of the most remarkable deals in American business history.

That left four teams accepted into the old league, the Pacers, Denver, San Antonio, and the Nets, who currently reside in Brooklyn after years in New Jersey. However, the terms were not friendly. Rather than be accepted into the league as equals from the start, the NBA put those teams at such a disadvantage it was almost impossible for them to win. They were treated more like expansion teams than previously existing teams.

The American Football League basically got the Super Bowl in its merger with the NFL and the American Basketball Association basically got the super shaft from the NBA.

As conditions of joining the NBA, each of the four ABA teams had to pay $3.2 million to the older league as "expansion" fees. The ABA teams were not permitted to draft college players for a year. The Nets had to pay the New York Knicks an additional $4.8 million for invading their territory. As part of the arrangement, too, the NBA refused to recognize any of the records attained by ABA players in the league. Future Hall of Fame players like Julius Erving had his achievements in the ABA eradicated by the NBA—at least as far as all-time NBA lists were concerned.

For three years the four ABA teams received no television rights shares and after that had to provide the St. Louis Spirits ownership with one-seventh of their TV payments in perpetuity. The breakup of the Spirits and the Kentucky Colonels resulted in their players being entered in a dispersal draft—but they could only be sold to older NBA teams, not to any of the four still-existing ABA teams. Essentially, the terms were hardly welcoming—almost as if the existing NBA owners were trying to make the ABA teams fail. It is almost miraculous that all four of those teams survived and remain in the league today.

The first season the Pacers were in the NBA, Bob Leonard invited his daughter, Terry, on a road trip to spend time with him. Terry was of college age by that time, and this is an incident she remembers vividly, although she said her father denies that the absent-mindedness implied ever occurred.

"This was a chartered flight for a game," Terry said, "so I could come along. It was a trip to Milwaukee [over Christmas break from college making it January 2, 1977 of the first NBA season]."

The Pacers had spent the night in a hotel and were going to take a team bus to the arena to play the Milwaukee Bucks before returning home. Terry planned to meet her father for the short bus ride, but when she called his room, the hotel desk attendant told her that he had checked out. She thought that was strange and so she called the room of trainer Davey Craig and was told he checked out. Then she tried to call George McGinnis.

"Everybody had checked out," Terry said. "The team bus was gone, and my dad had left me in the hotel. I had almost no money with me." She had suitcases and the need for a taxi cab, but little cash. She decided to telephone the Milwaukee Bucks offices and try to convince them she was telling the truth. "I'm thinking, *What a ridiculous story.*"

Terry made it to a special entrance of the arena, lugged her luggage inside, made her way to the Pacers locker room, and knocked on the door.

"Davey answered the door and he goes, 'Well, hi,'" she said. "He acted like nothing was wrong, and to this day my dad denies that he left me at a hotel. But he's heard it from plenty of people."

BOBBY LEONARD

We lost George McGinnis to Philadelphia because we couldn't pay him. George was offered $500,000, and that was a whole lot more than he was making with us. It was tough to lose George. He came to talk to me about it, but I said, "George, you've got to take it." The Pacers were having financial troubles, and there was no way the team could come up with the money to pay him what he was being offered.

To keep the Indiana Pacers in Indianapolis the struggle was on for us. Billy Knight became our biggest scorer, our go-to guy. He had some nights when he went for 50 points. Sometimes when we were playing San Antonio, he and George Gervin had shootouts. They had some real battles over who could score the most.

We picked up Dave Robisch from Denver and used him mostly off the bench. Bo Lamar came in from Southwestern Louisiana, and Bo could score. That was Dan Roundfield's first year, and he turned into an outstanding player. Danny Roundfield was a great story. He came out of Central Michigan. We took him in the second round of the draft.

Danny was a rookie, and he didn't look like a player who was going hard on the court, so I jumped all over him. Soon after that, it was on a Sunday afternoon, Nancy and I were at home and a car pulls into our driveway. It was Danny and his wife, Bernice. He was upset that I had gotten on him, and he didn't think I liked him. He wanted to let me know that he was trying and really cared about being on the team. We had a good conversation. I told him, "Danny, you could really be a player here." There was a gap between what I expected and what he thought I expected from him. I let him know I cared for him, but I told him I thought he could be a better player. While I was doing that, Nancy and his wife talked. After that talk, Danny made a big jump—from not starting to averaging almost 14 points a game, and then he made a lot of jumps from there.

He spent his first few years with the Pacers and then went to the Atlanta Hawks and Danny became a great NBA player. He was named to five All-Defense teams and was a three-time All-Star. Danny died fairly young, though, at 59. He and his wife were in Aruba on vacation, and he got caught in an undertow and drowned while saving his wife. When I heard that it was a big shock.

Bo Lamar was with us only for half a season, 35 games. We started seeing a lot of players coming and going. We couldn't pay the players what they wanted to make. We lost players because of financial reasons. That became my primary worry as the coach, that we couldn't hang on to the guys we needed to be building with.

Certainly, I wished that we still had the team from a couple of years before, so I knew it was going to be tough when we couldn't get the players we needed. I started having to rely on more players who didn't make as much money. We became more financially dependent in making up a roster.

There were a few rough stretches during the season, but we mostly held our own into February. Then we started losing. February was a bad month. We went 5–12 and we had two four-game losing streaks and two two-game losing streaks. We did a bit better in March, but in April we came into the playoffs after losing our last four games in a row, so we ended up with a losing record.

Things started to change pretty dramatically. The Pacers went from a team that was challenging for the title every year to a team that was finding it challenging to stay in business. And we weren't the only ones.

The merger with the NBA finally went through in June 1976, but it was a massacre what they did to us. We had no draft choices, no television money. We had caused them a lot of problems with players and they had to raise salaries and they hated the ABA. What they did was unbelievable. They really just tried to get rid of us.

They didn't accept Kentucky, and they were the most solid franchise around and had the great rivalry with us. I don't know why they wouldn't take them. Kentucky loves basketball. Look at the support for the University of Kentucky and the University of Louisville. I'm sure the rivalry with Indiana would only have gotten better.

It got to the point where our eight owners had decided they were going to have to declare bankruptcy and were not going to meet the payroll. That would have been the end of the team with all of the players becoming free agents. There probably never would have been a pro team in Indianapolis again. Market Square Arena, which pretty much existed because of the Pacers, stepped in and met the payroll.

There was a "Save the Pacers" campaign. We actually ran a telethon to promote buying Pacers season tickets. Nancy, who was part of a staff of 13 at the time in the Pacers' front office, worked on that and we sold enough season tickets to get the average attendance up to something like 10,800. But when we began playing a schedule in the NBA, the team wasn't the same. We were hurting for cash, and it was hard to get more players and improve.

Billy Knight was our top guy, and he averaged 26.6 points a game during our first year in the NBA. Then we added guard John Williamson in a trade. He only played 30 games for us, but Williamson was a remarkable talent who scored a lot of points wherever he went. He scored 20.7 points a game for us. Williamson could play. He could score. But he was a different kind of guy. He got a black belt in karate. He might have become a minister and he died of kidney failure when he was only 45. We traded him back to the Nets. We had a game against them in Indianapolis when he came back. Before the game he came up to our guys and said, "I'll get 50 points off you." And you know what? He did.

It was a wrestling match to coach John Williamson. Everybody knew that, even the clubs he was going to, but later he changed his whole life, his whole approach to life after he finished playing. He wasn't a bad guy.

That first year in the NBA our record was only 36–46, and we had a revolving door with players. Looking at the list of players on that roster, some of them stayed in Indiana for only a handful of games and I don't even remember coaching them. Darrell Elston played five games for us—that was his son Derek who just finished playing at Indiana. But Rudy Hackett and Clyde Mayes only played a few games. Len Elmore only played six games, so he must have been hurt that season. Some guys we liked but we had to trade them because their contracts were going to be up and we couldn't afford them.

Wil Jones, one of the Jones brothers, scored 13 points a game for us that year. Wil wasn't a bad player. At one point we had Ed Manning, Danny Manning's father.

From a business standpoint there is a lot going on over your head as coach, but you know what the impact is going to be on your roster.

You know I had always tried to stress the idea of a team as a family and when guys are going in and out so quickly, you don't get to know them as well. Mel Bennett was a 6'7" forward, and he was a little bit tough to coach. He thought he ought to be getting more minutes than he was. Everything became a battle. It wasn't like the old days when the players were tight.

Steve Green came off the bench for us for 70 games. Steve might have been Bobby Knight's first recruit for Indiana. He played in the ABA for a little while and then he became a dentist. He's got a great dental practice. Nancy and I go to him. Steve was a good shooter. Freddie Lewis was back with us for 32 games, and he scored seven points a game.

We did not make the playoffs our first year in the NBA with that 36–46 record. So we were part of the NBA, but there was a lot of resentment about what they did to the teams they took and the ones they left out. You look at the NFL and they didn't throw teams away.

In all of the years that have followed, you can look at what the NBA has done with all of its expansion and pretty much it just moved into the same cities that the ABA had first. Look at the teams and where they play now. The last year before they took the ABA teams there were 18 NBA teams. Then they added the four ABA teams. Now there are 30 teams.

In the East there is Miami, which used to have the Floridians. The Nets, who are in Brooklyn now but started out on Long Island. And there are the Pacers. There's also Charlotte, which once had the Carolina Cougars. In the West, there's San Antonio, Denver, and Memphis. Memphis had the ABA Tams and Sounds. The Utah team is in Salt Lake City and that's where the Utah Stars were. There are the Dallas Mavericks and there used to be the Dallas Chaparrals. Minnesota has the Timberwolves, and the ABA used to have the Muskies and the Pipers. There used to be a New Orleans Buccaneers in the ABA, and the NBA is in New Orleans, too. They just got back into those cities and pretty much expanded there.

One reason we resented what they did to us financially was that we felt we were better than they were at the time of the merger. Look at the exhibition games the last couple of years we played them before the merger. We were beating the NBA. The NBA made the right move. They knew we were in financial trouble, but they also knew we had the players that they needed. It was a down period for them. They didn't know that was about to change with Magic Johnson and Larry Bird coming in and then Michael Jordan. That was a few years away.

Going back to Danny Roundfield. After he got to be a very good player with us, his contract was up and we wanted to keep him. He was a heck of a player then. But when you're beaten down financially, you know you don't have the money to compete. Danny became a free agent. The Atlanta Hawks offered him $200,000, which we didn't have. Then the Phoenix Suns offered him $400,000, double. Then up steps Atlanta and offers him $450,000, and he went to Atlanta. We didn't have the $200,000. He went to Atlanta and had a great career there. Danny competed big-time on the basketball floor, but he was so soft-spoken off the court and such a nice person to the point where I almost thought he was putting me on. You'd talk to him and he would never get excited about things. I thought, "What kind of guy is this guy?" In later years, when I was doing the radio, every time we went down to Atlanta to do a game, Danny came over to see me.

Coaching and moving into the NBA from the ABA with the players we had at the time was a lot different than it would have been a few years earlier with the players the Pacers had then. And it was a lot harder when you didn't have money to go out and compete for new players.

CHAPTER 21

NBA STRUGGLES

Once accepted into the NBA, the Indiana Pacers had to sprint even harder to keep up with the competition since they were at such a disadvantage financially. With no television money coming in, drafting just five players for the 1977–78 season, and the franchise on the verge of bankruptcy, different people began wearing multiple hats.

The team asked Bob Leonard to become general manager as well as head coach. While that has been done in the NBA before and since, and in other professional sports, Leonard wanted nothing to do with desk work. He cared primarily about coaching and winning. He only really cared about personnel because that personnel affected coaching and winning. He was not a business person and did not want to handle business matters. So as a compromise he got his wife, Nancy, to handle the general manager duties. Nancy ran the office, and Bob supervised the stuff that focused most directly on the players, from their playing time to whether or not they would make the team and stay on the team.

At the time it was unheard of to place a woman in such a position of authority in professional sports, and for the most part the Pacers fudged it by putting Bob's name out front as the GM and hers as assistant GM. In reality, Bob and Nancy had a division of responsibility that she described this way— Bobby worked inside the lines of the court and she worked outside the lines of the court. Bob handled everything that went on inside the lines with the players. Everything that happened outside the lines was her responsibility.

That was pretty much how the Pacers operated between 1976 when the team became part of the NBA and 1980 when Bobby Leonard left coaching. Even prior to Nancy's appointment to a position of authority she had started the Pacers' dance group called the Pacemates. The team had cheerleaders, but this was an upgrade to dance cheerleaders.

"We practiced in the basement at our house in Carmel," Nancy Leonard said. "Yes, the Pacemates started in the basement. It was really funny because I'm trying to think how old Tommy and Timmy were when they got out of bed and snuck down the steps to watch the girls practice. They were probably three and six."

By the time the ABA merged with the NBA, Bob Leonard had been head coach for eight seasons, counting his partial year. The financial times had never been more perilous for the franchise, but there were also a number of changes going into effect because of the differences between the NBA and the ABA. The red, white, and blue ball was gone. The three-point shot was out for the time being. Nancy sensed that many in the Pacers' leadership group were a bit overwhelmed by the involvement in the NBA.

"I was totally not afraid of the NBA because Bob had been in it for all of those years," Nancy said. "I said, 'What are you worried about? There's a set of rules and regulations. Abide by their bylaws just the way you did ABA bylaws, and keep selling tickets the way you've been doing. There are going to be different referees.' They were treating it like the whole thing was doomsday. All of a sudden there was this big silence in the room. And they looked at me and said, 'Well, why don't you do it?'"

They meant taking care of the business end, the general manager's duties. "Then Bob said, 'She can do it.' No one thought this decision would go over well with the media, though, because I was the wife of the coach. So we came out with it [by] saying Bob would be general manager, and I would be assistant general manager. There was a lot of that coach/general manager stuff. That was normal in the earlier NBA days. It was often done that way."

But women did not have positions of responsibility with teams in the NBA in the late 1970s, and Nancy worried the local media would criticize her. Instead, she was pleasantly surprised when Indianapolis sports editor Bob Collins invited her to lunch and said he would do everything he could to help her—something she is grateful for even today.

From a practical standpoint, much of Nancy's responsibility came under the umbrella of what today would be called the chief executive officer. She attended league meetings, and she enjoyed working with the Celtics' Red Auerbach more than Bobby did.

"I guess I did everything other than coach, draft, and sign players," she said.

At one point in December 1978 when *Sports Illustrated* wrote a feature on Bob Leonard, saying he was about as closely identified with one team as any person ever, it touched upon Nancy's front-office work. The story called Bob the Katherine Hepburn of the pair for being "impertinent, charming, and stubborn" and called Nancy the Spencer Tracy of the pair and noted, "Few women in professional sports have achieved the front-office eminence that Nancy has."

For so many years Bob Leonard had considered his team to be family. Now the Pacers was actually the family business. One thing Nancy did was organize the office a bit, calling regular staff meetings when none had been held before. Also, knowing there was going to be skepticism about her role, she sought to embrace everyone and told the staff she couldn't do it all alone.

"I could hear people saying, 'Who do you think you are?'" she said. "But the NBA did have a lot of rules and regulations that the ABA didn't. In the ABA everything was real loose and casual. In the NBA you had to wear passes all of the time to go into the dressing room and things like that."

Once a business teacher, then a realtor, Nancy very much enjoyed working in pro basketball.

"I loved it," she said. "I had fun."

However, the Pacers didn't have as much fun as they had when they were winning titles. Bob wasn't having as much fun, either. He did a lot of wheeling and dealing, trying to rebuild the roster. The 1977–78 team was pretty high scoring. Adrian Dantley joined the team for 23 games and scored 26.5 points a game. Eight players, including those like Dantley and John Williamson, who did not play full seasons with Indiana, averaged at least 11.2 points a game. Yet the team's final record was 31–51, and the Pacers were shut out of the playoffs for the second year in a row.

In 1978, Larry Bird, who was from French Lick, Indiana, was attending Indiana State University where he was gaining national attention as an All-American. He was also eligible for the professional draft, what was known as a junior-eligible. However, he was still going to play one more year of college ball.

Nancy lobbied hard for the Pacers to draft Bird and then wait for him for a year to play. In the end the Boston Celtics did that very thing and by making that move out-maneuvered the rest of the NBA and gained the services of a future Hall of Famer. Before that Nancy pleaded the case for Bird to the board of directors. "Let us draft Bird," she said. "But we were in trouble financially and needed help right away. They said they couldn't afford to sit on him for a year. They didn't know if they would be able to meet his financial demands anyway. I didn't think we had anything exciting to sell and that would help. To this day I still get teased about it from members of the team administration who know I wanted us to draft Larry Bird."

The Pacers finished 38–44 in 1978–79 and 37–45 in the 1979–80 season. It felt as if the franchise was running in quicksand, unable to advance. Before that season ended Bob Leonard was no longer the coach.

"I did the job for four years, and then there was an ownership change," Nancy said. "It was stressful at the end for Bob. The new owners would send people in to overlook things, and they didn't know anything about basketball. Bob was stressed. The team had no money. The players were going. They were all going to [teams] where they could get better compensation. You couldn't blame them, but it was heartbreaking. We couldn't pay them."

Bobby Leonard

We had a lot of guys coming and going during the 1977–78 season. We got Adrian Dantley, who was a great scorer. We had him for 23 games, and he averaged 26.5 points a game. I traded him to the Los Angeles Lakers. I got along very well with Adrian. Adrian had a thing about him that some guys felt made him hard to coach. He and Jerry Sloan got into it in Utah. But I got Jimmy Edwards for him, the big center who was 7' tall, and we needed a big man.

James Edwards was an underrated player. That year he averaged more than 15 points a game, rebounded, and got better from there. He went to Detroit, and they won a world championship. He stepped up in Detroit. Boy, he was tough.

We had John Williamson for another half season, and we got Ricky Sobers from Phoenix. We traded Don Buse. Ricky did a good job for us, scoring more than 18 points a game.

We got Mike Bantom. Mike wasn't a bad player. He was a solid guy. We had a lot of guys who could play well but were not easy to blend into a team. Earl Tatum was there, Len Elmore was still around. Mike Flynn was there for a couple of years. And we had Johnny Neumann—there was a case. He averaged 40 points a game one year in college at Mississippi and led the country in scoring and he could shoot. He just mostly wanted to go his own way, and that's why he ended up going from team to team. It's hard to picture him as a coach, but he became one in Europe.

Johnny didn't score for us because he was on the bench. He was a funny guy. Johnny was a nut. One time we were on a road trip and he wore a suit made up like a Confederate general. He was something else. Everybody was laughing at him, but that's the way Johnny was. Later on he was coaching somewhere and wanted me to do a clinic with him. He was a scoring machine when he was young. He spent only 20 games with us. I might have thrown him into a deal somewhere. The players were coming and going.

It was driving me nuts is what it was doing. I was trying to put something together to win ball games, and things were changing by the minute with money. It was the toughest time of my career those last few years with the Pacers. For the 1978–79 season we got Johnny Davis who led us in scoring with more than 18 points a game. I got Johnny in a deal. I gave the Portland Trail Blazers our first pick in the draft, which they used on Mychal Thomspon, who never did turn into the player everybody thought he would coming out of Minnesota. I got several players out of that deal. We got Clemon Johnson. He had a heck of a good career. Good player. Clem was a good man. Corky Calhoun came in, too. We had Brad Davis out of Maryland, but he was too raw at the time. He's doing what I do, broadcasting games in Dallas. Johnny Davis played well for the Pacers for several years. He came out of the University of Dayton, and he's an assistant coach in the NBA now.

We got Rick Robey out of Kentucky, who had a long career. But we drafted him instead of taking Larry Bird with a future pick. With all of the wheeling and dealing, I got Alex English who was one of the great scorers and ended up in the Hall of Fame. But we lost him because of money. We couldn't afford to pay him what he was worth or what he could get.

Actually, we traded Alex with our first-round pick (which the Nuggets used on Carl Nicks—who played at Indiana State with Larry Bird) to Denver where he really blossomed, to get George McGinnis back. That was in February 1980, not long before I was finished coaching. George still scored in double figures for a couple of years, around 13 points a game, but he wasn't taking over a game like he used to do.

Before that we tried to get Larry Bird. I met with Larry, and the guy who has always been his agent and handled his money, over at the Hyatt Regency. Larry had another year left to play for Indiana State and wasn't going to leave early, but he was eligible for the draft because his class had graduated. That was the rule in those days. Larry came out of high school and was going to Indiana University, but he went home and went to work before he went back to school at Indiana State.

We sat down and talked about things. I asked him if he wanted a beer because I knew he drank beer. He said, "I like Heineken." Well, I knew he wasn't drinking Heineken over at Terre Haute. In Terre Haute I'm sure he was drinking cheap beer and now he wants a Heineken. So we sat there and talked and drank those beers. We were prepared to draft him and wait the extra year for him to play—that's what I told him. That's what I was ready to do. But we had an owner who didn't want to do that. He said, "We need a player now." And we did since we had just lost Danny Roundfield. But I thought Larry Bird was worth waiting for, and Nancy argued that case in a team board meeting. One of the board members had a daughter who went to the University of Kentucky, and in 1978 Kentucky had just won the NCAA tournament so she suggested that the Pacers draft Rick Robey. He said Kentucky had a player who was as good as Larry Bird.

We got out-voted on that deal, and that's how we got Rick Robey instead of Larry Bird. We would have been willing to wait for Bird. Bird would have been a Pacer. The other part of that was how would we have been able to pay him? We might have been able to pay him because we would have packed the joint with Larry on the team. But it didn't work out that way.

The Celtics did the same thing. They drafted Larry and waited for him. But they also had other first-round draft choices and we didn't, so they could afford to do it from that standpoint, too. Red Auerbach got the best of that situation, but I'm being frank here, I am not a big Red Auerbach fan at all. Somebody showed me something one day where Red said, "Leonard was a dog then, and he's a dog now." Where was he before he got Bill Russell? Bill Russell changed his life. Me and Red got into it more than once.

Once when I was in Baltimore and had Terry Dischinger, Red would stick Jim Loscutoff on Terry to rough him up. Jim played that role. Terry was just rolling up and down the floor. He had scored 15 points real quick, and Red went after him. Loscutoff hit Terry with his fist in the back of Terry's head, and it wasn't just a regular foul. This was intentional. The play was away from everything and boom! I knew what was going on because I had played against the Celtics in my time. I went right down to the Boston bench and said, "You get Loscutoff off of Dischinger or I'm going to beat your butt."

Sam Jones was right there and in these later years Sam and I play golf. He told me, "That was the funniest thing I've ever seen." Auerbach always played the tough guy, but you should have seen the fear in him. I am a lot bigger than him, but I don't like him. He always wanted to say something about me, and now I'm saying something about him.

Another time we got into it I was representing the Pacers near the end of it at an NBA Board of Governors meeting. Nancy and I were both down there. The meeting was at Amelia Island, one of those resorts in Florida. The three-point line was up for adoption. Angelo Drossos, who owned the San Antonio Spurs, said, "Slick, why don't you get up and talk about the three-point line?" I always liked it. I got up and said, "I don't think the basketball fans are any different in Boston, New York, or Philadelphia than they are in Denver, San Antonio, or Indianapolis. This is one of the greatest rules I've ever seen." Auerbach was the only dissenter. He said, "We don't want that goddamn three-point line." After the vote he came up to me and said that. "We don't want that." I said, "Well, Red, you made a living off of Bill Russell in the middle, and he didn't shoot three-pointers." He challenged me, and I answered. For that he's got to come out with his big mouth and say something about me. I'm not an Auerbach guy.

My last season was 1979–80, and we had seven guys who scored in double figures. Yet that team was only able to win 37 games. The leading scorer was Mickey Johnson. He only spent one year in Indiana, but that was the highest-scoring season he ever had. He was a very good player. He had played for the Chicago Bulls. This was another guy who had a bad rep about being hard to get along with. I took those guys. I worked with Mickey, but we did get into a fight one night.

He thought that in the last two minutes of every tight game that he could make the shot. Well, he shot us out of about three games in a row. So the next game when we got to the last two minutes—I think it was against Dr. J. when he was in Philadelphia—I took Mickey out of the ball game. And we went ahead and won the game.

At the beginning of the 1979–80 season, the Pacers signed me to a five-year contract. Frank Mariani and Sam Nassi ran the team. When I got the contract Nassi said something about wanting to make me a millionaire.

I was frazzled, and things were kind of crazy with the Pacers with all of those players going in and out and us not having enough money. I wasn't having as much fun as I was when we were winning, but I wasn't going to turn down a five-year contract if they were going to offer it. So I took it.

CHAPTER 22

END OF THE COACHING LINE

Bob Leonard's tenure coaching the Indiana Pacers ended during the 1979–80 season when the owners who had just given him a five-year contract extension fired him only months later and replaced him with Jack McKinney.

Leonard coached the Pacers from 1968–80 and compiled a record of 529–456. He won three American Basketball Association titles. He led the Pacers in 116 playoff games, winning 69 of those. In team history, the Pacers have employed 14 head coaches. Leonard was their second coach and he coached the most games, won the most games, and is the only coach to lead Indiana to a league championship.

After coaching the Chicago Packers/Zephyrs, the Baltimore Bullets, and the Indiana Pacers, Leonard never again coached in professional basketball. He had a big, fat cushion of a contract that he carried into coaching retirement—although there were eventually some hassles over that.

After all those years being devoted to the franchise, Leonard's family was none too happy about his dismissal. All of his children had grown up with professional basketball in their lives, and the majority of that time had been spent rooting for the Pacers, hanging out with Pacers' players, and having the run of the arena, whether it was the Fairgrounds Coliseum or Market Square Arena.

They had been part of the Pacers family as much as the Pacers players had been part of their own family—up until the previous couple of years when many of the mainstays retired or were traded.

When Bob went, Nancy went, too. She no longer served as general manager. Not hanging around with the team, though, also meant that she would not be hearing fans, players, and the like refer to her husband as Slick nearly as often.

"I don't really care for it," Nancy said. "I didn't really take it personally, but I have never called him that. I know that if mail comes to the house and it is addressed to 'Mr. and Mrs. Slick Leonard,' we don't really know them. He was Bobby at IU. I used to call him Bobby. More often I call him Bob now."

Tim, the youngest Leonard sibling, spent fewer of his formative years around basketball than his older brothers and sister. So it is perhaps not surprising that he did not remain a Pacers fan.

"I was 10 years old when my dad quit coaching," Tim said. "I just did not want to have anything to do with it. After he was fired and there was a field trip for kids with Jack McKinney as the coach, I just did not want to go. I think over the years maybe I've gone to five games."

Bill Leonard never shook his fandom, even after the Pacers were no longer his dad's team.

"I follow the Pacers big-time," Bill said. That translated to going to perhaps three games in person during the 2012–13 season and listening to all of the rest, either on radio or TV.

Tom Leonard, now in his mid-forties, continues to play recreational ball with the same group of friends he has been dribbling around with for about 20 years. He is also still a Pacers fan, though for a while he was a Philadelphia 76ers fan, too.

"When George McGinnis went to the 76ers, I rooted for them for a while," Tom said. "I do follow the Pacers, and I watch them on TV as much as time allows."

BOBBY LEONARD

We were at the league meetings in San Diego again. I think it was the second time I went to the league meetings. Sam Nassi calls me over and said could I come up to his suite. When I went up, he immediately went to the window and started looking outside. Sam was one of those guys who never looked you in the eye when he talked to you. Now he's looking out the window and talking to me.

"He said, 'Slick, I'm going to have to let you go.'" And I said, "You just signed me to a five-year contract." And he said that thing again about wanting me to become a millionaire. The Pacers had also just given me a lease on a Lincoln Town Car.

I was actually totally relieved about the job the way things had been going, though he didn't know that. For a few years it had been very tough financially. You're fighting all the odds. I had a bad case of burnout.

But I said, "Sam, I just got the lease on that new Lincoln Town Car." And he said, "Well, you can have it." See, he was scared that I was going to blow up on him when he let me go, and I just said, "Okay." If he was going to let me have the car, I wanted him to do it right away and not change his mind. So I asked him to get on the phone and call the office and tell them to sign the car over to me. He did call the accountant, Doug McKee, and said, "I want Slick to have that car." I walked out of that room just relaxed. I still had that five-year contract with more than four years to go on it, and I had the car.

That was a pretty hefty payout. After they thought about it a while, they tried to beat me out of the contract. Nancy and I went to court, and we won the court case, so they had to pay.

As much as I had loved coaching and being the coach of the Pacers, I was ready to step away from it. It had really taken its toll on me. I was 48 years old, and it was just time to get away from it and take a break. I didn't have a plan for the rest of my life or anything that I particularly wanted to do in a different career. I just wanted a break to start thinking about things. I was living in my home in Carmel, and I wasn't interested in jumping right back in and coaching somewhere else. At that point in my life I was like Jerry Sloan when he left the Utah Jazz. He said, "Don't call me because I don't want any coaching jobs." He was older and had done it for a longer time, but that's how I felt, too.

I did wonder how I would react if a team with a lot of money came along and asked me to coach. I felt a little bit lost for a bit. Actually, I did take a trip out to Denver and to meet with them. That was that summer after the season was over. The tough part of it with the Pacers for me was that the first several years were just terrific and the last three or so were tougher than nails. Money was the major factor with the franchise. Anyway, I talked to Denver and might have been more enthusiastic if two or three years had passed, but it felt too soon. I didn't really want to go back to coaching then.

You're trying and you're trying and you're trying but you're losing players because you can't pay them and it just got to the place where I dreaded going down to the office. We were even on the brink of Indianapolis losing the Pacers.

That telethon that Nancy was involved with was very big when they got the season ticket holders. That's one of the greatest things that have ever been pulled off: Save the Pacers! We were definitely in financial trouble. Sandy Knapp was a big player in that telethon. She was vice president for marketing and public relations, and then she became president of the Indiana Sports Corporation.

I wasn't really sure what I wanted to do. I had a background in basketball and a background in sales with Herff Jones. I had owned a restaurant that was successful, but not for too long. Nancy and I looked into buying an athletic lettering company. I went around, rounded up some business, and then I decided I didn't want to do it.

I went back to Herff Jones. I knew all of the people in the area, and I got a ton of business for them. Then I decided I didn't want to do that all over again. So I was just sitting around the house thinking.

It's funny because I do a lot of talking in public, on the radio and I used to give 30 or 40 speeches a year, that people think of me as very outgoing. I'm not. Nancy is the social person. I talk to people a lot if I'm close to them, but I don't go looking for company. I was searching for something that interested me after I left the Pacers. I wanted something that grabbed me.

I missed the game, but I didn't want to sit on that bench anymore. I wanted to stay around the game. The Pacers were paying me, and one day these TV guys showed up and they used the word "basketball." That was in 1985 when they asked me if I would do some color commentary on television. About five years had passed since I last coached, but I still loved basketball. Also, the Pacers had new owners. Frank Mariani and Sam Nassi weren't there anymore. In 1983, Herb and Melvin Simon bought the Pacers. Melvin has since passed away.

The TV people paired me up with Eddie Doucette to be an analyst on Pacers games. He was the play-by-play man for the Milwaukee Bucks for 16 years and worked for other teams and other sports. Eddie was the best guy to be around. I became his partner and did two years of television as the analyst starting in 1985–86. I didn't do every game, but I did a lot of them.

That was not a very good year for the Pacers. In fact, it was one of the worst. The team finished 26–56 and of course, didn't make the playoffs. Herb Williams was the high scorer at 19.9 points a game that year. There were some other good players—and some of them became very well-known Pacers—like Clark Kellogg, Wayman Tisdale, and Vern Fleming. But there weren't enough of them. Quinn Buckner, who became a very good friend, played a little bit on that team, too.

Television was interesting. It brought me back into the game. The interesting part was that it gave me an opportunity to see things on the court in a different way. I had seen everything that had come down the pike in basketball, from high school and college to the ABA and the NBA. I had seen everyone play, and I had my own opinions. I was one of the only guys who had been around that long, and I knew the former players, too.

The only one who is still announcing that has been around as long as me—almost, that is—is Tommy Heinsohn with the Boston Celtics. I think Tommy's a couple years younger than me. We both got into the league in 1956, but I had missed a couple of years that I might have played because of going into the army.

So now I was on television talking about the Pacers. I was back around the game of basketball, and it felt right. It wasn't my job to announce the game, only to say what I thought. I felt comfortable. Then the next year I was asked if I wanted to move over to radio. That was 1987. For some years after that in the 1990s, I did some radio and some TV, always as the color commentator.

Mark Boyle was the play-by-play man, the voice of the Pacers, and he worked alone. But Mark is a real pro—one of the best. He was just inducted into the Indiana Sportswriters and Sportscasters Hall of Fame in the class of 2013. I just throw in any old stuff. I make my comments and my baloney, and it works out.

Working with Mark was just smooth from the beginning. There was no adjustment for me. I didn't have to adapt at all. There wasn't much to it after I did those couple of years of television. Mark is right on top of every-thing. He does so much preparation. I don't have any preparation. I know every team in the league. I know every player. I know the moves they're going to make. I know the coaches. There's nothing I don't know about.

You get game notes so you look at those, and that gives you the lat-est information.

And when the time is right, when someone on the Pacers hits a three-point shot, I jump in there and say, "Boom, Baby!" I've got to get those "Boom, Baby!" lines in, but the way it works I can't just say it anytime. I'm at the mercy of the Pacers. They've got to hit the three-pointers. The fans like it. The fans want their "Boom, Baby!" lines. But the Pacers bet-ter make the three-point shots.

"Boom, Baby!" That became my trademark. I didn't set out to make it that, but that's what happened. Everyone loves to hear "Boom, Baby!" And I love to say it. The more I say it the better the Pacers are doing.

CHAPTER 23

BOOM, BABY!

Once Bob Leonard got himself situated behind a microphone, he discovered his new calling. It started with a few years of television color commentary and extended to the radio booth where, more than 25 years later, he is still at it with long-time play-by-play partner Mark Boyle, handling the ups and downs of Indiana Pacers fortunes in a totally different way than Bob did as the team's head coach.

Pacers fans have glued themselves to the radio for more than a quarter of a century waiting for the good-news signature call from Leonard confirming that one of their favorite players has nailed a three-point shot. The moment a long-range jumper nestles in the net, Leonard's explosive call of "Boom, Baby!" immediately rings out.

Leonard said his very first such call occurred when he was still coaching the team and guard Billy Keller threw down a timely jump shot from the corner in an ABA game. The Keller shot is the origin of Leonard's line, and although he did not use it in any regular manner when he was a coach, it came back to him as soon as he began broadcasting.

Keller, who played during the Pacers' championship years, said he was never aware that a shot of his gets credit for jump-starting the "Boom, Baby!" phenomenon.

When recently informed that one of his key jump shots is at the root of the phrase, he said, "I am? I don't think I ever knew that unless I just forgot. That's cool. That's terrific."

Although Boyle was used to working alone, he said adjusting to the arrival of Leonard as his partner was easy and they wouldn't still be working together after so many years if it wasn't a smooth partnership.

"It was a natural fit," Boyle said. "Fun is the right word for what we have. Our broadcasts are not traditional. I'm down the middle. I don't have my emotions on my sleeve like he does. Bob has the ability to bond with the average guy on the air."

Whether it is Leonard's slightly southern accent, his down-home manner, his obvious partisanship, or a combination of all three, which is likely, Leonard comes across as a friend watching and commenting on a game for the benefit of his listeners. He is not going to treat the players harshly, but he doesn't sugarcoat a bad night, either.

"He has a great passion for the game and for the Indiana Pacers," Boyle said.

Leonard—and his widely known nickname Slick—are just part of Pacer lore, a chunk of team history.

The funny thing for Boyle is that when he was first paired with Leonard for a game—a contest against the Boston Celtics—he was caught off guard when his partner loosed his first "Boom, Baby!" call.

"I didn't know about 'Boom, Baby!'" Boyle said. "I think Chuck Person hit a three-pointer. I started to describe it and all of a sudden I heard, 'Boom, Baby!' I didn't know what that was, and then I realized, 'Okay, this is his thing.'"

There is only a second's gap between a made Pacer three-pointer and a Leonard "Boom, Baby!" That tells the listener what happened. It's Leonard's form of play-by-play, and it definitely became his call. Fans totally identify with the exclamation. The use of "Boom, Baby!" hit new heights when future Hall of Famer Reggie Miller joined the Pacers for the 1987–88 season. The 6'7" Miller played 18 seasons with the Pacers and is regarded as one of the greatest jump shooters of all time. He made 2,560 three-pointers in the regular season during his career, more than enough to keep Bob Leonard busy on the "Boom, Baby!" front. Miller also let Leonard know he appreciated it when those announcements hit the airwaves.

"Reggie did get into it," Boyle said. "He liked it and he was making all of the threes."

Reggie Miller, one of those Pacers players with a retired jersey number, did enjoy every one of those "Boom, Baby!" descriptions. Although he didn't hear them live, he heard them on replays.

"It's such an iconic call," Miller said. "That's the signature. I thoroughly enjoyed it."

"Boom! Boom! Boom!" calls were like extra credit when Leonard awarded those on Miller's game-winning shots.

"Those are the things you always remember," Miller said. "In Indiana, we don't dunk as much, we shoot. 'Boom, Baby!' wouldn't be as good for dunks. It took on a life of its own. I think Slick and I and the shots will be [linked] together forever with 'Boom, Baby!'"

Miller so relished his connection to the phrase that when he retired from playing after 18 years with the Pacers he gained permission to name his new Los Angeles film-making company Boom Baby Productions.

A few years ago the Pacers made an exhibition road trip to China. As a demonstration of how the world has shrunk, Boyle had been in contact with some fans who followed the Pacers on the Internet, listening to the game broadcasts that he and Leonard handled. This group of Chinese fans showed up at the team hotel in Beijing and waited outside until Boyle walked out the door. Boyle grabbed Leonard and said, "Look at this," and pulled him outside where the fans made him aware that they knew all about "Boom, Baby!"

Anyone who has listened to the Pacers on the radio for even one game knows about "Boom, Baby!" According to Bob Leonard the younger, the coach's son who still gets called Slick Junior, "I love hearing it. I'm a big golfer, and when I make a putt, I go, 'Boom, Baby!' I don't listen to the Pacers on the radio when I'm home, but I catch Dad on the air when I'm traveling."

Tom Leonard used to listen to his father on Pacers games more often than he does now because he is busier now compared to past years. But like his brother Bob, if he is driving somewhere and the Pacers are on, he will click on the radio and listen to his father's voice on the game.

"I do listen to any game I can get," Tom said.

And he keeps his ear attuned to hear any "Boom, Baby!" calls that echo in the night.

Bill Leonard may be the most avid listener in the family, which makes sense since he is currently the biggest Pacers fan among the siblings.

"I listen to the radio all of the time with Dad and Mark," Bill said. "They're so much fun to listen to. I was going along in the car, listening to 1070-AM one night recently, and he just cracks me up. He just calls it like it is. One thing he said was, 'Basketball is just such an easy game if you do it the right way.'"

Above all, Bill listens for those Pacers' three-point shots.

"Boom, Baby!" he said. "It is a trademark."

BOBBY LEONARD

After a couple of years the Pacers gave me a choice between doing TV or radio. I chose radio because you don't have to look a certain way and you don't have to go through all of the stuff TV puts you through. But they had to get it approved by Mark because he worked alone. Mark said, "Yeah, let's take a shot at it." The rest is history. It worked out great.

Mark and I were compatible right away. We got along great. He's a real pro. He's one of the best play-by-play announcers I've ever heard. He's right on top of it all the time, and I just fit in. I'll make a comment once in a while, but I'm not going to interrupt what he's doing with the play-by-play. He got me going, and we've traveled together all of these years and have become good friends.

I think I talk mostly from a coaching perspective because that's what I was. And I have an entirely different voice than he has. I've got a little southern twang in mine. We get a lot of comments from people, and they seem to be pretty satisfied with the combination.

People come up to me all the time. Sometimes they tell me something they remember me saying on the air, but they also tell me they remember things that happened when I was coaching the Pacers.

Probably the best comments that I get say, "You really identify with the common man." That's important to me because most people can't. I don't set myself up on a pedestal or anything in the broadcast booth. I could say hello and talk to anybody, and I'm sincere about it. That's the way I coached, and that's the way I broadcast. My players knew that. I always said you can fool somebody for a week, a month, or six months, but sooner or later they're going to find you out if you haven't done it the right way. Then it's over.

When I walk around the concourse before a game and see the fans, they yell to me, "How many 'Boom, Baby!' calls are you going to do tonight?" I say, "I hope a bunch." "Boom, Baby!" really became popular with Reggie Miller. When Reggie got rolling and we were in the playoffs against the New York Knicks that time, that's when it really hit. Reggie had that spectacular stretch at the end of the game when he scored eight points in like 11 seconds, and two of them were three-pointers. "Boom, Baby!" And "Boom, Baby!" again. That's my favorite call in my broadcasting career, Reggie's explosion.

I remember in the 1990s during a playoff series when Nancy and I were driving to a Sunday afternoon playoff game. On the windows in a bank and other tall buildings in downtown Indianapolis, they had signs reading, "Boom, Baby!" It became very popular with everyone. I was a little bit surprised with how it took off. I know what it did for me when I was broadcasting. I'd get excited.

BOOM, BABY!

At first I didn't really know how it had caught on with other people, but then I went out and passed a yard here or a street there and the little kids were out shooting at the basket yelling, "Boom, Baby!" It's still alive. Reggie got into it. We'd be on the road getting on a bus after a game and he'd say, "How many 'Boom, babies!' did you give me tonight?"

I'd say to him that I thought I gave him a bunch. Reggie had an unbelievable number of game winners and when I knew the shot was a game winner and I knew it was going to be a three, I'd be ready and give him a "Boom! Boom! Boom!" It would be, "Boom, Baby! Boom! Boom! Boom!" And he knew about that. His friends must have told him because he wasn't listening on the radio—he was busy playing. So once in a while he would say, "Did you give me the 'Boom! Boom! Boom!?'"

It took off. There's no question about it. It's still one of the best ones going today among announcers because I've heard some of the other ones and they can't touch "Boom, Baby!" There's no question that one of the most exciting times of all was that day Reggie scored all of those points against the Knicks. I still call it the Miracle at Madison Square Garden.

That was such a spectacular run. He shocked them. One of those three-pointers, he had the ball inside the three-point line and he backed up beyond the line. It was right in front of Spike Lee who was trash talking. Reggie shocked New York, but he could do that. It seemed like he came up with the craziest games in New York.

One thing about being a full-time broadcaster with a professional sports team, especially the way the schedule is set up in the NBA, is that there is a lot of travel. Going back through my entire basketball career it was buses and trains and now it's chartered planes. It's so different than the way it was. Your luggage is all handled for you. It's such a soft way to travel. You're staying at the top hotels, the Ritz Carltons. It got better over a 20-year period.

It was still good from the beginning. When I started broadcasting, traveling was a lot better than it was when I was a player. You also develop relationships when you're traveling a lot, with the players, the TV people, the coaches. We always had a poker game, and I always played with the players. The players got to know me, but they never heard what I said because they never heard the radio broadcasts of their games. People would tell them sometimes, but it all worked out fine. I never had a problem with players for what I said on the air. They always knew I said it like it is. They never came back to me with any complaints. They knew what I would have said if they had come to me. I would have said, "I'm just telling what really happened, so don't try to hide from me."

I have always tried to stay as positive as possible. There's no question that I was a Pacers announcer. I was for the Pacers, period. For the most part Mark stays neutral. He's a Pacers guy, too, but we will both applaud somebody else on the other team if he does something really great. But we don't want to lose the ball game.

I remember Johnny Most with the Celtics from way back. Johnny wore his emotions on his sleeve. He was a Celtic through and through. I got to know him and he was okay. But he was more extreme, off the charts, with his support on the air. He used to yell that the Celtics were always getting beat up. But he was a guy who hit at the right time with the Celtics having Bill Russell and winning all of those championships. That makes you. It made him. He was loyal, loyal till the day he died.

In broadcasting, to some degree, you get into a routine because you're in the same home arena or the same road arenas that you've seen before all around the league. As time goes along, you're eating in the same places. Everybody finds his niche, and it just becomes a way of life. It's also a long season. With all of that travel, the further along I got in my career, the more the travel started bothering me.

One thing that became interesting to me was watching players develop over a few years, seeing the rookies come in and see how they progressed from their rookie year into their second and third years. While you're broadcasting, you get to see great play after great play. I saw Michael Jordan his whole career.

I saw John Stockton and Karl Malone. I saw Patrick Ewing. Right down the line from the time I was playing. I was right there playing against Wilt Chamberlain and Bob Cousy and Bill Russell. When you watch the players game after game when you are a broadcaster you get to the point where you know every move they're going to make, just like you did when you were coaching. Some guys are going to the right every time. Some guys can go right and left. You learn where they shoot from. You know their range. So that makes it easy when you're broadcasting a game. When you understand their tendencies, you rarely go, "I'll be darned."

There are still great players coming out of college every year so I get to see new guys. I enjoy seeing those kids play. And our team, the Pacers, has gotten better. I've been blessed. For that matter, Nancy and I have both been blessed to be able to stay around the game so long. She loves it, too. Nancy has always kept box scores, and she had scorebooks piled up for years worth of games. She never misses a home game. Nancy drives me to the arena. She's afraid of my driving.

When I'm broadcasting at Bankers Life Arena, we get there early and I go upstairs to the booth—we used to be at courtside, but they moved us. Nancy has a ticket on the floor, and she goes to the Locker Room restaurant and eats with her friends.

Nancy came with us when the Pacers went to China a couple of years ago. We got to visit the Great Wall. We went to Taipei and Beijing. That's when we met the Chinese fans. Mark grabbed me and goes, "Slick, come out here. You're not going to believe this." There were people of different sizes and ages, and they were holding up signs that said "Boom, Baby!" One of those young guys, Lee Holick, comes to Indianapolis and goes to games and brings us a gift every time. One time he gave me a beautiful letter opener, and he gave Nancy a keychain. Isn't that amazing, having Pacers fans in China? Small world.

For home games Mark and I meet at 5:30 PM and do our pregame. I like to get in the place early. I watch the guys doing their warm-ups.

If somebody's been hurt, I watch to see how he is shooting the ball. Of course, a guy could miss every shot in warm-ups and then connect and hit eight in a row in the game.

Sometimes I go down along the sideline while they're shooting and sit out there on the chairs watching them in the front row, and we chit-chat. I might congratulate them on how they're playing. It's pretty much a routine. Sometimes I see the other broadcasters. For a while, Tommy Heinsohn was with the Celtics, Johnny Kerr was with the Bulls, and Hot Rod Hundley was with the Jazz. Hot Rod Hundley retired, and Johnny's dead. Tommy doesn't go to all of the road games anymore. There's nobody doing it who is older than us.

Rod Hundley and I go way back. We were roommates with the Lakers. Rod was a real party guy who stayed out late, and sometimes he got into trouble. He used to tell stories a lot, and in those stories it would always be me starting fights and big drinking bouts and stuff like that—but it was Rod who was doing it all and he always brought my name into it. I don't think I ever did half of the things I have a reputation for doing because of what Rod told people.

After a while I get itchy sitting there before the games. I go out to the mezzanine. Right out behind me is the only place in the fieldhouse where they actually pop the popcorn fresh, and I get some. The game is probably still more than an hour away. I'm always waiting for them to play. It always bugs me. I'm thinking, *Let's go. Let's play.*

Once in a while I'll look around from the radio booth at the crowd and I'll see a sign here and there with "Boom, Baby!" It happens on the road, too, sometimes. They know about "Boom, Baby!" There is always a fan out there. "Boom, Baby!" was very popular. All of the broadcasters know who started it and where it came from. It was just one of those things. Other announcers have their thing. They even use "baby," but they don't use the "boom."

It's great for the fans who are listening on the radio because they can tell where the shot's coming from. Mark will say, "There's a shot for three." And I go, "Boom, Baby!" so they know it went in. You have to hit that "boom." The boom is what gets their attention. And then baby. You've got to let them know where it was shot—top of the key. So I always let the fan know where the shot was taken from.

For a while there were "Boom, baby!" sweatshirts for sale. They were around for quite a while. I probably could have done a lot more with it. At the time Nancy had it trademarked, since it was my trademark.

How's this one? I had this idea. You've got a woman who's having a baby, and you stop at the hospital gift shop and they sell pink balloons for a girl and blue balloons for a boy with "Boom, baby!" on it. That would work. Or you have little stuffed animals, other things for the little kids being born, in blue or pink depending if it's a boy or a girl, and they all say, "Boom, Baby!"

CHAPTER 24

As Serious as
a Heart Attack

Bob Leonard has had his share of body aches over the years. He has had back surgery, two hip replacements, and in 2003 while on a Pacers road trip as the radio analyst he suffered a heart attack in Portland. That ailment resulted in a stent being inserted into an artery.

However, far more serious was the second heart attack Leonard experienced on another Pacers' road trip, this one to New York on Sunday, March 13, 2011. Immediately after an Indiana–New York Knicks game at Madison Square Garden as the players and team personnel were loading up the buses to prepare for the flight home, Leonard was stricken in his seat.

On such road trips, Leonard and Quinn Buckner, the former player who handled Pacers TV commentary, usually sit together. Leonard was in the middle of a conversation with Buckner who was caught off guard when Leonard became non-responsive. Buckner shouted for assistance, and Pacers trainer Josh Corbeil and assistant trainer Carl Eaton were summoned. Leonard was laid out flat on his back in the aisle of the bus as they treated him and were later credited for saving Leonard's life.

"They were in the back of the bus," Leonard's radio partner Mark Boyle said. "At first we thought Quinn was kidding. Then it was very somber. Paramedics came in. It was sort of surreal. We didn't know how serious it was. It was frightening."

Leonard was treated at the scene and then rushed to Bellevue Hospital in Manhattan. He was mostly unconscious during this time period. Nancy was home in Carmel. She had just listened to the game on the radio from New York and was planning to stay up late to wait for Bob to return home.

"I'd done all my work, and I was going to watch something on TV," Nancy said. "I thought I'd put my feet up and enjoy myself because Bob wouldn't get home until 3:00 in the morning or something. Then the phone rang and it was Larry Bird and the first thing he said was, 'Now don't get excited.' I immediately thought, *Uh, oh.* He said, 'Now, listen. Bob's had a heart attack we think. But he's okay. He's awake now.' And then he went through the story about the bus and how they got him into an ambulance and that he was being taken to a hospital. I said, 'Well, Larry, what hospital?' He said, 'I don't know which hospital it is.' He said, 'I've got a call into the guys and they're to call me immediately when they know.' He called back and he said, 'It's Bellevue.' I said, 'Larry, you can't take him to Bellevue, that's the nut hospital!' That was the one in the movie *One Flew Over the Cuckoo's Nest.*

"I found out later from Donnie Walsh, who was the president of the Knicks at that time, that it happens to be the top trauma hospital in New York now and that Donnie was watching over everything. He knew exactly what was going on. But in the course of that evening, they didn't know for sure yet if Bob had a heart attack. Then they wanted to put stents in. Quinn was in the room with Bob. Quinn did not leave him. He never left for a second. They had all of these doctors running in and out. Finally, Quinn called and said, 'Here's what they want to do. They need to see if he's had a heart attack, and if he has, they want to put a stent in. They need permission to do it, and the doctor wants to talk to you.'"

Nancy was completely frazzled. She could barely understand the doctor, who had a thick foreign accent, and she worried that critical time was being wasted with all of the phone calls. "I was getting stressed," she said, "and I usually don't swear, but I said, 'Damn it, Quinn! Just tell them that you're his brother and tell them what to do.'"

Buckner began laughing, and Nancy couldn't figure out why he was laughing. "All of a sudden I realized what I had said," Nancy said. In the frenzy of the moment, she had forgotten that no one was going to fall for that claim since Leonard is white and Buckner is black.

The Pacers arranged for a plane to fly Nancy and Bob's youngest son, Tim, to New York. Nancy asked Tim to come because he is an occupational therapist and she figured that he would understand the medical terminology better than anyone else in the family. By the time Nancy and Tim landed, it was the next morning.

"I don't even know where they landed us," Nancy said, "and I don't know how we got to the hospital. I just know that it was a long way to his room, and I didn't know what I was going to find. We got to the room, and Bob was sitting up and leaning slightly forward. I said, "Why aren't you lying back on the pillow? He said, 'Because my back is burned.'" That's when I saw these burns on his back. It was from them trying to shock his heart.

"Then I saw Quinn sitting over in the corner on the floor, and he was holding Bob's slacks. He had taken Bob's slacks and shoes and everything. Bob doesn't carry a wallet and he carries all of his money wrapped up in his pocket. The minute I walked into the room, Quinn got something out of his pocket and threw this wad of money at me. He said, 'Here, I don't want the responsibility for this anymore.' Bob was just seeing me for the first time and he points a finger at me and says, 'I know every dollar that is in there.' He had won some of the money in a poker game."

Tim Leonard was used to seeing patients in distress, but he dealt with them as a professional, not as a relative.

"It was definitely traumatic," Tim said of getting to the hospital and seeing his father. "It's a little different when it's your dad. My dad has always been this big, strong, no-panic kind of guy. This was something serious. It's not what you want to see. His heart stopped. It was like he was dead.

"He may not remember this because he missed a lot of it being unconscious, but his back was hurting and his ribs hurt. He was in pain. When he had his first heart attack it was scary, but this was worse. It told you that he could be anywhere and it could happen again."

For a short period of time it was unclear if Bob was going to have to stay in the hospital in New York or if he could be flown back to Indianapolis, taken to a hospital there, and then receive further treatment.

"I was very, very worried," Nancy said. "They didn't know what they were going to do, and it seemed as if they were having some kind of disagreement over whether or not to put in a defibrillator or wait until he got back to Indiana. Would the flying in an airplane set everything off again? By then they could tell he had an irregular heartbeat. Then it got to be the last minute and it was decided that he was going. We had to call the Pacers and run around, trying to get ready."

No one ever wants to receive a late-night phone call informing them that a loved one has a major health problem, but the Leonards said that the Pacers organization quickly rallied to help Bob.

"I always tell anybody that if you ever get a phone call from Larry Bird and he says, 'Don't get excited,' don't pay one bit of attention to him," Nancy said. "Get excited. Go pack your bags because you're going somewhere in a hurry. Larry was terrific."

Bob was transferred to Indiana Heart Hospital, where he remained for a week or more. Thousands of well wishes were sent his way through the team. Former Pacers player Austin Croshere filled in for Bob on the air during the radio broadcasts. On April 8, 2011, Leonard returned to his job as the Pacers' color commentator—after missing just 13 games.

BOBBY LEONARD

I had a cardiac arrest right outside of Madison Square Garden. We had just won the game against the Knicks. When you come out of every arena, your buses are in the same place. There's a player's bus and a bus for the media, television people, and the trainers.

Quinn Buckner and I always sat together at the back of the bus. I said to Bucky, "Buck, see if you can get on your cell phone and see if you can find out who won the Doral Open golf." And he started pressing the buttons and told me who was leading. I've forgotten now, but when he did, Bucky said that I just kind of went forward a little bit and then just leaned back in my seat.

There was no pain, no nothing. I passed out. My heart stopped. I found out later that the percentage of survival of cardiac arrest is very low, less than 10 percent. I was out, but Bucky told me later what happened. The people around me pulled me out of the seat and lay me down on the floor and the assistant trainer, Carl Eaton, came over and gave me CPR. Well, to find out later, that just kept the blood flowing long enough to keep me from dying right then. Then the EMTs came with the defibrillators. They hit me with 350 volts. They hit me with one and they hit me with two. I'm lying on those metal strips that run down the aisle on that thin carpeting in the middle of the bus. The electrical volts from that defibrillator were burning me, burning my back. After two shots of that, the EMTs turned to Carl and said, "We've lost him."

But Carl wouldn't give up. He said, "No, hit him again." So they did it again and still it didn't do anything. Carl stayed right there and made them hit me a fourth time. Four times. And that one got me. That got my heart going. Then they got me to the Bellevue hospital and boy, they've got a great heart team there. Quinn rode with me in the ambulance and I think I woke up enough to have a few words with him there, but I really wasn't too aware of all that was happening to me.

They had to carry me out of the bus and took me past the other bus where the players were standing. Apparently some of the players were crying and praying. They took me to that hospital in the movie *One Flew Over the Cuckoo's Nest*, which used to be a big psychiatric hospital. It's not anymore. Quinn Buckner stayed with me the whole time. Larry got the private jet that the Pacers have to get Nancy and my son, Timmy.

I woke up in the hospital, and I did not have any pain. No pain. There was never any pain. I was fatigued and felt like I'd been through the ropes, and my back was really bothering me. The burns were pretty bad, actually. Nancy spent a lot of time taking care of my back because of those burns. She had to put ointment on my back for about two months.

They flew me back to Indiana, and I spent time in the Heart Hospital. If you want an endorsement for that hospital, we can provide it. Then I was sent home. Nancy and Timmy got me one of those hospital beds, and I stayed right there in the family room for quite a while. Nancy took care of me, but she says I objected at first. I didn't want any hospital bed, you know.

I spent another couple of weeks in the house, but then I was able to get back to work on the air and I returned to the arena for a game. The first game back it was great. You know the team or the fans put up a billboard in Indianapolis on Keystone Avenue. It just said, "Get well, Slick," and then there were signatures. I don't know how many thousands of names were on that thing—about as many as you could get on there because it was full.

Boy, that lets you know that people care about you. I couldn't have been treated any better by the Pacers, Larry Bird, Quinn Buckner, Susie Fischer, the public, the fans. The fans have always treated me great whether I was playing at Indiana or coaching for the Pacers. The fans of Indiana are my pals. Yeah, they're my pals.

They introduced me to the crowd that night and said that I was back, and they ran pictures of me on the big video board a few times.

That was my second heart attack. The first one was in Portland, Oregon, on December 16, 2003. I was on a road trip with the Pacers that time, too. I had just taken the elevator up to my room after playing in a poker game with some of the guys, and I had trouble breathing. I had to stay behind for a few days, and they sent a plane for me with my son, Bobby. That was an off day before a game.

I have to take pills every day, and I'm supposed to watch my diet and exercise. The first time I had a heart attack, they put one stent in. The second time they put two stents in. So I've got three stents. But you know, compared to football players who are older, I'm probably much healthier.

Some of those guys are really hurting by the time they retire. NFL guys, running backs—they can't get out of bed by themselves. In basketball you've got no pads, and the floor is a little bit harder when you hit it. Over an extended period of time you're beating yourself up a little.

I had two hip replacements over the last 10 years, and I had a back operation three years ago. I have an aortic aneurysm, which is like having a flat tire, a blown tire, and it gets so big they've got to cut you open and put a net around that. I've lived a hard life, but I've reached 80 and beyond.

So after the heart attack in New York, I was able to go back on the air and pick up my Pacers broadcasting that same season. I was lucky to be able to do that. But at the end of that season, I thought I was going to retire. I had a good ride, and I thought it might be time to give it up. I didn't want to retire, but I thought it might be the time to do it.

When the 2011 season ended, I thought I may have called my last Indiana Pacers game, and that's how I viewed it heading into the summer. But then Larry Bird came up with a good idea, which I loved.

EPILOGUE

BROADCASTING
FOREVER

More than an hour before the Indiana Pacers were scheduled to tip off against the Detroit Pistons for an NBA game at Bankers Life Fieldhouse in February 2013, Bob Leonard took a walk through the concourse at the arena considered perhaps the best in the league.

As Leonard strolled, many fans on their way to their seats greeted him with, "Hi Slick," as they passed. Many others stopped him and asked him to pose for pictures. Some middle-aged fans with children posed them together. Leonard smiled and posed, smiled and posed.

Leonard paused and looked into one of the glass cases preserving memorabilia from the early days of Indiana basketball. Someone sidled up next to him and asked, "Did you play them?" The "them" was the Indianapolis Olympians, which had departed the local scene 60 years earlier. It would not have been impossible.

Occasionally, one dad would tell his too-young-to-know child, "This is Bob Leonard, one of the best players IU ever had." Another dad would tell another child, "This is the best coach the Pacers ever had."

Bob Leonard, wearing a black sport coat over a red turtleneck, seemed relaxed during the lead-up to his on-air performance when it would be up to the Pacers' long-distance shooting accuracy to determine how many times he declared, "Boom, Baby!" during the game. During his relaxation time on weekdays, Leonard may lounge around in a sweatshirt and a base-ball cap. On game days his light-colored hair is perfectly coiffed, if thinning.

One of the things that keeps Leonard fresh more than a quarter of a century into his Pacers' broadcasting role is watching the young talent come into the league. On this night he commented about the improvement of Detroit center Greg Monroe, the Cleveland Cavaliers' explosive Kyrie Irving, and the point guard for the Portland Trail Blazers, Damian Lillard.

Ever the optimist, Leonard thought that his Pacers might win a division title and be in top-notch shape for a good playoff run. Winning in the postseason, as Leonard has said, was what it's all about in the NBA. David West was a real pro, he noted, young players like Paul George and George Hill were getting better, and the Pacers had to overcome the loss of high-scoring Danny Granger to do well.

After Leonard's pregame consult with partner Mark Boyle, he adjourned to The Legends, the bar and hot food buffet location that is open to patrons who have paid for a certain type of ticket. Before all home games, Leonard sits in the same seat at the bar and chats with bartender, Steven, and eats a fairly light pregame meal.

This was still true during the 2012–13 season because Leonard was still broadcasting Pacers' games. The idea of giving up the job after the New York heart attack ended with a compromise. Larry Bird, who is the team's president of basketball operations, suggested that Leonard stay with the Pacers and only handle home games. It would be less strenuous than traveling all over the country all winter. Leonard asked for Boyle's blessing, got it, and stayed on under those conditions.

His family is glad that he did.

"I hope he never gives up the announcing," Tim Leonard said. "He's a great fit. I definitely have people in my life who want me to say, 'Boom, Baby!' They'll go, 'C'mon, just say it once.' I say it around my three kids."

Leonard has been nominated for inclusion in the Naismith Basketball Hall of Fame, and Reggie Miller is not the only member of that Hall who believes Bob should be inducted.

"It's a shame he's not in the Hall," Miller said. "He was so far ahead of the game with the Pacers. He is a Hall of Fame coach, a Hall of Fame broadcaster, and a Hall of Fame person."

Bob Leonard gets plenty of attention simply walking around Bankers Life Fieldhouse, but he is also recognized when he is anywhere else, too. He doesn't seek out the attention, but it comes his way.

"He doesn't really want people to recognize him," Bill Leonard said. "But I've been out with him where people go, 'Hi Coach,' maybe 20 times. I think it's good for him to keep broadcasting."

Tom Leonard definitely wants to keep hearing those "Boom, Baby!" calls, too.

"I think my dad is still the same person who came out of Terre Haute to go to IU," Tom said. "But he's become a big part of the fabric of the city of Indianapolis."

Every night that Bob Leonard settles into his seat above the court to pull on his headphones and broadcast a home Pacers game, he can be reminded of his place in team lore. If he glances back over his head, he can see a handful of banners with retired numbers hanging from the rafters. There are a small number of players—most of whom he coached— and there is one for the coach, too. Since Leonard never played for the Pacers, he never wore a numbered uniform jersey, but the team figured out a way to honor him in the same fashion. The Bob Leonard banner features a totally different kind of number. It reads "529," representing the number of games his Pacers teams won.

BOBBY LEONARD

I did think of retiring after my heart attack, but Larry Bird and I are buddies and he said to me, "Slick, just don't go out on the road." He was right. He said just do the home games. That was 41 games plus the playoffs, and that's plenty. It keeps you just active enough.

A lot of people ask me if I was scared of dying when I had the heart attack. I mean, my heart stopped. But I was not scared because I made it all the way through it. I said, "The Lord just wasn't ready for me yet." You think that way when you've beaten something like that.

In my mind I had beaten that when I got out of New York when I was headed home to Indiana. You never really beat those things, though. I've got a defibrillator pacemaker, and I'm taking all kinds of medications. But you're still very fortunate. Nancy and I will be 81. I hope we get to our 60th anniversary in 2014. This all means I'm doing a whole lot better than a lot of folks. Let's face it, we've been blessed. And I was able to go back to doing what I had been doing.

When Larry first said that I could just do the home games and not travel, I wanted to hear what Mark said. I wanted to see if it was okay with him since he had to go out on the road and do all of the games. Mark did some of them by himself, and Austin Croshere did some with him. I felt I had to get Mark's approval to just do home games. But he was okay with it. Everybody was just so good to me. It was unbelievable.

They still wanted me around. Or maybe they just felt sorry for me. I want to keep up the broadcasting as long as I can. I'll go as long as I can, as long as my health holds up. I expect to be back for the next season and as many seasons as I can make it. As long as I can do a quality job, and as long as my health is okay, I want to do it. Some people look forward to retiring and just hanging around. I don't ever want to retire. I don't look forward to it.

I have had a great life in so many ways, with Nancy beside me all of the way. I owe just about everything to Indiana University. I was the first basketball player inducted into the Indiana University Sports Hall of Fame. They picked an IU 100th anniversary team, and I was on that. When you start thinking of 100 years of basketball and you're one of 12 or 15 guys, that's pretty good. It all lets you know that you accomplished something in your life.

Not long ago they had the members of the 1953 championship back for a reunion and introduced us to the crowd. It was a good day. I mean, a great day. Here you go to a university like IU for four years and you walk out of there and years later they call you back and put you in a Hall of Fame. When I went back for the team anniversary, they treated us like it was yesterday. They just opened up their arms, and everything was magnificent. I told the athletic director Fred Glass, "Boy, you just made a bunch of 80-year-olds feel like a million dollars." Indiana University has just been such a big part of our lives, Nancy and I.

At this age, with my schedule going into Indianapolis for all of the Pacers games, I don't get to Bloomington much to see the Hoosiers live. I don't like crowds much. But I do watch IU on TV every game and root for them. When we were there for the anniversary of our NCAA win, we met the whole team and shook hands with them. We took some pictures with the ball club.

I've had a few governors of Indiana have me in for things. Governor Mitch Daniels gave me the Sagamore of the Wabash award. That was the second time I got it. Governor Edgar Whitcomb gave it to me, too, and he gave me a license plate that read, "ABA–1." I am also a Kentucky Colonel.

Over the years I have been nominated for the Naismith Basketball Hall of Fame in Springfield, Massachusetts. But I have a certain feeling about that. I feel that the Basketball Hall of Fame is for players. I don't feel as if it should be for coaches and broadcasters. I know they have a category for contributors, too, but I feel it should be all about the players. If my being a college All-American, the Most Valuable Player in the East-West All-Star game, and my playing career in the NBA can't get me in there, then so be it.

Some sports memorabilia collectors remember me. I get mail all the time from around the country and even foreign countries asking me to sign things. That's one thing that's changed over the years. Now when the players are coming out of their hotels, the bus is there but there are barriers to keep the autograph seekers away. The players think all of them are just selling them. If you see the same faces in different cities, which you do in a lot of places, and they want autographs, you know they're selling them. You hope they still give the autographs to the kids and when they're getting pictures personalized, they're not selling them.

I get up really early in the morning, around 5:00 AM, and read the paper, but I try to keep up my fitness. I go to a racket club. I take steams, and they have a lot of workout equipment. They've got weights and everything, all kinds of machines. It's like what all of the major hotels have in their fitness centers now when you travel. It wasn't like that in the 1950s when we stayed at the old Paramount Hotel in New York or the other flea bags we stayed in. Now I'll be ahead of most 80-year-olds, or as fit as 75-year-olds, or maybe even a 70-year-old. But the old life, it takes it out of you when you get up there.

If someone had told me when I was 14 years old and playing basketball that I would still be involved in the game when I was 80, I couldn't have imagined it. Except for the military and selling class rings for Herff Jones, the rest of it has been basketball. I think I've been one of the fortunate few to be able to stay involved with the sport to this point in life. Others have done it, but Tommy Heinsohn in Boston is the only other one that I know of in the pro game now. Tommy and I are a different breed.

I still like being around the game of basketball after all these years. I don't want to be sitting around the living room by myself, watching the games and saying, "Boom, Baby!" to an empty room. I'd rather be saying, "Boom, Baby!" to Pacers fans.

APPENDIX

Terry Leonard's letter to Jack Dolph regarding scheduling Pacers games on Christmas Day, and the responses she received from Thurlo McCrady and Jack Dolph.

October 20, 1971

Mr. Jack Dolph
1700 Broadway
New York, New York   10019

Dear Mr. Dolph:

I am writing this letter in regard to the Indiana Pacers-versus-Utah
Stars game on Christmas Day.

Before I begin this letter, maybe I had better identify myself so that
you will not throw this letter out, thinking it is from a fan who really
has nothing to lose whether the game is on Christmas Day or not. I
do have something to lose-- my father! I am Terry Leonard and my father,
Bobby Leonard, is the coach of the Indiana Pacers. He has never been
gone on Christmas before and I think it is absolutely disgusting that
he has to be gone this year just because the person who scheduled the
games thought he had the right to schedule this one on Christmas. I
don't believe anyone has the right to take a father away from his family
on this religious holiday unnecessarily. You cannot tell me that this
game is necessary to be played on Christmas.

I am fifteen and I have four younger brothers, two of which are four
years and seven months. Timmy is the seven-month-old. This will be
his first Christmas. Tommy, who is four, is just beginning to learn
the meaning of Christmas and I'm sure that he'll really miss Dad because
fathers play a very important role on Christmas Day. They are just
naturally there on Christmas morning when the family goes to church and
then comes home to open the gifts and discovers that Santa has been
there. As for the rest of us, we realise that Dad has his job but this
is going a little bit too far. Sure it's his job, he gets paid for it,
and he enjoys it, but not on Christmas. He's gone half of the year
anyway. I would think you would have enough feeling to let him be home
with his family on Christmas.

I'm sure my father does not want to be in some unfamiliar town in a
motel on Christmas either. Not only are you involving our family, you
are involving all the players on the team and their families, too.
Most of the players' children are under the age of six and will probably

261

2

wonder where Daddy is when they wake up Christmas morning and go running in to get him to come and see what Santa brought.

Christmas is a time for families and you will destroy Christmas Day for many families if you keep this game scheduled as is.

If all this does not phase you, maybe you could look at the religious part. Do you actually think that Christmas is a time for screaming fans, locker rooms and strange, lonely hotel rooms? No. Christmas is a religious holiday when people are supposed to celebrate the birth of Christ. This means in church with your family, not in a sports arena.

I hope you will decide to re-schedule this game. If you do, you will make a lot of people very happy.

Respectfully yours,

Terry Leonard
Daughter of Pacer Coach Bobby Leonard

TLL:lmr

American Basketball Association

1700 Broadway
New York, N.Y. 10019
(212)765-6880

October 27, 1971

Miss Terry Leonard
c/o Indiana Pacers
638 East 38 Street
Indianapolis, Indiana 46205

Dear Terry:

Commissioner Dolph has asked that I answer your recent letter relative to the Indiana Pacers game at Utah on Christmas Day. First, may I say that I am responsible for the making of the ABA schedule but also for about twenty years, I was a college coach and I know how much my wife and four children regretted my being away on Christmas Day for the various Christmas tournaments down through the years.

Each individual team in the ABA gives me the date for their 42 home and then it is necessary for me to guarantee them an opponent each of those dates. If I recall, during the process of making the schedule this last year, it was necessary for Utah to play on Christmas Day. In fact, three of the teams are playing on Christmas Day which means that six ABA teams are involved in games that day. I am sure not only your Daddy but the other coaches and the players on each of the teams do not look forward to this part of their schedule. To alleviate this problem, the League might pass regulation prohibiting games on Christmas Day, but I do know that various other religious holidays, including some of the Jewish religious days, would also have to be taken into consideration

I am sure that both you and I feel this day to be more important than almost any other holiday, and I wish that I could tell you that the Pacers or any other team will not be playing on Christmas Day in the future. It might even be possible for the Pacers to catch a very early flight out of Indianapolis and get to Salt Lake City in time for the 3:00 game, but at this time of the year weather conditions are not always the best and the team might miss the game.

Thank you for your letter, and if you should see the Pacers' coach around at any time, give him my best wishes for a successful year.

Best regards,

Thurlo E. McCrady
Executive Director

TEM:da

American Basketball Association

1700 Broadway
New York, N.Y. 10019
(212)765-6880
Jack Dolph/Commissioner

October 29, 1971

Miss Terry Leonard
c/o The Indiana Pacers
638 East 38th Street
Indianapolis, Indiana   46205

Dear Terry:

I know that Mr. McCrady wrote you a letter
but I would like to add my thoughts.

I'm really sorry that your Dad won't be
home for Christmas but I think you ought
to remember that he is one of the best
basketball coaches in the country and
being a coach means he has to be away a
lot more than he wants. Don't forget though
that after the season he's home a lot more
than most Dads.

You may be right about scheduling games on
Christmas. I don't believe we can change
the game this season, but I promise you that
we will give it careful consideration in the
future.

Sincerely,

/maf

SOURCES

PERSONAL INTERVIEWS

Harley Andrews
Larry Bird
Mark Boyle
Don Buse
Mel Daniels
Terry Leonard Grembowicz
Jerry Harkness
Darnell Hillman
Bobby Howard
Billy Keller
Bill Leonard
Bobby Leonard
Bob Leonard
Nancy Leonard
Tim Leonard
Tom Leonard
Clyde Lovellette
George McGinnis
Reggie Miller
Bob Netolicky
Paul Poff
Jimmy Rayl
Burke Scott

BOOKS

Hiner, Jason. *Mac's Boys: Branch McCracken and the Legendary 1953 Hurryin' Hoosiers*. Bloomington, Indiana: Indiana University Press, 2006.

Indiana Pacers 2011–12 Media Guide.
National Basketball Association Guide, 1965–66.
Indiana University Men's Basketball 2010–11 Media Guide.

MAGAZINES

Sports Illustrated, "Slick Gets In His Licks," Bruce Newman, December 18, 1978.

NEWSPAPERS

Minneapolis Star-Tribune, "Happy Anniversary: Lakers Survive Crash," Jerry Zgoda, January 18, 2010.

FILMS

Film documentary, *Undefeated: The Roger Brown Story*, Ted Green producer, 2013.

ABOUT THE AUTHORS

Bobby Leonard is a former high school, college, and professional basketball star originally from Terre Haute, Indiana, who was given the nickname "Slick" early in his career. He was a member of Indiana University's 1953 NCAA basketball championship team and was a two-time All-American guard for the Hoosiers. A professional player in the NBA, Leonard then led the Indiana Pacers to three American Basketball Association championships as coach, and has served as a broadcaster for the franchise for more than 25 years. He and his wife, Nancy, live in Carmel, Indiana.

Lew Freedman is the author of 60 books about sports and Alaska, and as a veteran journalist for the *Anchorage Daily News*, *Chicago Tribune*, and *Philadelphia Inquirer*, he has won more than 250 awards. A graduate of Boston University, Freedman owns a masters degree from Alaska Pacific University. He and his wife, Debra, live in Indiana.

INDEX

6th Armored Division, 79
76ers, 89, 93, 211, 232

A

AAU, 82, 154, 161
Abdul-Jabbar, Kareem, 112, 117, 157, 163
Albany State, 194
Albert, Raymond, 3
Alford, Steve, 45
All-American Sports Camp, 168
Allen, Phog, 18, 49, 58
Allen, Steve, 75
Ameche, Alan, 130
Amelia Island, 228
American Basketball Association, x, 77, 141, 144, 147, 153, 166-67, 180, 189, 196, 199, 211, 214, 231
American Basketball League, 112
American Football League, 148, 199, 214
Andrews, Arley, 11-12
Andrews, Harley, 11-12
Arizin, Paul, 90
Arizona State, 143
Armstrong, Warren, see also Warren Jabali, 157
Arnzen, Bob, 194
Aruba, 216
Assembly Hall, ix, 41, 52, 186
Athletics, 171
Atlanta, 89
Auburn, Indiana, 34
Auerbach, Red, 22, 104, 118, 126, 135, 223, 227-28
Australia, 89
Averitt, Bird, 207

B

Bacall, Lauren, 119
Bahamas, 173
Bainbridge, Indiana, 168
Baker, Jerry, 150
Balfour Award, 49
Baltimore, 130
Ball State University, 30
Bankers Life Arena, x, 244
Bankers Life Fieldhouse, 146, 208-9, 255, 257
Bantom, Mike, 225
Barkley, Charles, xii
Barnes, Kathie, 29
Barnett, Dick, 197

Barnhill, John, 162-63, 175
Barry, Rick, 150, 157-58, 161, 180, 186
Baylor, Elgin, xi, 89, 103-5, 111-16, 118, 164-65
Beard, Ralph, 25, 80-81, 83
Bears, 127, 183
Beaty, Zelmo, 176, 184, 194
Bedford, Indiana, 27, 68
Bee, Clair, 83
Bellamy, Walt, 121-23, 125, 127, 129, 172
Bellevue Hospital, 247-48, 251
Bemoras, Irv, 50
Bennett, Mel, 219
Bennett, Tony, 103
Berry, Raymond, 130
Bianchi, Al, 77, 92-93, 192
Biasone, Danny, 88, 93
Big Ten, ix, 30, 34, 37, 39, 45-50, 52-53, 56-57, 60-61, 65, 67, 69-70, 85, 91, 165, 180, 183
Bird, Larry, vii-viii, xii, 1, 78, 157, 182, 220, 224, 226-27, 248, 250, 252-53, 256-57
Black Cats, 12
Blackhawk, 22
Blattner, Buddy, 115
Bloomington High School, 75, 79
Bloomington, Indiana, ix, xiii, 25, 27-28, 31-34, 41, 45, 50, 56, 61, 67, 71, 73-75, 79, 85, 180, 259
Bobby Leonard's All American Scoreboard Restaurant, 203
Bockhorn, Arlen, 136
Boilermakers, 67
Boom Baby Productions, 239
Boone, Pat, 119, 150
Boone, Ron, 184
Boozer, Bob, 136
Borgia, Sid, 133
Bosse, Evansville, 13, 20
Boston Garden, 135
Bowling Green, 92
Boyle, Mark, 236-39, 247, 256
Bradley, Bill, 197-98
Branch McCracken Court, 63
Braun, Carl, 90
Braves, 134
Bredar, Jimmy, 50
Brewer, Ronnie, 17-18
Brickhouse, Jack, 61
Brooklyn, 111, 214, 219

Brown County State Park, 41
Brown, Hubie, 207
Brown, Jeff, 7
Brown, John Y., 213
Brown, Larry, 173, 206
Brown, Phil, 7
Brown, Roger, xi, 143, 149-51, 153-54, 157-58, 160, 168, 175, 177, 189-90, 192, 194, 196, 198, 200, 202
Bryant, Kobe, 112, 116
Buccaneers, 219
Buckner, Quinn, 235, 247-52
Bucks, 215, 235
Building Trades Union, 195
Bullets, x, 73, 83, 116, 122, 128, 130, 132, 138, 162, 231
Bulls, 48, 91, 213, 228, 245
Buse, Don, 189, 191-92, 196, 200, 203-5, 207, 211, 225
Butler Fieldhouse, 21, 60, 82
Butler University, 60, 65, 98, 141, 150

C

Cadet Colonel, 79, 124
Cain, Carl, 67
Calhoun, Corky, 226
California, 106, 111-12
Calvin, Mack, 164
Cardinals, 115
Care Group, 23
Carmel High, 98
Carnesecca, Lou, 180
Caroline, 17
Carroll, Iowa, 99, 107-9
Carson, Johnny, 76
Case, Everett, 24
Case, Otto, 39
Castellani, John, 111
Cavaliers, 91, 256
Celtics, viii, 2, 22, 80, 88-90, 94, 100, 104-5, 115-16, 118, 125-26, 134, 157-59, 163, 196, 223-24, 227-28, 235, 238, 243, 245
Central Indiana, 138
Central Michigan, 216
Chamberlain, Wilt, xi, 90, 103, 112-13, 116-18, 244
Chambers, Goethe, 39
Champaign-Urbana, 50
Chaparrals, 143, 189, 201, 219
Charleston, 101
Cheaney, Calbert, 45
Chicago Stadium, 60, 128

Chuck Taylor All-Star, 67
Cincinnati Gardens, 136-37
Cincinnati, 89, 123, 136
Cipriano, Joe, 129
Civilian Conservation Corp, 6
Claws, 212
Clem, 226
Clinton High School, 14
Clippers, 116
Collins, Bob, 223
Colonels, 155, 164, 168,
 175, 181, 194, 202, 207,
 213-14
Colonels, 155, 164, 168, 175,
 181, 194, 202, 207, 213-
 14, 259
Colts, 130, 138, 181
Columbia University, 81
Combes, Harry, 50
Combs, Glen, 176
Conley, Gene, 134
Conseco Fieldhouse, 208
Cooz, 135
Copacabana, 103
Corbeil, Josh, 247
Costello, Larry, 77, 89
Cougars, 164, 219
Cousy, Bob, xi, 89, 100, 113,
 116, 118, 134, 137, 244
Covenant Club, 126
Cowboys, 22, 129
Cox, Johnny, 128
Craig, Davey, 171, 181-83, 215
Crean, Tom, 62
Crispus Attucks High
 School, 78
Crooked Stick, 80
Crosby, Bing, 119
Croshere, Austin, 250, 258
Curtis, Glenn, 13
Cushman, 17

D
Dallas, 200, 226
Dampier, Louie, 164, 194-
 95, 207
Daniels, Governor Mitch, 259
Daniels, Mel, xii, 148-51,
 154-55, 157-58, 163, 168,
 170, 177, 189, 191, 193,
 196, 200-201, 203, 207
Dantley, Adrian, 224-25
Dartmouth, 90
Davies, Bob, 89
Davis, Brad, 226
Davis, Deacon, 67
Davis, Johnny, 226
Davis, Ralph, 121, 123
Day, Doris, 119
D-Day, 8, 39
DeaKyne, Jim, 39
DeBusschere, Dave, 197
DeFur, Don, 38
Dellafield, Larry, 67

Delta Tau Delta, 33
Dempsey, Jack, 76
Denver, Colorado, 173, 183,
 186, 201, 204, 228, 234
DePaul, 49, 57, 59-60, 85,
 102
Derek, 218
Detroit, 87, 89
DeVoe, Chuck, 201
Dischinger, Terry, 122-23,
 125, 127-29, 172, 227-28
Dixie Limited, 3
Dixon, Spike, 88
Dodgers, 111, 118
Don Maneely High School, 21
Doucette, Eddie, 235
Downing, Steve, 181
Drake University, 201
Drossos, Angelo, 228
Drucker, Norm, 133
Dukes, Walter, 93
Duquesne University, 123

E
Eakins, Jim, 157
Eastern Division, 94
Eastern Kentucky, 164
East-West College All-Star,
 51, 74, 76-77, 259
Eaton, Carl, 247, 251
Eckrich Meat Packing, 40
Eckrich, Marge, 37, 40
Eddy, Ray, 67-68
Edwards, James, 225
Edwards, Jimmy, 225
Eisenhower, Dwight, 71
Elgin, xi, 89, 103-6, 108,
 111-16, 118, 164-65
Elmore, Len, 203, 211, 218,
 225
Elston, Darrell, 218
English, Alex, 226
Erskine Park Golf Club, 74
Erving, Julius (Dr. J), 154,
 161, 213-14, 229
Esposito, Sammy, 30, 34,
 39-40, 61, 82
Evansville Bosse, 13, 20
Evansville, Indiana, 13, 20,
 189, 191-92
Ewing, Patrick, 244

F
Fairgrounds Coliseum, 150,
 156, 158, 165, 168, 184,
 186, 201, 204, 208, 231
Fargo, North Dakota, 92
Farley Bridge, 32
Farley, Dick, 25, 32, 37,
 39-40, 46, 62, 66, 70,
 77, 79
Felix, Ray (Baby Ray), 116
Ferrari, Al, 67
Ferry, Bob, 129

Final Four, 21, 48, 50, 57, 60,
 103, 129
Finley, Charlie, 176
Fischer, Susie, 252
Fleming, Vern, 235
Florida, 228
Floridians, 148, 150, 219
Flynn, Mike, 225
Fontanet Beantowners, 21
Ford, Lee, 51
Fort Benning, Georgia, 79
Fort Leonard Wood, Missouri,
 75, 79, 85
Fort Wayne, 62, 81, 87-88,
 90, 94, 111
Foust, Larry, 90, 101, 105, 109
Frazier, Walt, 197
Freeman, Donnie, 189, 191-
 92, 196, 200-201
Freeman, Robin, 67
French Lick, Indiana, viii, 224
Fulks, Joe, 90, 104
Furimsky, Paul, 185

G
Gardner, Wee Willie, 78
Garmaker, Dick, 67, 85, 90, 105
Garrett, Billy, 18, 39, 46-47
General Motors, 154
Generals, 78
George Washington High
 School, 181
George, Jack, 136
George, Paul, 256
Georgia, 79, 194
Germany, 118
Gervin, George, 161, 173,
 203, 216
Giants, 70, 111
Gilmore, Artis, 161, 193, 195,
 207, 213
Glasgow, Kentucky, 3, 41
Glass, Fred, 63, 259
Gola, Tom, 90, 136
Goodrich, Gail, 112
Gophers, 67, 85, 91, 106
Granger, Danny, 256
Grant, Travis, 212
Great Wall, 244
Green Bay, 138, 208
Green, A.C., 157
Green, Cornell, 129
Green, Sihugo, 121, 123, 129
Green, Steve, 219
Greer, Hal, 89
Grembowicz, Terry Leonard,
 86
Gretzky, Wayne, 208
Groh, Red, 88
Groza, Alex, 25, 83
Guadalcanal, 8
Guerin, Richie, 77, 90
Gushue, Joe, 133
Gustavus Adolphus College, 88

Index

H

Hackett, Rudy, 218
Hagan, Cliff, 25, 77, 89, 114
Hall of Fame, viii, 80, 121, 128, 130, 153, 157, 161, 173, 186, 193, 198, 203, 207, 214, 226, 236, 256-59
Hamilton, Steve, 91
Hannum, Alex, 173, 183
Harkness, Jerry, 143
Harlem Globetrotters, 67, 73-74, 76-77, 82, 117, 123
Harry, Dancing, 205
Hartman, Sid, 79-80
Hawkins, Connie, 161
Hawkins, Roger, 161
Hawkins, Tommy, 109
Hawks, 2, 88-90, 94, 99, 105-6, 114-16, 119, 136, 176, 216, 220
Heat, 149
Heiney, John, 38
Heinsohn, Tommy, 89-90, 134, 235, 245, 260
HemisFair Arena, 204
Hepburn, Katherine, 223
Highlands Cemetery, 23
Hightower, Wayne, 164
Hill, George, 256
Hill, Tony, 47
Hillman, Darnell, 177, 179, 181, 189, 191, 196, 200, 211
Hinkle Fieldhouse, 21, 60
Hinkle, Tony, 60, 141
Hoffman, Paul, 130
Holick, Lee, 244
Hoosier Classic, 60
Hoosiers, ix, 30-31, 37-38, 45-47, 51-52, 55-57, 60, 65-68, 73, 143, 156, 159, 174, 177, 259
Howard, Bobby, 38, 41
Howell, Bailey, 129
Huff Gym, 50
Hulman, Rose, 176
Hulman, Tony, 176
Hundley, Hot Rod, 86, 90, 101-2, 105, 111, 113-14, 123, 245
Hunter, Les, 129

I

Idaho, 128-29
Illinois, 1, 39, 51
Indiana Basketball Hall of Fame, 11, 13, 78
Indiana Central, 181
Indiana Heart Hospital, 250, 252
Indiana High School All-Star Game, 32
Indiana Medical Center, 173

Indiana Mr. Basketball, 47
Indiana Sports Corporation, 234
Indiana Sportswriters and Sportscasters Hall of Fame, 236
Indiana State Fairgrounds, 141
Indiana State Teachers College, 13
Indiana State University, 1, 3, 184, 224
Indiana University Sports Hall of Fame, 258
Indiana University, ix, xi, xiii, 16, 26-27, 30, 37, 45, 73, 121, 131, 141, 143, 177-78, 227, 258-59
Indiana, vii-xii, 1-3, 11, 13, 15-16, 18-19, 21-27, 29-32, 34, 37-38, 41-42, 45-47, 49-53, 55, 57, 60, 62, 65-68, 70, 73-75, 78-80, 82, 85-88, 98, 109, 121, 125, 129, 131, 138-39, 141-44, 148, 150-51, 153-54, 156, 159, 161-69, 172-73, 175, 177-82, 184, 189-93, 197, 199-201, 203, 208, 211-12, 215, 217-19, 221, 224, 226-28, 231, 234, 236-39, 247, 250, 252-53, 255, 258-59
Indiana-Kentucky All-Star, 40
Indiana-Kentucky, 40, 196
Indianapolis 500, 4
Indianapolis Athletic Club, 174
Indianapolis City Council, 154
Indianapolis Motor Speedway, 4
Indianapolis, vii, 1, 23, 41, 61, 78, 82-83, 131, 141, 150, 165, 172, 175, 180-81, 183, 185, 197, 199, 205, 208, 215, 217-18, 223, 228, 234, 241, 244, 250, 252, 257, 259
Iowa City, 66, 69-70
Iowa, 48, 65, 67, 69-70, 99, 107-9, 116, 125
Irving, Kyrie, 256
Islanders, 202
Issel, Dan, 161, 193, 195, 207
Italy, 193
IU Fieldhouse, 52
IU Hall of Fame, 187
Iwo Jima, 8

J

Jabali, Warren, see also Warren Armstrong, 157-58, 175
Jackson, Phil, 112
Jayhawks, 57

Jays, 7
Jazz, 233, 245
Jeffersonville, 38-39
John, Tommy, 12-13, 91
Johnson, Andy, 121, 123
Johnson, Clemon, 226
Johnson, Emerson, 18
Johnson, Gus, 128-29, 172, 192, 196
Johnson, Magic, xii, 112-13, 220
Johnson, Mickey, 228
Johnston, Neil, 90, 136
Jones, Caldwell, 194
Jones, Herff, 138-39, 147-48, 186, 234, 260
Jones, Jimmy, 184
Jones, K.C., 89-90, 117
Jones, Sam, 80, 89-90, 117, 137, 228
Jones, Wally, 83, 129
Jones, Wil, 207, 218
Jordan, Michael, xii, 91, 104, 192, 220, 243
Joyce, Kevin, 203

K

Kalafat, Ed, 67, 85, 90
Kansas City Municipal Auditorium, 59
Kansas City, ix, 57, 61, 89
Kansas State, ix, 18, 49, 53, 55, 57-61, 65, 117
Kansas, 2
Karl, George, 204-5
Keeneland Race Track, 25
Keller, Billy, 153-55, 163, 170, 175-77, 183, 189, 191-92, 196, 200, 203, 206, 211, 237
Kellogg, Clark, 235
Kennedy, President John F., 122
Kentucky Derby, 172
Kentucky Wesleyan, 164
Kerner, Ben, 136
Kerr, Johnny, 48, 50, 76-77, 89, 92, 173, 245
Kiel Auditorium, 136
King's Island Amusement Park, 169
Kings, 89
Knapp, Sandy, 205, 234
Knicks, 78, 82, 88, 90, 97, 103, 111, 197, 200, 214, 241-42, 247-48, 250
Knight, Billy, 203-5, 211, 215, 218
Knight, Bobby, 47, 53, 174, 219
Kojis, Don, 129
Kokomo, Indiana, 22, 39, 86, 131, 138, 143, 147
Korean War, 23, 42, 71

Kraak, Charlie, 28, 33, 39, 71, 77
Krause, Moose, 24
Krebs, Jimmy, 90, 116
Kundla, John, 92-93, 97, 100, 105-6, 111

L

Lakers, x, 2, 18, 67, 73, 77-80, 83, 85-91, 93-94, 97-99, 102-3, 105-7, 110-16, 119, 121-23, 131-33, 137, 155-58, 164, 172, 197, 201, 225, 245
Lamar, Bo, 212, 216
Lancaster, Harry, 24
Lane, Frank, 126-27, 130
LaRue, Bernie, 183
LaRusso, Rudy, 90, 99, 106, 114, 116
Las Vegas, Nevada, 76
LaSalle, 90
Lebanon, Indiana, 23, 175
Lee, Spike, 242
Leno, Jay, 76
Leonard, Bill, 112, 122, 168, 232, 240, 257
Leonard, Bob, vii-ix, xi-xii, 1, 11, 27, 38, 46, 55, 65, 85, 97-100, 111, 121, 141-43, 153, 156, 168, 170-71, 178, 189-91, 200, 211-12, 214, 221-24, 232, 237, 239, 255, 257
Leonard, Darlene, 3
Leonard, Hattie Mae, 3
Leonard, Nancy, 27-31, 33, 37-40, 45, 55, 63, 65, 70, 73-76, 79, 85, 105, 109, 112, 122, 130, 138, 143, 148-49, 173, 185, 187, 195, 203, 216-17, 219, 221-24, 227-28, 232-34, 241, 244, 246, 252, 258-59
Leonard, Terry (Grembowicz), 86-87, 105, 122, 142, 168, 214-15
Leonard, Tim, 167, 190-91, 222, 249, 251-52, 256
Leonard, Tom, 167-69, 190, 222, 232, 240, 249, 257
Lewis, Freddie, 143, 150-51, 159, 162, 175, 177, 186, 189, 191-92, 196, 200-201, 203, 219
Lexington, Kentucky, 24-25
Lillard, Damian, 256
Little League, 7, 59
Lombardi, Vince, 59
Long Island, New York, 187, 219
Los Angeles Coliseum, 77, 113

Los Angeles Memorial Sports Arena, 113
Los Angeles, 89, 106, 110-14, 116, 118-19, 164, 176, 239
Loscutoff, Jim, 90, 227-28
Loughery, Kevin, 129
Louisiana State, 49, 57, 66, 69-70, 193
Louisville, 11, 24, 65, 123, 164, 217
Lovellette, Clyde, xi, 1-2, 18, 49, 85, 93, 101, 126, 141-42, 144, 201
Loyola, 129, 143
Lucas Oil Stadium, 208
Lucas, Maurice, 157
Luckman, Sid, 127
Lugar, Richard, 208

M

MacArthur, Douglas, 71
Macauley, Ed, 89
Madison Square Garden, 77, 81-82, 102-3, 133, 135, 242, 247, 250
Madison, Wisconsin, 34, 67
Malone, Karl, 244
Mama Leone's Italian Restaurant, 102
Manning, Danny, 218
Manning, Ed, 218
Mantle, Mickey, 118
Maravich, Pete, 193
March Madness, 49, 62
March of Dimes Telethon, 211-12
Marchetti, Gino, 130
Mariani, Frank, 229, 235
Marines, 8-9
Market Square Arena, 156, 168, 190-91, 204, 208-9, 217, 231
Martin, Slater, 77, 88, 90
Martinsville, 13, 19, 61
Maryland, 203, 226
Massachusetts, 52-53, 259
Masters, Bobby, 47
Mavericks, 118, 219
Mayes, Clyde, 218
McCarthy, Babe, 202
McClain, Ted, 207
McCracken, Branch "Emmett B.", ix, 18-19, 23, 25, 27, 30-31, 38-39, 45-47, 55, 63, 66, 70, 173-74
McCracken, Mary Jo, 41, 52
McDuffy, Dick, 17
McGill, Bill, 125, 164
McGinnis, xii, 78, 154, 157, 170, 177-78, 180-81, 189, 191, 193, 196, 200, 204-6, 211, 215, 226, 232
McHale, Kevin, 157

McKee, Doug, 233
McKinney, Bones, 164
McKinney, Jack, 231-32
McMahon, Jack, 122, 124
McMillan, Buck, 14
Mencel, Chuck, 61, 67, 85, 90
Meredith, Don, 22
Michigan State, 67
Michigan, 173, 216
Mikan, George, xi, 77, 85, 87-88, 90-91, 98, 101-2, 179-80
Mikkelsen, Vern, 77, 91, 101, 105
Miller, Larry, 164
Miller, Reggie, 238-39, 241, 256-57
Minneapolis Star-Tribune, 79
Minneapolis, 92-93, 98, 103,105-6, 109, 111-12, 122, 131
Minnesota, 48, 57, 61, 67, 85, 88, 91, 106, 111-12, 114, 148, 179, 200, 202, 219, 226
Miranda, Sammy, 47-48
Missouri, 79
Moe, Doug, 157, 161
Molinas, Jack, 81
Monday Night Football, 22
Monroe, Earl, 130
Monroe, Greg, 256
Monrovia High School, 46
Montana State, 65
Morehead State, 91
Morgantown, 101
Most Valuable Player, 49, 74, 77-78, 259
Most, Johnny, 115, 135, 243
Mount, Charlie, 7-8
Mount, Rick, 23, 175-77, 183, 195
Mountaineers, 111
Mouse, Mickey, 88, 182
Mullaney, Joe, 173
Murphy, Audie, 71
Muskies, 148, 200, 219

N

Naismith Memorial Basketball Hall of Fame, viii, xi, 80, 121, 153, 256, 259, see also Hall of Fame
Naismith, Dr. James, 52-53
Nashville House, 41-42
Nassau County Coliseum, 187
Nasser, Billy, 23
Nassi, Sam, 229, 232, 235
National Anthem, 82, 113
National Basketball Association Guide, 82
National Basketball League, 82, 88

INDEX

Nationals, 88-89, 93
Naulls, Willie, 90
NBA Board of Governors, 228
NBA Hawks, 176
NBA Players Association, 199
NCAA, 1, 48, 58-59, 103, 129, 191
Nelson, Don, 125
Netolicky, Bob, 143, 149-50, 155, 158, 160, 163, 168-70, 175, 177, 179-80, 189, 196, 200-201, 203, 211-12
Nets, 180, 186, 201-2, 213-14, 218-19
Neumann, Johnny, 225
New Albany, Indiana, 55
New Castle, Indiana, 11, 19, 39
New Jersey, 91, 214
New Orleans, 219
New York City, 81, 102, 153
New York, 75-76, 81-82, 97, 100, 102-3, 111, 133, 135, 187, 197-98, 202, 228, 242, 247-50, 253, 256, 258, 260
Newell, Pinky, 183
Newton, Bill, 193
NFL, 148, 199, 214, 219, 253
Nick the Greek, 171
Nicks, Carl, 226
Nitschke, Ray, 186
Normandy, 8, 39
Norris, James, 128
North Carolina State, 24, 35
North Carolina, 58, 80, 164, 204
North Dakota, 92
North Station, 97, 135
Northwestern, 65, 67
Notre Dame, 14, 24, 33, 49, 57, 59-60, 65-66, 69-71, 77, 109, 147, 194-95
Nowitzki, Dirk, 118
Nuggets, see also Rockets, 205, 213, 226

O

O'Neal, Shaquille, 112
Oakland, 161, 164
Oaks, 150-51, 157, 164, 169
Ohio State, 67, 130
Ohl, Don, 129
Oliver, Jerry, 174
Olmpians, 82-83, 150, 255
Olympic, 2, 67
Olympics, 89, 154
Oregon State, 65
Oregon, 252
Orioles, 130
Orwig, Bill, 173-74
Overbrook High School, 117

P

Paar, Jack, 75
Pac-10, 49
Pacemates, 222
Pacers, vii-viii, x, 22-23, 48, 82, 139, 141-44, 146-51, 153-57, 159, 161, 163, 165-70, 174-78, 180, 182-83, 187, 189-91, 194, 199-201, 203, 207-9, 211-24, 226-29, 231-41, 243-44, 247, 249-53, 255-57, 259-60
Packers, x, 121-24, 131, 231
Pan American Games, 208
Paramedics, 247
Paramount Hotel, 100, 260
Parish, Robert, 157
Parker, Jim, 130
Patton, George, 71
Paultz, Billy, 186
Paxson, Jim Jr., 91
Paxson, Jim Sr., 91
Paxson, John, 91
Pearl Harbor, 7-8, 53
Penn State, 69-70
Pennsylvania Station, 97, 100, 135
Peoria, Illinois, 51
Person, Chuck, 238
Pettit, Bob, 49, 57, 69, 77, 94, 114
Philadelphia Convention Center, 135-36
Philadelphia, 97, 117, 215, 228-29
Phipps, Junior, 39
Pipers, 158, 179, 200, 219
Pistons, 81, 87, 89, 94, 105, 111, 114, 119, 128-29, 255-56
Podres, Johnny, 118
Poff, Paul, 55-56
Pollard, Jim, 77, 111, 121
Popovich, Gregg, 147
Pro Football Hall of Fame, 130
Pros, 176
Purdue University, 23, 52, 60, 67-68, 122, 141, 175-76, 183
Purdue, 150, 153

R

Racers, 208
Rams, 118
Ramsey, Frank, 25, 77, 80
Rangers, 106
Ravens, 62, 70
Ray, William, 112
Rayl, Jimmy, 22, 143-44
Red Sox, 134
Reed, Willis, 197
Robbins, Red, 194

Robertson, Oscar, xi, 78, 89, 113, 118, 136, 154, 161, 182, 200
Robey, Rick, 226-27
Robinson, Brooks, 130
Robinson, Ermer, 77
Robisch, Dave, 212, 216
Roche, John, 186
Rockets, see also Nuggets, 173, 180, 183, 186, 191, 194, 207, 213-14, 216, 219
Roosevelt, President Franklin D., 4
Root, Nancy, 27
Rose Polytechnic Institute, 7
Rose-Hulman Institute of Technology, 7
Rosenthal, Dick, 60, 69, 77
ROTC, 74, 79, 124
Roundfield, Bernice, 216
Roundfield, Danny, 212, 216, 220, 227
Roy, Robert, 98
Royals, 2, 89, 101, 136
Rudolph, Mendy, 133
Rupp, Adolph, 24-25, 49
Russell, Bill, xi, 89-90, 105, 113, 116-17, 125-26, 134, 172, 227-28, 243-44

S

Sagamore of the Wabash, 259
Sails, 212
Salt Lake City, 164, 184, 219
San Antonio, 205, 216, 219
San Diego, 206, 232
San Francisco, 89, 111-12
San Jose State, 177, 181
Santa Clara, 90
Saperstein, Abe, 77
Sauldsberry, Woody, 121, 123
Schaus, Freddy, 111, 119
Schayes, Dolph, 89
Schlundt, Don, 42, 45-46, 48-49, 55-56, 60, 62, 65-66
Schooley, Jim, 33-34, 39
Scott, Burke, 40, 42, 56, 58-59, 66
Scott, Lou, 39
Sears, Kenny, 90
Seattle University, 103
SEC, 49
Selvy, Frank, 77, 106, 113-14, 123
Seton Hall, 93
Sharman, Bill, 89-90, 117, 133, 158, 164, 173, 176
Sharpe, Howard, 13-14, 17, 23-24, 26
Shelbyville, 18, 39
Short, Bob, 106
Shue, Gene, 90, 129

273

Silas, Jimmy, 203
Siler, Billy, 14
Silna, Dan, 213
Silna, Ozzie, 213
Simon, Melvin, 235
Simpson, Ralph, 205
Skoog, Whitey, 93
Skoronski, Bob, 138, 186, 208
Sloan, Jerry, 225, 233
Smith, Dean, 57-59
Sobers, Ricky, 225
Sounds, 176, 203, 212
South Bend, Indiana, 24, 27, 29, 42, 73, 79, 86, 195
South High Street, 41
Southeastern Conference, 49
Southern California, 164
Southern Methodist, 90
Spirits, 213-14
Sports Illustrated, 223
Sportscasters Hall of Fame, 236
Springfield, Massachusetts, 52, 259
Spurs, 147, 201, 204-5, 213-14, 228
Squires, Virginia, 173, 192, 213
St. John, 180
St. Louis, 97, 99, 135
St. Peter, Minnesota, 88, 91
Stags, 121
Stars, 158, 164, 176, 180, 194, 212, 219
State Fairgrounds Coliseum, 168
Staverman, Larry, 141, 143, 147, 149, 157
Stevens, Denny, 17-18
Stockton, John, 244
Stokes, Maurice, 89
Stone, George, 176
Storen, Mike, 141-42, 144, 147, 161-62, 175
Strickland, Jim, 41
Strom, Earl, 133
Sullivan, Ed, 75-76
Sullivan, Ma, 8
Sullivans, 6-8, 13-14, 22
Suns, 192, 203, 220, 225
Super Bowl, 62, 70, 208, 214
Sycamores, 1
Syracuse War Memorial Auditorium, 135
Syracuse, 92, 97, 133, 136

T

Tams, 176, 219
Tatum, Earl, 225
Tatum, Goose, 77-78
Taylor, Chuck, 67, 168
Taylor, Ron, 39, 56
Terre Haute Garfield, 1, 18

Terre Haute Gerstmeyer Technical High School, Ix, xi, 11-13, 17-18, 26, 131
Terre Haute, Indiana, 1-4, 7, 16-18, 21-23, 26-27, 33, 41, 45, 58, 61, 82, 85, 87, 91, 141, 184, 190, 201, 227, 257
Texas, 22, 106, 205
Thacker, Tom, 163
The Ed Sullivan Show, 75-76
The Fieldhouse, 29
The Tonight Show, 75
Thompson, David, 35, 173
Thomspon, Mychal, 226
Thorn, Rod, 101, 129
Thornberry, Joe, 7-8
Tigers, 70
Timberwolves, 219
Tisdale, Wayman, 235
Touchdown Jesus, 195
Trager, Dave, 126-27
Trail Blazers, 226, 256
TriDelt House, 33, 37
Twyman, Jack, 89, 136
Tyra, Charlie, 123

U

UCLA, 90, 141, 153
Union City, 39
United States Army, 73
University of Cincinnati, 163
University of Dayton, 91, 154, 226
University of Illinois, 189
University of Indianapolis, 181
University of Kansas, 2
University of Kentucky, 83, 164, 194, 217, 227
University of Louisville, 217
University of Minnesota, 57, 85, 106
University of Pittsburgh, 203
University of South Carolina, 203
University of Washington, 49, 129
Unseld, Wes, 130
USA Today, 212
Utah State, 125, 129
Utah, 171

V

Valle, John, 16
Valparaiso, 60
Vanek, John, 133
Vigo County, 21
Virginia, 5

W

Wabash River, 1
Wabash Valley Tournament, 12, 19

Wabash Valley, 1, 12, 21
Walsh, Donnie, 248
Walton, Bill, 117, 157
Wampler, Freddy, 14
Warriors, 88, 111
Warriors, 88-90, 111, 117, 136, 161
Washington Clay High School, 42
Washington, 61
Watson, 38-40, 174, 178
Watson, Lou, 38-40, 174, 178
West Virginia University, 101
West Virginia, 102
West, David, 256
West, Jerry, xi, 101, 111-16, 118, 123, 137, 164-65, 192
Western Division, 94, 176, 196, 201
Western Kentucky, 164
Whitcomb, Governor Edgar, 259
White Sox, 30, 35, 126
White, Dick, 42, 46, 58
Wildermuth Intramural Center, 29
Wilkens, Lenny, 114
Wilkes, Jamaal, 112
Williams, Herb, 235
Williamson, John, 218, 224-25
Wilson, Clarence, 77
Winslow, Indiana, 31, 39
Wisconsin, 34, 67
Wise, Willie, 164, 176, 184, 194
Wizards, 122
Wooden, John, 1, 13, 141
Works Project Administration, 6
World Golf Hall of Fame, 80
World Hockey Association, 208
World Series of Basketball, 76
World War II, 5, 7, 30, 46, 71, 82, 106-7
Worthy, James, 112, 157
Wright, Jackie, 39

Y

Yankees, 171
Yardley, 89
YMCA, 53
York, Bill, 168
Youngan, Keith, 17-18

Z

Zephyrs, x, 122-26, 128, 131, 141-42, 231
Zinkoff, Dave, 117